AF835122

IoT Cybersecurity

Internet of Things (IoT) systems create a massive attack surface with billions of connected devices that often have weak default credentials and limited security capabilities, making them easy targets for cybercriminals to exploit at scale. Compromised IoT devices can serve as entry points for attackers to access valuable network resources, steal sensitive personal and business data, or launch large-scale botnet attacks that disrupt critical infrastructure. Without proper security measures, IoT vulnerabilities can lead to serious consequences, including operational disruptions, safety hazards in critical systems like healthcare and transportation, and significant financial and legal penalties from regulatory noncompliance. *IoT Cybersecurity: Trends, Challenges, and Solutions* addresses the significant knowledge gap between rapidly deployed connected devices and understanding their unique security challenges. Highlights include:

- An efficient lightweight cryptography technique for enhancing IoT security
- Machine learning approaches for IoT network threat detection and security optimization
- Using AI to enhance IoT-based intrusion detection systems
- A study on emerging threats and vulnerabilities

This book presents research and insights into practice that explore security holes and effective solutions in the realm of IoT cybersecurity. Covering the evolving threat landscape in IoT environments, it sheds light on the intricacies of cybersecurity patterns and addresses the challenges that arise. This book is a resource offering innovative solutions, research findings, case studies, and practical insights related to securing IoT ecosystems.

Advances in Computational Collective Intelligence

Series Editor: Dr. Subhendu Kumar Pani

Using AI to Develop Sustainability Strategies for a Changing Global Economy
Edited by A.V. Senthil Kumar, Ankita Chaturvedi, Atul Bansal, and Rohaya Latip

Artificial Intelligence, Geographic Information Systems, and Multi-Criteria Decision-Making for Improving Sustainable Development
Edited by Sujoy Kumar Jana, Kamalakanta Muduli, Indrajit Pal, and Purushottam Meena

Advanced AI and Data Science Applications
Edited by Dr. D. Sivabalaselvamani, Dr. G. Revathy, and Dr. Ranjit Singh Sarban Singh

Intelligent Business Analytics
Edited by Nitendra Kumar, Lakhwinder Kaur Dhillon, Mridul Dharwal, Elena Korchagina, and Vishal Jain

Augmented Reality and Sustainability: Goals and Challenges
Edited by Sonal Trivedi, Vishal Jain, Balamurugan Balusamy, Subhendu Pani, and Danish Ather

Patient-Centric 6G: A New Era in Smart Healthcare
Edited by Rajeev Kumar, Ankush Joshi, Preeti Bajaj, and Danila Parygin

Generative AI Tools: From Algorithms to Applications
Edited by Priyanka Sharma, Senthil Kumar AV, Monika Jyotiyana, and Adnan Alrabea

IoT Cybersecurity: Trends, Challenges, and Solutions
Edited by Laxmi Shaw, D. Ajitha, Chinmay Chakraborty, and S.M. Prabin

https://www.routledge.com/Advances-in-Computational-Collective-Intelligence/book-series/ACCICRC

IoT Cybersecurity
Trends, Challenges, and Solutions

Edited by
Laxmi Shaw, D. Ajitha, Chinmay Chakraborty, and
S.M. Prabin

CRC Press
Taylor & Francis Group
AN AUERBACH BOOK

Designed cover image: Shutterstock

First edition published 2026
2385 NW Executive Center Drive, Suite 320, Boca Raton FL 33431

and by CRC Press
4 Park Square, Milton Park, Abingdon, Oxon, OX14 4RN

CRC Press is an imprint of Taylor & Francis Group, LLC

© 2026 Taylor & Francis Group, LLC

Reasonable efforts have been made to publish reliable data and information, but the author and publisher cannot assume responsibility for the validity of all materials or the consequences of their use. The authors and publishers have attempted to trace the copyright holders of all material reproduced in this publication and apologize to copyright holders if permission to publish in this form has not been obtained. If any copyright material has not been acknowledged please write and let us know so we may rectify in any future reprint.

Except as permitted under U.S. Copyright Law, no part of this book may be reprinted, reproduced, transmitted, or utilized in any form by any electronic, mechanical, or other means, now known or hereafter invented, including photocopying, microfilming, and recording, or in any information storage or retrieval system, without written permission from the publishers.

For permission to photocopy or use material electronically from this work, access www.copyright.com or contact the Copyright Clearance Center, Inc. (CCC), 222 Rosewood Drive, Danvers, MA 01923, 978-750-8400. For works that are not available on CCC please contact mpkbookspermissions@tandf.co.uk

For Product Safety Concerns and Information please contact our EU representative GPSR@taylorandfrancis.com. Taylor & Francis Verlag GmbH, Kaufingerstraße 24, 80331 München, Germany.

Trademark notice: Product or corporate names may be trademarks or registered trademarks and are used only for identification and explanation without intent to infringe.

ISBN: 9781032958781 (hbk)
ISBN: 9781032960753 (pbk)
ISBN: 9781003587859 (ebk)

DOI: 10.1201/9781003587859

Typeset in Adobe Garamond Pro
by codeMantra

Contents

About the Editors

Laxmi Shaw is a data scientist and researcher specializing in artificial intelligence, machine learning, and biomedical signal processing. She is currently working as a postdoctoral researcher in the Information Systems and Analytics Department at the McCoy College of Business, Texas State University, and also serves as a senior postdoctoral fellow at the Dell Medical School, The University of Texas at Austin.

She holds a Ph.D. in Electrical Engineering from the Indian Institute of Technology Kharagpur (2019), an M.Tech. in Instrumentation and Electronics Engineering from Jadavpur University, Kolkata (2010), and a B.E. from Sambalpur University (2006). She has over 6 years of industry experience as a senior data scientist with leading multinational corporations, including Samsung Research Lab, Bangalore, and other global firms in Hyderabad.

Her research interests include pattern recognition, cognitive and computational neuroscience, IoT-based cloud computing, computer vision, and AI-driven predictive modeling for healthcare and smart energy systems. She has authored three internationally published books and over 40 peer-reviewed research papers in reputed IEEE, Springer, and Elsevier journals and conferences.

She actively contributes to the scientific community as a reviewer for top-tier journals and holds lifetime professional memberships in ISTE and ACM.

D. Ajitha is working as an associate professor in the School of Computer Science and Engineering (SCOPE), VIT, Vellore. She earned a B.Tech. from JNTU, Hyderabad, in 2006 and an M.Tech. in VLSI System Design from JNTUA, Ananthapuramu, in 2009. She obtained her Ph.D. from the Department of Electronics and Communication Engineering, JNTUCEA, Ananthapuramu, India. She has lifetime professional memberships in IETE and ISTE. She has published more than 38 papers in international conferences and journals. Her areas of research interest are digital logic circuits in the nano-field, low-power VLSI, and reversible logic.

Chinmay Chakraborty is currently serving as an associate professor and the head of COIR in Medical Technology at KIIT Deemed to be University, India. He received a postdoctoral fellowship at the Federal University of Piauí, Brazil, and has been a visiting fellow at the University of Malta, Europe, and Chongqing University of Technology and Business, China. His core research interests include the Internet of Things, artificial intelligence and machine learning, and health informatics.

He has been consistently ranked among the Top 2% Scientists worldwide in artificial intelligence and image processing by Stanford University (2021–2025). He is the recipient of the Marie Skłodowska-Curie Actions Europe Fellowship Grant under Horizon 2023 and was nominated as a Prominent Young Researcher by INAE (SERB), Government of India. He has received multiple accolades including the ANRF-INAE Startup Competition Prize (2025), BIT Faculty Appreciation Award (BITFAA;24), Highest Citation Awards (2023–2024), and recognition as an AICTE-Distinguished Professional (2025).

S.M. Prabin is working as an assistant professor senior grade in the Department of Computer Science and Engineering at Vellore Institute of Technology, Vellore. He earned his bachelor's degree from Anna University, Chennai, and his master's degree from PSNA College of Engineering and Technology, Dindigul. He earned his Ph.D. from Anna University, Chennai. He has more than 13 years of teaching experience, and his areas of interest are artificial intelligence and its applications, cryptography and network security, wireless networks, machine learning, and deep learning. His profile includes more than 14 SCI and Scopus publications. He also published various papers in international conferences, and he is also a reviewer for various journals.

Contributors

D. Ajitha
Department of Software Systems
School of Computer Science and Engineering (SCOPE)
Vellore Institute of Technology
Vellore, India

Gayathri Ananthakrishnan
School of Computer Science Engineering and Information Systems
Vellore Institute of Technology
Vellore, India

Nikil Aventhiha G
Department of Cybersecurity and Internet of Things, Sri Ramachandra Faculty of Engineering and Technology (SRET)
Sri Ramachandra Institute of Higher Education and Research
Chennai, India

Baiju Babu Vimala
School of Computer Science and Engineering
Vellore Institute of Technology
Vellore, India

Shatarupa Bandyopadhyay
Department of Software Systems
School of Computer Science and Engineering
Vellore Institute of Technology
Vellore, India

Priya Boopalan
Electronics Division
ZF Active Safety and Electronics
Farmington Hills, Michigan

Anil Kumar Chikatimarla
Department of Computer Science
A.G. & S.G. Siddhartha Degree College of Arts & Science
Vuyyuru, India

Kinny Garg
Department of Electronics and Communication Engineering
AMC Engineering College
Bengaluru, India

Bilas Haldar
Department of Artificial Intelligence & Machine Learning
St. Thomas' College of Engineering & Technology
Kolkata, India

Hari Kalva
Department of Electrical Engineering and Computer Science
Florida Atlantic University
Boca Raton, Florida

Niranjan Kannanugo
Department of Electrical and Electronics Engineering, Jain (Deemed to be University)
Bengaluru, India

Manivannan Karunakaran
School of Computer Science and Engineering
JAIN (Deemed-to-be University)
Bengaluru, India

Priyan Malarvizhi Kumar
Information Science
University of North Texas
Denton, Texas

Sumit Kushwaha
Department of Centre for Research and AI Development Learning Ecosystem (CRADLE) Cell
Chandigarh University Uttar Pradesh
Uttar Pradesh, India.

Malini S
Department of Electronics and Communication Engineering
AMC Engineering College
Bengaluru, India

Partha Kumar Mukherjee
Department of Computer Science and Engineering
The Neotia University
Sarisha, India

Pavithraa D
Department of Cybersecurity and Internet of Things, Sri Ramachandra Faculty of Engineering and Technology (SRET)
Sri Ramachandra Institute of Higher Education and Research
Chennai, India

S. M. Prabin
Department of Information Security
School of Computer Science and Engineering (SCOPE)
Vellore Institute of Technology
Vellore, India

Priyadharshini P
Information Technology
PSNA College of Engineering and Technology
Dindigul, India

Raghu N
Department of Electrical and Electronics Engineering Jain (Deemed to be University
Bengaluru, India

Sree Ranjani Rajendran
Department of Electrical Engineering and Computer Science
Florida Atlantic University
Boca Raton, Florida

Akhil Raju
Department of Forensic Science
University of Calicut
Tenhipalam, India

Jaya Subalakshmi Ramamoorthi
Department of Software Systems
Vellore Institute of Technology
Vellore, India

Roshini B
Department of Cybersecurity and Internet of Things, Sri Ramachandra Faculty of Engineering and Technology (SRET)
Sri Ramachandra Institute of Higher Education and Research
Chennai, India

Himadri Nath Saha
Department of Computer Science
SNEC, Calcutta University
Kolkata, India

G. Senbagavalli
Department of Electronics and Communication Engineering
AMC Engineering College
Bengaluru, India

Shanthi D
Computer Science and Engineering
PSNA College of Engineering and Technology
Dindigul, India

Laxmi Shaw
Dell Medical School
University of Texas at Austin
Austin, Texas

Somasundaram R
Department of Cybersecurity and Internet of Things, Sri Ramachandra Faculty of Engineering and Technology (SRET)
Sri Ramachandra Institute of Higher Education and Research
Chennai, India

Ben Othman Soufiene
PRINCE Laboratory Research
ISITcom
Hammam Sousse
University of Sousse
Sousse, Tunisia

Suresh K
Computer Science and Engineering
PSNA College of Engineering and Technology
Dindigul, India

Thamizharasan S
School of Computer Science Engineering
Vellore Institute of Technology
Vellore, India

Velvizhi V A
Department of Electronics and Communication Engineering
Sri Sairam Engineering College
Chennai, India

Chapter 1

An Efficient Lightweight Cryptography Technique for Enhancing IoT Security

Bilas Haldar, Partha Kumar Mukherjee, and Himadri Nath Saha

1.1 Introduction

The Internet of Things (IoT) refers to a system of interconnected physical devices embedded with sensors, software, and communication technologies. Through the interconnection of these devices over the Internet, automation, real-time decision-making, and enhanced functionality across a variety of sectors are enabled. IoT systems can operate autonomously or interact with users, providing insights and improving efficiency in everyday tasks and industrial operations. The IoT has transformed modern industries by enabling seamless communication and data transformation among interconnected devices. The goal of IoT is to automate tasks, enhance efficiency, and provide real-time insights by allowing devices to communicate with each other and make decisions based on the data they collect and process. Its applications span diverse domains, including healthcare, smart cities, and industrial automation. Its applications span various industries, from healthcare to transportation, smart city, smart home, hospitality and tourism, smart agriculture, smart education, and industrial automation making it a key driver of innovation in today's world. Figure 1.1 provides the application of IoT in

DOI: 10.1201/9781003587859-1

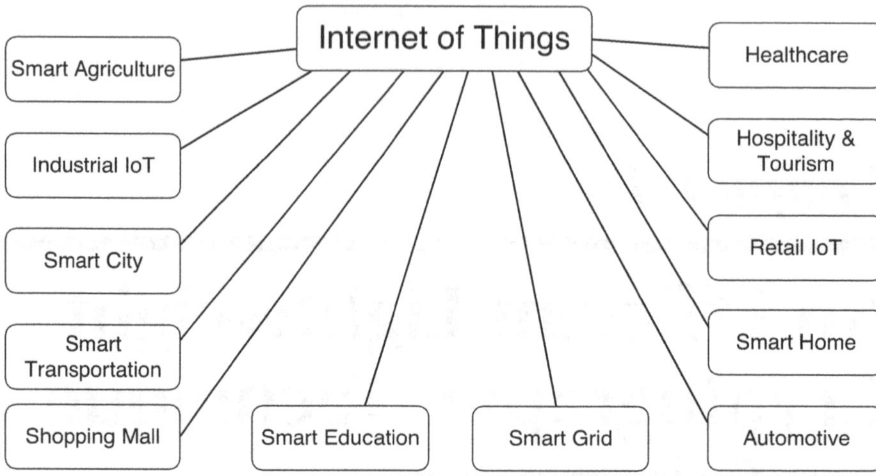

Figure 1.1 Applications of IoT across various domains and highlighting its broad impact on diverse industries.

various sectors. It enables remote monitoring and control of home systems, improving convenience and energy efficiency. IoT devices enable interactive learning through smart boards, connected projectors, and real-time monitoring of student progress. The powered checkout IoT systems allow customers to purchase items without traditional checkouts by automatically detecting items and charging them. IoT devices monitor equipment conditions in factories, predicting failures before they happen, thus reducing downtime and repair costs.

However, the rapid growth of IoT networks has introduced significant security challenges, particularly due to the constrained memory, computational power, and energy resources of IoT devices. The major security issues in IoT systems are denial of service (DoS) attacks, unauthorized access, information disclosure, and distributed denial of service (DDoS) attacks. Figure 1.2 showcases the security vulnerabilities of the IoT devices. The lack of authorized access enables hackers to infiltrate IoT devices and networks that belong to others. Unauthorized data tampering and device control, together with resource misuse, are potential outcomes. The unauthorized exploitation of bandwidth, power, and processing capabilities through unauthorized access reduces the performance of legitimate devices. The distributed nature of IoT device data storage and transmission stretches across several systems. Data becomes vulnerable to privacy breaches whenever it is not properly secured. The server becomes overwhelmed when attackers send numerous requests at once, which results in denying service access to legitimate users. A robust method for securing IoT systems by combining elliptic curve cryptography (ECC) with a one-time key approach is introduced [1]. The security method delivers protection against crucial IoT operating system weaknesses, including memory heap penetration and address modification attacks. This paper provides an extensive review of

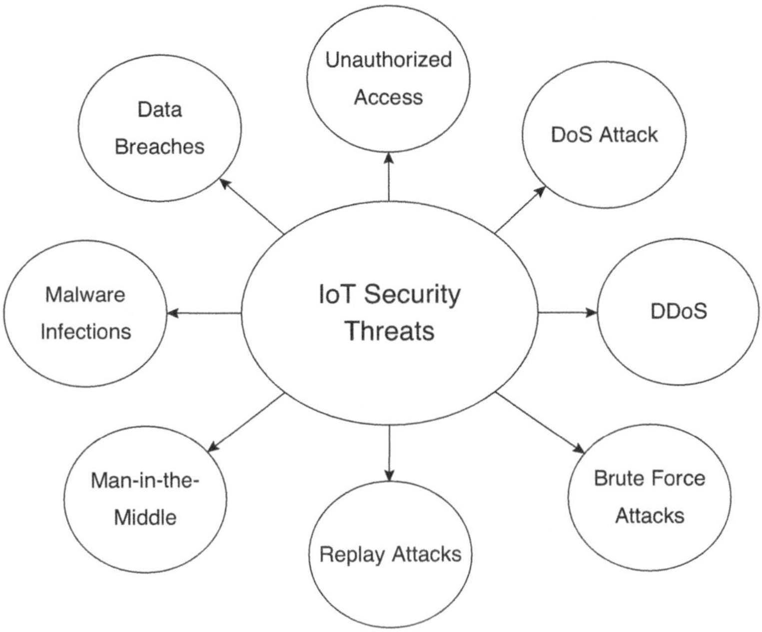

Figure 1.2 Illustration of key IoT security threats and emphasizing the vulnerabilities associated with IoT ecosystems.

IoT network security problems while discussing the IoT system vulnerabilities in detail [2]. A breakthrough framework for IoT system security is created [3] and presented. A security framework introduced Software Defined Network controller systems coupled with blockchain controllers that operate through a Cloud-based Software Defined Network architectural design to manage 100 mobile IoT nodes and an OpenFlow switch. A scheduling approach for IoT systems combines a three-dimensional S-box solution with the logistic map algorithm, as described [4]. A complete security package featuring Combined Elements targets IoT devices with minimal resources used in smart homes. The scale of DoS attack increases through DDoS because attackers implement (botnets) multiple compromised systems to deliver coordinated attacks targeting one system or the entire network preventing user access. The current security challenges demonstrate that IoT systems demand individual security protocols designed specifically for their particular weaknesses and boundaries.

This chapter introduces a new lightweight cryptographic method based on Message Authentication Codes (MACs), which provides strong security protection to IoT systems. The traditional cryptographic methods, which work well in standard computing environments, fail to match the particular security needs of IoT systems. The development of lightweight cryptography (LWC) became essential research because robust security features must work efficiently across IoT device limitations. LWC provides strong security options and low operational resource needs, thus making IoT systems proficient in defense operations with optimized performance levels. Data protection is achieved through an efficient method of key creation and MAC generation and authentication systems. The proposed solution achieves secure data protection by applying streamlined algorithms with a creative design method protecting data integrity and privacy and verification features. A protected infrastructure framework defends IoT systems against common dangers and defends against wiretapping and replay assaults together with unauthorized access attempts. The suggested approach underwent comprehensive tests across multiple IoT systems, which proved enhanced speed and resource efficiency and attack resistance against traditional cryptographic methods. The final data results indicate that this stripped-down security approach establishes an effective defense system for the upcoming IoT implementation frameworks. The methodology delivers workable and scalable security measures that protect shopping malls and smart homes and educational smart environments.

1.1.1 Objective of the Work

1. The research examines security concerns affecting IoT systems, particularly targeting unauthorized entry, data degradation, resource exploitation, information leakage along with DoS and DDoS attacks on IoT devices.
2. Design and propose a novel lightweight cryptographic technique tailored to meet the security needs of IoT devices while considering their computational, memory, and energy constraints.
3. The system requires optimization of ECC algorithms for key generation, MAC generation, and MAC verification to achieve robust security.
4. Introduce a robust cybersecurity framework to protect IoT networks from prevalent cyber threats like eavesdropping, replay attacks, and unauthorized access, ensuring a holistic security solution.
5. Demonstrate the applicability of the LWC solution in securing IoT applications across various domains ensuring confidentiality, integrity, and authentication.

1.1.2 Primary Contributions

This research provides a significant contribution toward developing efficient and scalable cryptographic solutions for IoT security. The authors introduce an optimized cryptographic approach leveraging ECC for secure key generation, MAC generation, and MAC authentication tailored for resource-constrained IoT devices. The work develops a security framework to mitigate common cyber threats in IoT networks. The authors conduct extensive performance analysis across different IoT environments, measuring key metrics such as key generation time, MAC generation time, and MAC verification time, to validate efficiency. The work demonstrates the practical relevance of the proposed cryptographic methodology for securing IoT applications.

1.1.3 Chapter Organization

This chapter is organized as follows. Section 1.2 introduces the literature review and existing challenges in IoT security. The proposed methodology for the LWC technique and cybersecurity framework is presented in Section 1.3. The results of the proposed MAC methodology are discussed in Section 1.4. The performance evaluation and comparison of the suggested methodology are introduced in Section 1.5. Security analysis and applications of the MAC techniques are introduced in Section 1.6. The last Section 1.7 concludes with a summary of key findings and directions for future research.

1.2 Literature Review

The increasing interconnectivity of devices on the IoT has brought forth new challenges in securing these systems from various cyber threats. Researchers have proposed using different cryptographic techniques and emerging technologies to solve security issues known to exist in IoT systems. Security solutions focus on confirming the confidentiality along with integrity and availability of data as they optimize the resource capacity of IoT devices. Mabodi et al. [5] introduced a hybrid cryptography approach to enhance security in IoT systems, specifically targeting the Multi-level trust-based intelligence schema for securing of IoT. This approach was evaluated through extensive simulations in the NS-3 environment, demonstrating its effectiveness in mitigating security risks within IoT networks. Kumar et al. [6] conducted a comprehensive literature analysis of post-quantum cryptography for IoT networks. The research identifies obstacles and benefits of implementing quantum-proof cryptography solutions, which protect real-time resource-limited devices. Their work explores ways to develop lightweight post-quantum cryptographic defensives, which guard IoT devices against quantum attack vulnerability, and examines viable quantum-resistant algorithms suitable for IoT implementations. The IoTSpotter framework developed by Jin et al. [7] functions to resolve safety problems in mobile IoT applications. Mobile IoT applications work as supporting tools that assist IoT devices through these applications. The framework identifies essential artifacts like IoT devices, which operate under the apps together with specific IoT libraries used for extensive security examination of mobile IoT ecosystems. Panagiotou et al. [8] presented a cryptographic solution based on Advanced Encryption Standard in various modes of operation, including Electronic Code Book and Cipher Block Chaining, to secure electronic data, texts, and images in IoT applications. These modes provide strong encryption and integrity verification, making the proposed system highly suitable for securing IoT systems, which often handle sensitive data and require efficient encryption techniques to run on resource-constrained devices.

Sadhukhan et al. [9] established an IoT communication authentication system using ECC, which incorporated three-factor remote user authentication. The implementation of various authentication elements makes IoT communication security robust by enhancing protection for IoT devices and service accessibility in privacy-demanding applications. Khan et al. [10] developed a secure framework for authentication and encryption using improved ECC for medical sensor data in IoT systems. Medical data security during transmission from IoT-enabled sensors to healthcare institutions exists within a proposed framework of protection. The work presented by Verma et al. [11] illustrates how blockchain integration with advanced cryptographic techniques maximizes the security features for IoT deployments. The combined system of IoT and blockchain technology establishes an unbreakable, decentralized protection, which tackles various security risks for IoT systems without compromising data tracking safeguards. Patnaik et al. [12] revealed key security challenges of IoT by outlining its communication problems with specific vulnerabilities to attack. The authors proposed new cryptography approaches combined with strong network infrastructure design and effective policies to defend IoT systems against cyberattacks. Prasanalakshmi et al. [13] analyzed data transmission performance and protection strategies in IoT frameworks when managing medical data. The proposed model addresses both security needs when protecting data transmission, as well as achieving fast data transfer speeds. An experimental work by Hasan et al. [14] analyzed cryptographic protocols used in IoT applications through symmetric and asymmetric encryption classification. Researchers examined prevalent cryptographic algorithms to measure their functionality through studies of decryption speed and encryption duration and guessing attack immunity. Hashim et al. [15] introduced an IoT security mechanism that depends on Henon mathematical algorithm-controlled random sequences to defend against assaults.

The research work of Sittampalam et al. [16] introduced an innovative Random Secret Key method to elevate the security performance of symmetric lightweight cryptographic algorithms operating in IoT environments. This performance optimization method allows strong security measures to coexist with IoT device requirements. An urban transportation-oriented IoT deployment secure data sharing mechanism was introduced by Bi et al. [17] through their hybridized cryptographic integrated steganography cryptographic-embedded steganographic approach. The implementation of fusion cryptography merges encryption with data nesting and produces protected security together with stealth storage capabilities that resist access by unauthorized viewers while preventing predatorial exposure. Thakor et al. [18] analyzed security threats affecting IoT primitives, such as Radio Frequency Identification (RFID) tags, combined with sensors and smart cards, due to their power-operational and processing-storage limitations. The research, while demonstrating LWC benefits, validates the combination of security with performance and affordability to direct future studies of optimized encryption for IoT devices with limited capabilities. A comprehensive survey of IoT weaknesses and exploitable attacks together with defensive measures was presented by Jurcut and colleagues [19] while analyzing technological aspects and architectural structures in IoT ecosystems. The authors present solutions that restore compromised security as well as risk mitigation strategies alongside preventive service measures along with suggested improvements for IoT systems against continuing cyberattacks. Shamala et al. [20] investigated security needs and threats that exist within IoT cryptography by presenting a detailed analysis of available security solutions with their key challenges. Because of restricted device capabilities, this paper examines how IoT systems should achieve security-performance equilibrium.

Dankan et al. demonstrated blockchain technology as a solution to boost IoT systems' security management operations [21]. The research work examined IoT device applications throughout all sectors. Blockchain technology improves security through its decentralized storage system that creates transactions automatically resistant to alteration. The research introduced LRECC as a hybrid security method, which combines Logistic Regression and ECC to enhance the IoT systems' defense capabilities. Security threats receive detection and prevention together with threat mitigation through the hybrid solution, which employs an ECC-based key generation and distribution model. Dhamodharan et al. [22] designed an improved cryptographic solution, which merged ECC along with TwoFish to boost IoT system protection. The combined approach utilizes ECC for its efficient key generation while incorporating TwoFish algorithm protection for IoT communication systems offering greater operational scalability and security strength despite resource constraints. Qasem et al. [23] established a complete analysis of cloud-based IoT systems and examined the encryption algorithm difficulties found across both environments. The research evaluates different encryption methods while analyzing the security obstacles and optimization requirements of such systems. Research by Dhar et al. [24] dedicated itself to exploring how blockchain and quantum cryptography mechanisms protect audio, video, and image data in IoT applications. Research works show quantum key distribution represents an advanced encryption choice, which betters standard cryptographic methods to combat modern cyber dangers. The development of a secure resilient IoT-based Smart Grid ecosystem for dependable energy delivery in the face of growing digital risks was explained by William et al [25]. The work addresses potential vulnerabilities in the system, such as unauthorized access and cyberattacks targeting critical infrastructure, by focusing on the secure communication of IoT devices within the smart grid. Chinbat et al. [26] evaluated the performance of various machine learning models and lightweight cryptographic algorithms for message encryption and classification in healthcare IoT devices. Arunachalam et al. [27] proposed a malware detection and prevention framework to enhance secure data transmission among IoT devices. Table 1.1 provides a summary of the literature review on previous research efforts.

Table 1.1 Summary of the Literature Review

Author`	*Methodology Used*	*Limitations and Future Work*
Mabodi et al. [5]	Hybrid cryptography approach	The approach requires further optimization to reduce energy consumption and mitigate malicious attacks on the Internet of Things.
Sittampalam et al. [16]	Random secret key	Security and performance need improvement.
Bi et al. [17]	Hybridized cryptographic integrated steganography	Future work involves integrating a human cognitive interface framework for system stabilization.
Dankan et al. [21]	Blockchain technology	Security enhancements are necessary to address current vulnerabilities in the application of blockchain.
Arunkumar et al. [28]	Logistic regression and elliptic curve cryptography	The methodology presents high complexity and will require further optimization to improve its efficiency.
Dhamodharan et al. [22]	Elliptic curve cryptography and the TwoFish algorithm	The method leads to increased time complexity, requiring further work to reduce processing delays.

The reviewed literature highlights the ongoing efforts for reducing vulnerabilities of IoT systems, which focused on both cryptographic solutions and optimized frameworks for data protection. Approaches such as hybrid cryptography, lightweight encryption schemes, and multilevel security mechanisms are critical to addressing the unique challenges of securing IoT devices, especially those with limited resources. However, the development of an innovative, robust security methodology is required to improve the security of IoT devices. There is a need for research focused on reducing energy consumption and addressing the vulnerabilities of malicious attacks, particularly in resource-constrained IoT environments. A potential research gap lies in the development of novel key management protocols that can enhance security, while optimizing computational efficiency, particularly in real-time applications. This work proposed an innovative LWC to prevent cyber threats in IoT devices. The work developed a robust security framework using an ECC-based MAC generation technique. The work suggested key generation, MAC generation, and MAC authentication using ECC methodology. It improves the security of the IoT systems and optimizes the time efficiency.

1.3 Proposed Methodology

The proposed LWC using MAC is a cryptography construct used to ensure the integrity and authenticity of a message over the network. The sender can prove that the message has not been altered by the attackers. It originates from a legitimate source by generating a MAC. The ECC provides a secure approach to implement MACs with efficient performance. The strong mathematical security properties of elliptic curves ensure the integrity of the data, while requiring shorter key lengths compared to traditional cryptography methods. Finite fields over elliptic curves are used in public key cryptography as the basis for ECC. It provides high levels of security with relatively small key sizes, making it particularly well-suited for resource-constrained environments in IoT devices. The proposed MAC operates with a security key length of 256 bits. The compact size of keys leads to improved security performance during IoT operational systems. Standard MAC algorithms contain lightweight versions that provide message integrity protection alongside authenticity features using limited computational processing power. The algorithms exist to serve IoT networks and devices that require authenticating signals and conserving power supply simultaneously.

IoT healthcare security and smart agriculture, together with smart home and smart educational platforms, require strict data authenticity and integrity systems for patient protection and information security. The proposed MACs establish cryptography protocols that maintain the authentication and integrity of IoT data by validating both source authenticity and data integrity. The lightweight deployment of ECC for MAC implementation provides both high security capabilities and efficient computational performance that suits health service environments with limited resources. The proposed lightweight cryptographic solution provides important benefits to IoT through its reduced key complexity and enhanced computational speed and secure processing. These attributes are crucial for securing sensitive data transmitted between IoT devices. The suggested LWC solutions are implemented to overcome the issues of resource-constrained devices without sacrificing security. Their computational efficiency, low memory usage, and minimal energy consumption make them ideal for embedded systems, IoT devices, and other resource-constrained applications. The use of ECC-based lightweight MAC for IoT ensures secure and authenticated communication, safeguarding data and operational integrity.

1.3.1 Key Generation

The key generation technique provides authentication keys for IoT systems. The proposed key generation method relies on an ECC-based lightweight MAC technique, methodology for its operation. The proposed method produces security keys for private key exchange between entities during communication. Every IoT device generates a unique private key. The corresponding public key is derived from the private key and shared securely with authorized entities. The key generation methodology in ECC-based lightweight MAC schemes is introduced in Algorithm 1.1.

Algorithm 1.1

A finite field is denoted by the symbols *Fp*, where *p* is a large prime number. The geometric points on the elliptic curve (EC) are represented by the variable $G=(x_G, y_G)$, where x_G and y_G are the coordinates on the *x*-axis and *y*-axis, respectively. The private key of the IoT device is denoted by the symbol *d,* with the corresponding public key represented as *Q*. Similarly, the private key of the control system is denoted by the symbol *e*, and its public key is represented by *R*.

Step 1. Generate ECC Parameters:

- Select an EC: Choose a suitable EC defined over a finite field *Fp*, where *p* is a large prime number.
- Choose a Base Point *G*: Select a base point $G=(x_G, y_G)$ on the EC with prime order *n*.

Step 2. IoT Device (Sender) Key Generation:

Private Key Generation:

- Generate a Random Integer: Choose a random integer *d* from the interval [1, *n*–1].

Public Key Derivation:

- Compute the Public Key *Q*:
  - Compute $Q=d{\cdot}G$ .... (1) // It performs EC point multiplication between *d* and *G*.
  - *Q* is the public key for IoT. It is a point on the EC.

Step 3. Control System (Recipient) Key Generation:

Private Key Generation:

- Generate a Random Integer: Choose a random integer e from the interval [1, *n*–1].

Public Key Derivation:

- Compute the Public Key *R*:
  - Compute $R=e{\cdot}G$ .... (2) // It performs EC point multiplication between *e* and *G*.
  - *R* is the control system's public key. It is a point on the same EC. The value of *e* and *d* must be different.

Step 4. Key Distribution:

- Distribute the public key *Q* to other entities with whom secure communication is intended.
- Securely store and manage the private key *d* to prevent unauthorized access and ensure its confidentiality.

SECURITY ANALYSIS OF KEY GENERATION TECHNIQUE

- **Key Size:** The security of the ECC-based lightweight MAC scheme depends significantly on the size of the EC parameters (e.g., curve order n) and the randomness of the private key d.
- **Randomness:** Ensure that the private key d is generated using a cryptographically secure random number generator to resist brute-force attacks.
- **Storage and Management:** Implement secure storage and management practices for private keys to prevent key compromise and unauthorized access.

1.3.2 Lightweight Message Authentication Code Generation

The lightweight MAC generation technique leverages the Elliptic Curve Digital Signature Algorithm (ECDSA) to securely authenticate messages in IoT networks. The methodology enables security measures by providing message verification and originality checks through an approach that suits resource-limited IoT system requirements. The algorithms specified in Algorithm 1.2 describe the process for creating lightweight MACs.

Algorithm 1.2

Step 1. Message Hashing: A hash function is applied to the message to generate a fixed-length digest $H(m)$, which uniquely represents the content of m. This step is crucial for compressing the message data into a manageable format for cryptographic operations while ensuring resistance to tampering and collisions.

Step 2. Signature Creation: Using its private key, the IoT devices generate an ECDSA signature:

- Private key d is generated during key generation.
- Selects a random number k and computes a point $(x1, y1) = k \cdot G$ on the elliptic curve, where G is the base point.
- Computes the signature components r and s, where $r = x1 \bmod n$ and $s = k^{-1}(H(m) + d \cdot r) \bmod n$. .... (3), Here, H(m) is the hash of the message, d is the IoT private key, and n is the order of the curve.
- The MAC is constructed by concatenating r and s with the original message m.

Step 3. MAC Calculation: The final authenticated message is created by combining the ECDSA signature (r, s) and the original message m. This ensures the integrity and authentication of the IoT systems. Any modification to m will result in a mismatch during verification. The signature (r, s) proves that the message originates from the legitimate IoT device with knowledge of the private key d.

The ECC-based lightweight MAC generation algorithm that implements ECDSA creates a solid method for validating electronic messages within IoT deployments. The combination of ECC's capabilities with its robust security properties enables secure sensitive data exchange between entities that need protection against access violations and data tampering risks. The algorithm experiences appropriate testing under different operational conditions to verify its practical usefulness in real IoT implementations.

SECURITY ANALYSIS OF MAC GENERATION TECHNIQUE

- **Forgery Resistance:** The security of ECC ensures that it is computationally infeasible for an attacker to forge a valid MAC without knowledge of the IoT's private key.
- **Efficiency:** ECC provides strong security with shorter key lengths, resulting in reduced computational overhead and faster processing times.
- **Scalability:** The scheme is scalable and can be adapted to various network sizes and configurations.

1.3.3 Lightweight MAC Authentication

The method defines a simplified authentication system based on ECC (ECC) for protecting message authentication across IoT networks. The objective focuses on achieving maximum security, combined with optimal resource utilization for IoT devices in processing sensitive data. The authentication procedure includes three fundamental processes of Signature Extraction, followed by Message Hashing, and completed with Signature Verification steps. The framework carries out the processes in sequence to prove message integrity alongside authenticity checks. The written procedure for MAC authentication is documented in Algorithm 1.3.

Algorithm 1.3

Step 1. Signature Extraction: The first stage of the verification process requires the recipient to obtain signature elements r and s from the received message. Message signing through execution of the ECDSA enables the sender to create signature components r and s.

Step 2. Message Hashing: The recipient implements a cryptographic hash function to measure the digest of the received message. A cryptographic hash function transforms the input message into a unique $H(m)$ hash output that represents the entire message with a fixed size. A hash function transforms any message change into a completely different digest, which lets users detect message alterations efficiently.

Step 3. Signature Verification: The verification process checks message integrity through an ECC operation, which uses the sender's public key. A sequence of steps for performing this process follows:

Step 3.1. Compute the Modular Inverse: Computes $w = s^{-1}\ mod n$, ... (4), where n is the order of the elliptic curve. w represents the multiplicative inverse of s modulo n, and it plays a key role in the verification formula.

Step 3.2. Calculate Intermediate Values: Calculate $u1 = H(m).\ w\ mod n$, ... (5), where $H(m)$ is the message hash. Calculate $u2 = r.w\ mod n$, ... (6), where r is the first signature component.

Step 3.3. Determine Elliptic Curve Point: Determines the point $(x2,\ y2) = u1 \cdot G + u2 \cdot Q$ .... (7), where Q is the sender's public key and G is the generator point of the elliptic curve.

Step 3.4. Validate the Signature: Validates that $r \equiv x2$ mod n. .... (8), If the condition is true, the signature is valid, confirming the integrity and authenticity of the message. If not, the message has been tampered with or is from an unauthorized source.

SECURITY ANALYSIS OF MAC AUTHENTICATION TECHNIQUES

The ECC-based MAC scheme provides strong security features appropriate for healthcare infrastructure:

- **Strong Authentication:** ECDSA ensures that only authorized IoT with the correct private key can generate valid MACs.
- **Data Integrity:** The cryptographic hash function guarantees that any tampering with the message will be detected.
- **Efficiency:** ECC's efficient computation and smaller key sizes minimize computational overhead, ideal for real-time healthcare applications.
- **Public Key Verification**: Ensure the authenticity of Q to prevent man-in-the-middle attacks.

1.3.4 CyberSecurity Framework for IoT Devices

The proposed cybersecurity framework is designed to prevent common IoT threats like spoofing, unauthorized access, and data breaches using lightweight MAC technique. The approach illustrated in Figure 1.3 utilizes authentication features with encryption technologies along with key management capabilities for protecting IoT devices against cyberattacks. The protective measures that secure IoT devices operate best when adopting this method to manage their particular constraints and establish both robust defense mechanisms and security efficiency. Lightweight MAC security systems serve as suitable solutions for protecting IoT devices that have constrained resources.

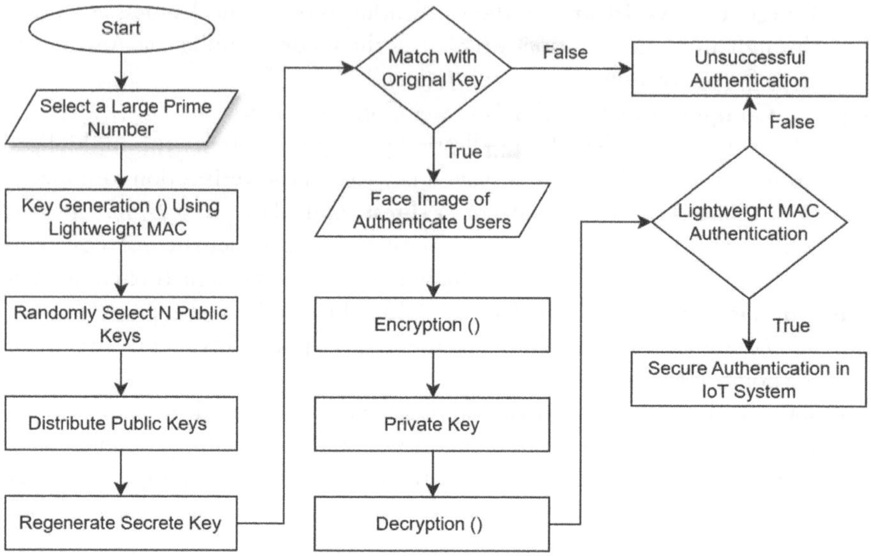

Figure 1.3 A cyberattack prevention framework utilizes MAC technologies for IoT devices.

1.3.4.1 The Functionality of Proposed Cybersecurity Framework

1. **Key Generation and Distribution:**
   - **Prime Number Selection:** The process begins with the selection of a large prime number, which serves as the foundation for secure cryptographic operations.
   - **Key Generation Using Lightweight MAC:** A lightweight MAC enables the efficient generation of cryptographic keys, which works well for IoT devices that have limited computational capabilities.
   - **Public Key Selection and Distribution:** To establish secure communication, users receive a random selection of N public keys that are distributed to their participating devices.
   - **Secret Key Regeneration:** The distributed public keys are used to regenerate a secret key for authentication and encryption.
2. **Authentication Process:**
   - **Matching Keys:** An authentication procedure validates the generated key by comparing it against the original master key. The verification process fails when authentication keys do not match their original form.
   - **User Identity Verification:** The framework verifies user identity through biometric data, starting after key verification is accomplished.
3. **Secure Communication:**
   - **Encryption and Private Key Utilization:** User data encryption occurs through the private key system after users complete their successful verification process.

  - **Decryption:** Authorized entities maintain exclusive ability to decrypt messages, which protects the data secrecy when messages move through the system.
4. **Lightweight MAC Authentication**
  - **Backup Authentication Mechanism:** The security framework uses lightweight MAC authentication as an extra procedure to verify user identity.
  - **Result Validation:** Failing outcome from this process results in authentication denial. The system receives a security certification when the authentication process remains successful.
5. **Outcome**
  - **Unsuccessful Authentication:** An unsuccessful execution of any framework step leads to the denial of access from unauthorized users, while safeguarding the IoT network.
  - **Secure IoT System:** A secure authentication state becomes established when every step in the process succeeds, thus providing reliable defense against cyberattacks.

1.4 Results and Discussion

The results of the suggested methodology for IoT security in various sectors are presented in this section. The work evaluates the key generation times for IoT devices and the control system based on varying sizes of prime numbers. Table 1.2 presents the key generation time for IoT devices and the key regeneration time for the control system based on the number of digits of a prime number. These times were measured in seconds and varied according to the length of the prime number used in the cryptographic operations.

It has been observed from Table 1.2 that there is a clear trend of increasing key generation time, as the number of digits in the prime number increases. IoT devices show a gradual increase in key generation time, with times starting from 0.9931 seconds for a 4-digit prime number, and reaching up to 10.7705 seconds for a 13-digit prime number. The increase in key generation time is relatively moderate for smaller prime numbers (4–6 digits). As the number of digits increases, the time required for key generation increases significantly. This exponential growth is expected due to the increased computational complexity. Key generation time in IoT devices is limited by their hardware capacity and affects the duration. A growing key size requires more resources, which in turn results in delayed computational times. A 4-digit prime number enables key generation in 1.0681 seconds, but when extended to a 13-digit prime number, the process requires 11.8964 seconds according to the control system. Key regeneration times for the control system exceed those of IoT systems, which points toward potential distinctions in hardware

Table 1.2 Key Generation Time for IoT Devices and Control System Based on the Number of Digits of a Prime Number

Number of Digits of a Prime Number	*Key Generation Time for IoT Devices (second)*	*Key Regeneration Time for the Control System (second)*
4	0.9931	1.0681
5	1.2452	2.0026
6	1.9045	2.8549
7	2.8231	4.2873
8	4.0573	6.6431
9	6.3701	7.9272
10	7.2837	8.8067
11	8.0176	9.6801
12	9.9245	10.7443
13	10.7705	11.8964

strengths or processing performance differences between these systems. Analysis of key generation and regeneration times for IoT devices and smart control systems establishes their fundamental significance. The increasing computational demand with larger prime numbers necessitates careful consideration of key sizes to ensure optimal performance without compromising security.

Table 1.3 demonstrates the time performance of ECC-based lightweight MAC generation and verification operations, using the proposed methodology during simulations with varying IoT device counts. The rising number of Internet-connected devices causes corresponding delays during the MAC generation and verification process. Existing resources allocate additional processing requirements to handle more devices in the IoT system, which results in this measured time increase trend. One IoT device requires 0.8346 seconds to generate MACs, which progressively increases to 8.2568 seconds for 13 IoT devices. The verification time for lightweight MAC becomes faster at approximately 1.4237 seconds during the initial test of one IoT device, but jumps significantly to about 11.5617 seconds for 13 IoT systems. The time needed for generations tends to grow longer with an increasing number of IoT devices and network elements. The process of producing lightweight MACs demands proportional increases in computational resources when networks grow in size. Network complexity directly has an impact on the duration of generation operations. MAC verification takes longer than generation because it requires multiple additional verification computations beyond the MAC generation processes.

Table 1.3 Lightweight MAC Generation Time and Verification Time Using the Proposed ECC-Based MAC Methodology

Number of IoT Devices	*Lightweight MAC Generation Time (second)*	*Lightweight MAC Verification Time (second)*
1	0.8346	1.4237
2	1.4321	2.5721
3	1.5426	2.8976
4	2.7094	4.0148
5	2.9238	4.1039
6	3.25473	5.1146
7	4.3942	6.6417
8	4.5163	7.2757
9	5.8641	8.7819
10	6.0131	8.9014
11	6.4706	9.2157
12	7.6702	10.0412
13	8.2568	11.5617

Research findings demonstrate that ECC-based lightweight MAC methods scale well across IoT networks, even though time requirements grow with rising device numbers. Healthcare applications require fast responses; hence, MAC operation duration needs appropriate balancing according to application requirements. When using between one and five IoT devices, the proposed methodology delivers execution times that remain reasonable, thus demonstrating effectiveness for deployments with small product counts. When operating larger IoT deployments, efficiency optimization techniques become essential to preserve workflow performance.

1.5 Performance Analysis and Comparison

This section presents the performance analysis of the proposed techniques for IoT devices. The performance analysis of the results presented in the research work regarding key generation for IoT devices and control systems depends on the number of digits in the prime number, as shown in Figure 1.4

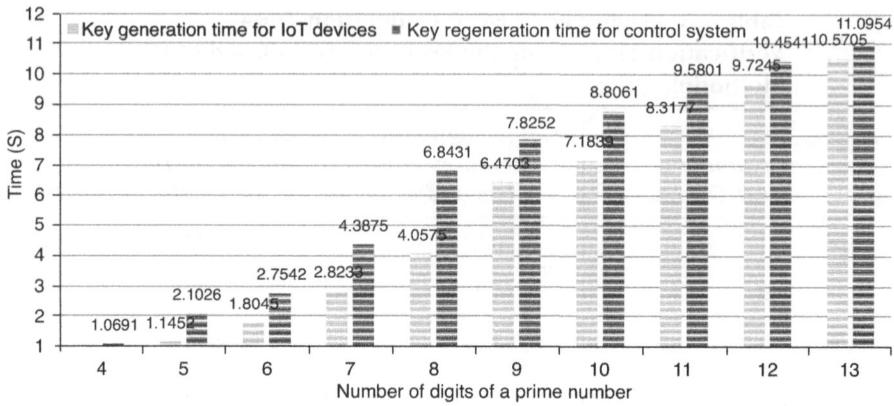

Figure 1.4 Key generation time for IoT devices versus control system time of the lightweight MAC algorithm.

The number of digits in the prime numbers determines key generation duration for IoT devices and the key regeneration duration for the control system, as shown in Figure 1.4. The diagram features separate bars: the blue column reflects IoT device key generation timing, while the orange column shows control system key regeneration periods in this figure. Prime numbers with additional digits extend the duration required for both IoT device key generation and control system key renewal. The timing reveals exponential behavior, particularly at high-digit configurations. Throughout all digit counts, the control system's key regeneration time surpasses the key generation time of IoT devices. The gap between key generation times for IoT devices and control systems widens prominently with increasing digit quantity of prime numbers, which creates additional computational challenges for control systems dealing with large primes. The graph illustrates the scalability challenges associated with ECC-based lightweight MAC key generation and regeneration. While IoT devices maintain relatively efficient key generation times, control systems face increasing computational demands with larger prime numbers.

Figure 1.5 illustrates the relationship between the number of IoT devices and the time required for MAC generation and verification using the proposed lightweight ECC-based MAC methodology. The graph includes two lines. The green color columns represent the MAC generation time, and the orange color columns represent the MAC verification time. The linear increase in MAC generation time indicates that the system scales efficiently with an increasing number of IoT devices, although the cumulative time can become significant as the number of IoT devices grows. Verification time, while also linear, shows a steeper slope, highlighting a scalability challenge that needs to be addressed for larger deployments. The consistent

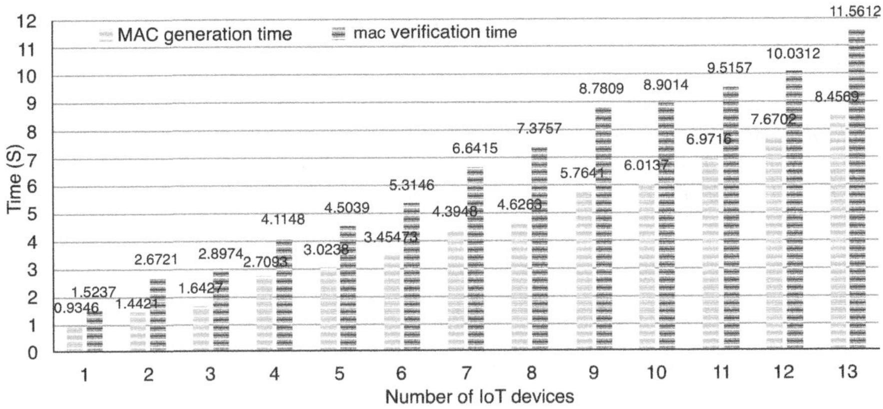

Figure 1.5 Number of IoT devices versus lightweight MAC generation time and verification time.

gap between generation and verification times underscores the additional computational effort required for verification.

This gap widens slightly with an increasing number of IoT devices, suggesting that optimization efforts focus more on improving verification efficiency. Implement adaptive security measures where the complexity of MAC operations can be adjusted based on the system's real-time requirements and the number of active IoT devices. Dynamically balance the trade-off between security and performance based on operational context. The analysis of Figure 1.5 showcases the importance of optimizing MAC generation and verification times for scalable deployment of IoT devices. While the system performs efficiently with a small number of IoT devices, the increasing computational load for verification, in particular, poses a scalability challenge. Addressing this through algorithmic improvements, parallel processing, hardware acceleration, and adaptive security measures will be crucial to maintaining both security and performance. This optimization will ensure that IoT devices can effectively support real-time, secure operations in healthcare settings.

Table 1.4 presents a comparison of key generation and regeneration times between the proposed methodology and the modified ECC [29]. The comparison is based on the number of digits in the prime number used for key generation and regeneration. According to the comparison results, the proposed methodology consistently shows lower key generation time compared to modified ECC, suggesting better efficiency. Key regeneration time is also significantly lower in the proposed approach, which is critical for secure and fast reauthentication in IoT and control systems. As the number of digits in the prime number increases, both key generation and regeneration times increase for both methods, but the proposed method scales more efficiently. The table provides empirical evidence that the proposed methodology is superior in both key generation and regeneration times, making it a more efficient choice for IoT security and control systems.

Table 1.4 Comparison of Key Generation and Regeneration Time Between Proposed Methodology and Modified ECC

Number of Digits of a Prime Number	*Key Generation Time for IoT Devices (second)*	*Key Generation Time (second) [29]*	*Key Regeneration Time for the Control System (second)*	*Key Regeneration Time (second) [29]*
4	0.9931	1.1034	1.0681	1.5781
5	1.2452	1.4301	2.0026	2.4265
6	1.9045	2.6247	2.8549	3.0358
7	2.8231	3.0186	4.2873	4.8837
8	4.0573	4.7569	6.6431	6.9013
9	6.3701	6.9905	7.9272	8.2092
10	7.2837	8.0541	8.8067	9.4178
11	8.0176	8.9867	9.6801	10.5673
12	9.9245	10.4251	10.7443	11.1952
13	10.7705	11.5604	11.8964	12.5426

1.6 Security Analysis and Application of IoT in Healthcare

IoT security in healthcare focuses on implementing robust measures to protect sensitive information, ensure operational integrity, and safeguard patient safety. Some key applications and considerations of IoT in the healthcare sector are patient monitoring and assistance, data integrity and privacy, threat detection and mitigation, secure remote access, and resilience against attacks. It is important to confirm that only authorized personnel can access IoT operations through the authentication and MAC verification techniques. Guaranteed communication protocols joined with access rules defend sensitive cargo from both unauthorized actions and interception attempts. ECC-based key generation together with message authentication protects patient records against unauthorized modification by ensuring healthcare data integrity. IoT devices feature detection systems that combine with security responses to protect against threats. Healthcare personnel use remote access capabilities to take command of IoT devices so they can perform patient diagnosis and telemedicine operations. Remote sessions remain protected through protected encryption-based systems that prevent attackers from accessing session data while in progress. The security features integrated at production time generate protection for IoT devices from common malware incidents and guard against DoS attacks and attacks targeting physical device modification attempts. Standard secure boot procedures with firmware update capabilities together with physical safety measures build the foundation that security systems require. Billions-In-Play Practice maintains essential health records since strong security integrated into IoT devices protects patient data while preserving infrastructure continuity and IoT system implementation choices of hospital executives.

This ECC-based MAC system provides lightweight protection for message operations when healthcare networks send IoT hardware devices during their transport phase. The designed system blocks unauthorized modifications of essential data and commands while maintaining reliability in medical operation. IoT devices and healthcare systems authenticate messages through the system's protective management of legitimate communication processing. It protects IoT devices from spoofing attacks while enabling exclusive communication by authorized and trusted sources. The implementation of ECC-based MAC technology enables network components to trace IoT device actions to their original sources, so disputes about source identities can be prevented. Medical application functions must have natural workforce participation together with organizational alignment of communication abilities to ensure adequate patient care. The security framework provides a reliable defense framework that protects IoT devices from multiple cyberattacks. The techniques described here strengthen IoT device cybersecurity protection when healthcare systems use them in their implementations. The proposed solution introduces standardized security protocols, which enable secure communication among operational IoT device infrastructure networks. The communication framework implements secure wire-based and wireless protocols to build encrypted paths for data transfer that stop passive inspections. The non-repudiation features of ECC technology track all IoT device activities, maintaining evidence of their authentic operations. Such capability stands essential for ensuring healthcare accountability. The proposed methodology is adaptable to a wide range of industrial IoT applications, including smart agriculture, smart cities, smart transportation, smart homes, and smart education, among others.

1.7 Conclusion

Momentum-based developments in modern industries result from the IoT technology that creates meaningful device automation as well as superior decisional effectiveness and functional improvement. These benefits from IoT systems, such as energy optimization, predictive maintenance, and interactive learning, are burdened by major security challenges due to device resource limitations, which expose IoT systems to advanced cyber threats and unauthorized access, data tampering, and DoS/DDoS attacks. This chapter introduces a novel set of cryptographic techniques using ECC technology, which specifically targets IoT system resource-constrained environments to handle current security challenges. The proposed security framework implements optimized cryptographic methods, which establish dependable protection systems that preserve power and computational power while developing enhanced key systems and MAC processing mechanisms. The evaluation demonstrates that this security methodology works well to protect data securely by using strong authentication, improving encryption speed, reducing resource use, and achieving better security strength than traditional cryptographic methods. Performance benchmarks of multiple IoT platforms indicate good results due to verification efficiency improvements and lower power usage. The suggested techniques provide protection against standard IoT security threats, such as eavesdropping, unauthorized access, and replay attacks.

Through implementing a cybersecurity framework, scientists can better protect IoT networks against potential threats, like eavesdropping, unauthorized entry, and replay attacks. The advanced security solution enables practical scalability implementation, which enables organizations to establish effective IoT security measures for enterprise and industrial applications. Research outcomes demonstrate that lightweight cryptographic approaches provide efficient security solutions for modern IoT environment requirements. The introduced ECC-based MAC authentication method would confront scalability limitations when used in extensive IoT networks that consist of numerous devices. When network size increases, it can lead to various performance problems, including authentication delays together with increased computational needs and limited capacity of low-power IoT devices that affect both authentication and real-time communication quality. Future security solutions will need both efficient optimization strategies and adaptive key management mechanisms because they will help decrease the challenges IoT devices currently face. The analysis of large-scale IoT deployment scalability for the proposed methodology along with assessment of system performance in dynamic network environments represents needed future research directions. Additionally, exploring its compatibility with emerging IoT architectures and communication protocols will enhance its adaptability across diverse applications. Further investigations should also assess the potential integration of this cryptographic approach with AI-driven security surveillance systems, enabling intelligent threat detection and adaptive security mechanisms.

Acronyms

AES	Advanced Encryption Standard
CBC	Cipher Block Chaining
DDoS	Distributed denial of service
DES	Data Encryption Standard
DoS	Denial of service

ECB	Electronic Code Book
ECC	Elliptic curve cryptography
ECDSA	Elliptic Curve Digital Signature Algorithm
HCIS	Hybridized cryptographic integrated steganography
IDS	Intrusion detection systems
IoT	Internet of Things
LWC	Lightweight cryptography
MAC	Message Authentication Code
MTISS-IoT	Multi-level trust-based intelligence schema for securing of IoT
OTK	One-time key
QKD	Quantum key distribution
RSA	Rivest-Shamir-Adleman
RSK	Random secret key
SDN	Software Defined Network

References

1. Khalifa, M., Algarni, F., Khan, M. A., Ullah, A., & Aloufi, K. (2021). A lightweight cryptography (LWC) framework to secure memory heap in Internet of Things. *Alexandria Engineering Journal*, *60*(1), 1489–1497.
2. Litoussi, M., Kannouf, N., El Makkaoui, K., Ezzati, A., & Fartitchou, M. (2020). IoT security: challenges and countermeasures. *Procedia Computer Science*, *177*, 503–508.
3. Velmurugadass, P., Dhanasekaran, S., Anand, S. S., & Vasudevan, V. (2021). Enhancing Blockchain security in cloud computing with IoT environment using ECIES and cryptography hash algorithm. *Materials Today: Proceedings*, *37*, 2653–2659.
4. Rahman, Z., Yi, X., Billah, M., Sumi, M., & Anwar, A. (2022). Enhancing AES using chaos and logistic map-based key generation technique for securing IoT-based smart home. *Electronics*, *11*(7), 1083.
5. Mabodi, K., Yusefi, M., Zandiyan, S., Irankhah, L., & Fotohi, R. (2020). Multi-level trust-based intelligence schema for securing of internet of things (IoT) against security threats using cryptographic authentication. *The Journal of Supercomputing*, *76*, 7081–7106.
6. Kumar, A., Ottaviani, C., Gill, S. S., & Buyya, R. (2022). Securing the future internet of things with post-quantum cryptography. *Security and Privacy*, *5*(2), e200.
7. Jin, X., Manandhar, S., Kafle, K., Lin, Z., & Nadkarni, A. (2022). Understanding IoT security from a market-scale perspective. In *Proceedings of the 2022 ACM SIGSAC Conference on Computer and Communications Security* (pp. 1615–1629), Los Angeles, USA.
8. Panagiotou, P., Sklavos, N., Darra, E., & Zaharakis, I. D. (2020). Cryptographic system for data applications, in the context of internet of things. *Microprocessors and Microsystems*, *72*, 102921.
9. Sadhukhan, D., Ray, S., Biswas, G. P., Khan, M. K., & Dasgupta, M. (2021). A lightweight remote user authentication scheme for IoT communication using elliptic curve cryptography. *The Journal of Supercomputing*, *77*(2), 1114–1151.

10. Khan, M. A., Quasim, M. T., Alghamdi, N. S., & Khan, M. Y. (2020). A secure framework for authentication and encryption using improved ECC for IoT-based medical sensor data. *IEEE Access, 8*, 52018–52027.
11. Verma, R., Dhanda, N., & Nagar, V. (2023). Analysing the security aspects of IoT using blockchain and cryptographic algorithms. *International Journal on Recent and Innovation Trends in Computing and Communication, 11*(1s), 13–22.
12. Patnaik, R., Padhy, N., & Srujan Raju, K. (2021). A systematic survey on IoT security issues, vulnerability and open challenges. Edited by Suresh Chandra Satapathy, Vikrant Bhateja, B. Janakiramaiah, Yen-Wei Chen. In *Intelligent System Design: Proceedings of Intelligent System Design: INDIA 2019* (pp. 723–730). Springer Singapore.
13. Prasanalakshmi, B., Murugan, K., Srinivasan, K., Shridevi, S., Shamsudheen, S., & Hu, Y. C. (2022). Improved authentication and computation of medical data transmission in the secure IoT using hyperelliptic curve cryptography. *The Journal of Supercomputing, 78*(1), 361–378.
14. Hasan, M. K., Shafiq, M., Islam, S., Pandey, B., Baker El-Ebiary, Y. A., Nafi, N. S., … & Vargas, D. E. (2021). Lightweight cryptographic algorithms for guessing attack protection in complex Internet of Things applications. *Complexity, 2021*(1), 5540296.
15. Hashim, M. M., Rhaif, S. H., Abdulrazzaq, A. A., Ali, A. H., & Taha, M. S. (2020). Based on IoT healthcare application for medical data authentication: Towards a new secure framework using steganography. *IOP Conference Series: Materials Science and Engineering, 881* (1), 012120.
16. Sittampalam, G., & Ratnarajah, N. (2020). Enhanced symmetric cryptography for IOT using novel random secret key approach. In *2020 2nd International Conference on Advancements in Computing (ICAC)* (Vol. 1, pp. 398–403). IEEE. Colombo, Sri Lanka.
17. Bi, D., Kadry, S., & Kumar, P. M. (2020). Internet of things assisted public security management platform for urban transportation using hybridised cryptographic-integrated steganography. *IET Intelligent Transport Systems, 14*(11), 1497–1506.
18. Thakor, V. A., Razzaque, M. A., & Khandaker, M. R. (2021). Lightweight cryptography algorithms for resource-constrained IoT devices: A review, comparison and research opportunities. *IEEE Access, 9*, 28177–28193.
19. Jurcut, A. D., Ranaweera, P., & Xu, L. (2020). Introduction to IoT security. In *IoT Security: Advances in Authentication* (pp. 27–64). Edited by Madhusanka Liyanage, An Braeken, Pardeep Kumar, Mika Ylianttila. John Wiley & Sons.
20. Shamala, L. M., Zayaraz, G., Vivekanandan, K., & Vijayalakshmi, V. (2021). Lightweight cryptography algorithms for internet of things enabled networks: An overview. *Journal of Physics: Conference Series, 1717* (1), 012072.
21. Gowda, V. D., Kawale, S. R., Prasad, K., Kumar, N. A., Reddy, N. S., & Ashreetha, B. (2023). Technologies for comprehensive information security in the IoT. In *2023 International Conference for Advancement in Technology (ICONAT)* (pp. 1–5). IEEE. Goa, India.
22. Sandoya, F., Dhamodharan, D., Hilario Rivas, J. L., Choque Flores, L., & Thaddeus, S. (2021). Embedding elliptic curve cryptography and twofish algorithm to improve data security in Internet of things. *Advances in Mechanics, 9*(3), 971–978.
23. Qasem, M. A., Thabit, F., Can, O., Naji, E., Alkhzaimi, H. A., Patil, P. R., & Thorat, S. B. (2024). Cryptography algorithms for improving the security of cloud-based internet of things. *Security and Privacy, 7*(4), e378.

24. Dhar, S., Khare, A., Dwivedi, A. D., & Singh, R. (2024). Securing IoT devices: A novel approach using blockchain and quantum cryptography. *Internet of Things, 25*, 101019.
25. William, P., Chowdhury, S., Falah, A., Hussain, A., Kumar, R., & Rao, A. L. N. (2024). Security enhancement in Iot based smart grid system using cryptographic techniques. In *2024 4th International Conference on Innovative Practices in Technology and Management (ICIPTM)* (pp. 1–6). IEEE. Noida, India.
26. Chinbat, T., Madanian, S., Airehrour, D., & Hassandoust, F. (2024). Machine learning cryptography methods for IoT in healthcare. *BMC Medical Informatics and Decision Making, 24*(1), 153.
27. Devi, R. A., & Arunachalam, A. R. (2023). Enhancement of IoT device security using an Improved Elliptic Curve Cryptography algorithm and malware detection utilizing deep LSTM. *High-Confidence Computing, 3*(2), 100117.
28. Arunkumar, J. R., Velmurugan, S., Chinnaiah, B., Charulatha, G., Prabhu, M. R., & Chakkaravarthy, A. P. (2023). Logistic regression with elliptical curve cryptography to establish secure IoT. *Computer Systems Science & Engineering, 46*(1), 2635–2645.
29. Haldar, B., & Jha, P. K. (2023). Securing mobile robots multi-party authentication technique using modified elliptic curve cryptography. In *2023 International Conference on Advanced Computing & Communication Technologies (ICACCTech)* (pp. 104–109). IEEE. Banur, India.

Chapter 2

Enhancement of IoT-Based Intrusion Detection Systems by AI and ML Methodologies

Shatarupa Bandyopadhyay and
Jaya Subalakshmi Ramamoorthi

2.1 Introduction

The Internet of Things (IoT) has become an integral part of the present industrial scenario across various domains, such as transportation, healthcare and agriculture, fuelled by the need for ensuring seamless connectivity across devices. However, this rapid interconnectivity has expanded the attack surface area, leading to increasing security concerns against cyberattacks and other malicious threats. Intrusion Detection Systems (IDSs) have been developed to answer such concerns in real time while protecting sensitive data, making them very important for secure IoT systems. However, traditional methods have been found to be inadequate due to diverse applications and the dynamic nature of IoT environments. The advent of AI and ML into cybersecurity offers a promising alternative to available solutions, since such frameworks can autonomously detect anomalies as well as learn patterns by processing and analysing tremendous and varied volumes of data. Several approaches have been put forward to mitigate threats and adapt to evolving cyberattacks. However, issues like imbalanced datasets, lack of computational power, overfitting risks and lack of awareness of new attacks are still prevalent, especially

 DOI: 10.1201/9781003587859-2

in IoT environments, which are even more vulnerable to such risks. Given the widespread applications of IoT systems in various industries, it is imperative to focus on mitigating such risks and developing secure networks.

2.1.1 Chapter Scope and Contributions

The scope of this chapter is limited to a review of current IDS solutions for IoT and a conceptual proposal of an IDS framework. It presents a review of a collection of ML methods, a high-level comparison of their usefulness for IDS, datasets used for training, testing and evaluation of these models, and prevalent AI methodologies implemented in IDS for IoT systems, along with the research gaps in the current literature. Furthermore, it proposes a theoretical framework with a hybrid approach that aims to overcome these gaps to develop a real time and adaptable system, and compares these models to current works.

2.1.2 Chapter Organisation

The structure of the chapter is as follows: Section 2.1 presents a general introduction to IDS in IoT networks and the need for research focus in this area. Section 2.2 provides an overview of typical IoT architecture, its advantages, applications, types of IDSs and the challenges faced by them in IoT systems. Section 2.3 offers an overview and comparison of some supervised, unsupervised and self-learning ML models for IDS. Section 2.4 presents an overview and comparison of datasets used for preprocessing, training and evaluation of these models. Section 2.5 is the literature survey for some AI-based IDS in IoT networks, as well as the research gaps present in them. Section 2.6 presents the proposed architecture and a theoretical comparison with current AI solutions. Finally, Section 2.7 concludes the chapter by discussing the future directions for AI approaches in IDS for IoT environments.

2.2 Internet of Things (IoT) and Intrusion Detection Systems (IDS)

2.2.1 Internet of Things (IoT)

Technology has, over time, gradually expanded from large-scale industrial machinery to minute devices used in everyday life – home appliances, wearable devices, vehicles, etc. IoT technology represents such an advancement that allows for new ways to collect, exchange and act on data. It consists of an interconnected network of "things" or physical objects which are embedded with sensors/actuators/software, etc., and gathers data, processes it, connects to the internet, and performs

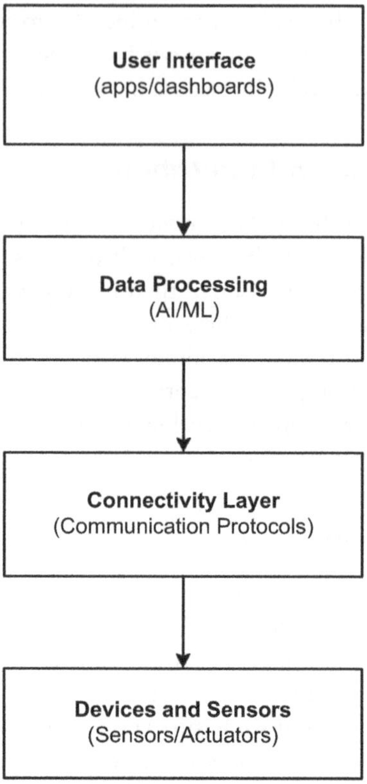

Figure 2.1 Architecture of a generic IoT system.

many other applications. It has resulted in the development of "smart" systems, which can even perform real-time operations like processing, decision-making, etc. Health monitors, electronic fitness trackers, voice assistants, etc., form some common examples of IoT systems that are used in everyday life. The following subsections describe the key components of this technology, which are also summarised in Figure 2.1.

2.2.1.1 Sensors and Actuators

These are two of the main components of an IoT system, as they interact with the environment to either collect data or perform some actions based on that data. Sensors obtain data from the environment and convert it to digital signals that can be further processed and transmitted, while actuators perform the reverse – convert from digital signals to physical motion. Examples include temperature, light, motion and humidity sensors.

2.2.1.2 Connectivity

Several protocols are used for transmitting and receiving data across devices or to a server (or typically, the cloud). Some examples are –

1. **Short-Ranged Communication:** Wi-Fi, Bluetooth and Zigbee are the protocols used especially for low-power scenarios.
2. **Long-Range Connectivity:** 4G/5G connectivity, widely used for mobile applications.
3. **LPWAN:** These are typically used for industrial applications for example, smart agriculture.

2.2.1.3 Data Processing and Storage

Data processing can happen either locally (edge computing) or via a central server system. More complex cases are usually handled by cloud servers, a popular solution. Analysis of data can be done using AI/ML methodologies to generate insights or automate related processes by taking decisions. Furthermore, a user interface enables humans to control, configure and interact with the entire IoT network remotely.

2.2.2 Advantages

The primary advantage of IoT technology lies in its ability to collect, analyse and share data seamlessly in real time. As a result, errors due to human intervention are minimised, leading to better resource management, reduction in costs and the automation of routine tasks, thereby increasing efficiency. Furthermore, it enhances convenience and accessibility by enabling remote connectivity, monitoring and control. Hence, it helps make data-driven decisions and improves the quality of life.

2.2.3 Applications

The applications of this technology span a diverse range of fields, from smart homes to agriculture, healthcare, production procedures, maintenance, etc. For instance, smart appliances like thermostats, lighting or voice assistants can be controlled remotely and thus improve the quality of life. Furthermore, use cases in healthcare consist of smart medical tools that can monitor vitals or provide alerts in real time. It can be also used for smart traffic management and monitoring pollution levels in urban areas, while in agriculture it could be used to monitor soil, weather and crop conditions. Hence, IoT forms a versatile technology with a high potential. Therefore, it is essential to maintain the security and integrity of such networks to prevent the loss of sensitive information.

2.2.4 IDS in IoT Networks

Even though IoT systems have several benefits, they also come with certain drawbacks. Some prevalent concerns are data security and privacy. This is typically due to the vast amounts of sensitive information that may be generated from sensor data. For example, patient health data generated from electronic health monitors is highly confidential in nature, and a data breach in such cases could be very harmful. Furthermore, managing and processing large amounts of data can also be challenging. In addition, the security systems of such frameworks are often difficult to integrate due to the varied protocols that they use, which can cause incompatibility between them and result in interoperability issues. Compact devices further limit the power, processing, and memory capabilities, thereby reducing their effectiveness. Hence, focus must be placed on strengthening the security of such environments to prevent risks of system failures, potential downtimes, data breaches and associated financial losses. In such a scenario, IDSs prove to be highly beneficial as they can help detect malicious attacks, raise alarms and thus help in responding quickly to the situation. These systems can identify abnormal traffic flow, and when combined with AI, they can further work with highly diverse attack types in dynamic environments. Therefore, IDSs prove to be essential for protecting sensitive data, identifying and responding to threats in real time, particularly in such vulnerable IoT environments.

2.2.5 Types of IDS

The modern digital landscape comprises interconnected networking systems with a variety of integrated technologies. However, these advancements have also increased the range and variety of attacks that occur on such networks. Especially for interconnected systems like IoT that consist of many devices, sensors and actuators, the attack surface is a lot higher, making them vulnerable to such network intrusion attacks.

In such a scenario, it is imperative to detect network intrusions in real time and take immediate response. Intrusion detection involves monitoring as well as analysing activities within a network to identify suspicious behaviours, detect unauthorised access and other such potential security breaches. An IDS is essentially a system that collects information from different network sources and analyses this information for threats. These systems safeguard the confidentiality, integrity and availability of network systems by detecting malicious activity.

IDSs can be classified into the following –

1. **Host-Based IDS (HIDS):** HIDS operates on standalone devices ("hosts"), observing activities like changes made to files, application behaviour and system logs. They are particularly effective in detecting attacks targeting a specific system or device. For example, log analysis tools and anti-malware software.

2. **Network-Based IDS (NIDS):** NIDS monitors network traffic for suspicious patterns, examining data packets based on signatures of known attacks. These systems are often deployed at critical network points like at network borders to detect and prevent unauthorised activities in real time. For example.: Snort and Suricata.
3. **Signature-Based IDS:** This approach relies on predefined signatures or patterns of known threats. While effective in identifying previously documented attacks, signature-based systems struggle against novel or unknown threats.
4. **Anomaly-Based IDS:** Anomaly-based IDS are somewhat similar to NIDS, detecting malicious activity by using attack signatures. However, these systems try and establish a "baseline" of normal behaviour using statistical, heuristic or ML-based approaches. Hence, any deviations from such behaviour allows them to detect unseen attacks. However, such IDSs have a tendency to suffer from higher false-positive rates.
5. **Hybrid IDS:** These IDSs can be thought of as a combination of signature-based and anomaly-based approaches, leveraging their strengths to balance accuracy and adaptability. They offer a more robust defence by leveraging the strengths of both approaches.

2.2.6 Challenges of IDS in IoT Environments

Despite their critical role in securing network systems, traditional IDS approaches face several limitations in todays' dynamic environments. These range from scalability and generalisability issues to resource constraints. Some challenges faced by such systems are discussed below –

1. **Scalability Issues:** IoT environments typically deal with large volumes of data generated by its diverse interconnected devices. Traditional IDS may struggle to scale effectively, leading to performance bottlenecks.
2. **High False Positive Rates:** Many anomaly-based IDS generate excessive false positives due to the difficulty in defining the baseline behaviour across heterogeneous IoT systems. This can overwhelm security teams and delay genuine alerts and incident response.
3. **Evolving Threats:** Cyberattackers continually develop sophisticated and evasive techniques, such as zero-day exploits and polymorphic malware. Signature-based IDS, in particular, fail to detect these unknown threats.
4. **Resource Constraints:** It is usually difficult to implement an IDS on an IoT network, as such networks typically suffer from limited resources like power, memory and processing abilities.
5. **Data Heterogeneity:** The diversity of data types and communication protocols in IoT networks complicates the creation of effective IDS models that can generalise across all environments.

To overcome such limitations, several AI and ML methodologies have been integrated into traditional IDS methods to create robust and generalisable systems. The following section discusses some common ML methodologies.

2.3 Machine Learning Techniques

Machine Learning refers to a system's ability to learn and improve from some given data without any human interference or explicit programming. ML models follow several strategies for different types of problems. Some of these methods are broadly discussed in the subsequent sections –

2.3.1 Supervised Learning

Supervised learning uses a labelled dataset, i.e., where both the input and target variable are labelled, for training and testing. As a result, the model learns to associate the input with its respective output label. There are several kinds of supervised learning algorithms –

2.3.1.1 Linear Regression

It is commonly used for dealing with continuous variables. This model tries to fit a line through the given data points by reducing the discrepancy between the predicted output and the actual values and optimising a cost function, typically mean-squared-error. Equation 2.1 describes its formula as follows:

$$y = \beta_0 + \beta_1 * x_1 + \beta_2 * x_2 + \cdots + \beta_n * x_n + \varepsilon \tag{2.1}$$

where y is the target variable referring to the prediction results, $\{x_1, x_2, \ldots, x_n\}$ are the independent variables that influence the target, and β_0 refers to the 'y'-intercept, i.e., the baseline value of the target when all the independent variables are zero. Furthermore, $\{\beta_1, \beta_2, \ldots, \beta_n\}$ in Equation 2.1 represent the coefficients or weights assigned to each independent variable. The higher the value of a particular coefficient, the greater the influence of its corresponding variable on the predicted outcome. In addition, an error term, ε is added to the equation to account for the variation in the target variable that is not caused by the independent variables, i.e., randomness and measurement errors.

Any error function can be used in place of 'ε' in Equation 2.1, depending on the requirements of the problem at hand. The mean-squared-error function, as described in Equation 2.2, is commonly used and it computes the Euclidean distance between the predicted and actual data points. It can be defined as below –

$$\varepsilon = (1/n) * \Sigma(y_i - \hat{v}_i)^2 \tag{2.2}$$

where, n represents the number of data points observed, y_i refers to the true value of the ith data point, and $\hat{y}_i$ is the value of the target variable predicted by Equation 2.1.

2.3.1.2 Logistic Regression

This type of regression is typically utilised for binary classification tasks (usually class 1 or 0). It is performed using the sigmoid function, which converts a numerical value into a number between 0 and 1. The formula is:

$$P(y = 1 \mid x) = 1/\left(1 + \exp\left(-(\beta_0 + \beta_1 * x_1 + \cdots + \beta_n * x_n)\right)\right) \tag{2.3}$$

Here, in Equation 2.3, the output represents the likelihood of the instance being in class = 1, which is typically the convention. The other notations have the same connotations as in linear regression above.

2.3.1.3 Support Vector Machines (SVMs)

This model is effective in high-dimensional spaces and can perform complex classification tasks. The optimisation problem in Support Vector Machine (SVM) involves finding the hyperplane that minimises classification errors while maintaining a maximum margin between the closest data points of different classes.

2.3.1.4 Decision Trees

Both classification and regression tasks can be performed by this model. It works by repeatedly dividing the dataset based on features that cause the most significant reduction in a measure of impurity (e.g., Gini Impurity or Information Gain). The tree structure is further updated by selecting the most relevant features to split at each node, ultimately classifying or predicting outputs based on the feature values.

2.3.1.5 Random Forests

This technique merges multiple decision trees to improve the accuracy and robustness of predictions, essentially an ensemble method. This aggregation of results allows it to reduce overfitting and variance compared to individual decision trees. Each tree is trained using a random sample of the data/features, with the final result being derived by averaging the predictions (regression tasks) or through a majority vote (classification tasks) from all the trees.

2.3.2 Unsupervised Learning

Unsupervised learning works with datasets where the target labels are unknown. It aims at identifying inherent structures or patterns in the data. This methodology is particularly useful for determining clusters, anomalies, or relationships between data points. Some techniques of implementing unsupervised learning are as follows -

2.3.2.1 K-Means Clustering

This algorithm uses similarity as a basis for partitioning data into '*K*' distinct clusters/groups. Initially, centroids for each cluster are chosen, and each data point is assigned to the closest centroid. The centroids are then recalculated as the average of all the points in their respective clusters. These iterations take place until the algorithm converges. The goal of *K*-means is to minimise the Euclidean distances (usually) between each data point and its corresponding cluster centre, as shown in Equation 2.4 –

$$J = \Sigma\,\Sigma\left\| x_i - \mu_k \right\|^2 \tag{2.4}$$

where J is the total sum of squared distances between each data point and its corresponding cluster centroid, μ_k represents the centroid of cluster k and x_i represents a data point in cluster k.

2.3.2.2 Density-Based Spatial Clustering of Applications with Noise (DBSCAN)

This model is also used for clustering however it doesn't need the number of clusters to operate. Instead – unlike *K*-means – it groups points based on the density of data points in the feature space. Density-based spatial clustering of applications with noise uses two key parameters:

- ε – the radius of the neighbourhood, i.e., the distance up to which points are considered for a specific cluster
- minPts – the minimum number of points necessary to form a cluster.

Density-based spatial clustering of applications with noise is particularly useful for identifying clusters of arbitrary shapes and detecting outliers in the data. It defines a cluster as a group of dense points that is specified by the above two parameters. Every cluster should have a "minPts" number of points within a radius of ε to be considered a cluster.

2.3.2.3 Principal Component Analysis (PCA)

Dimensionality reduction is its most widespread application, i.e., maintaining variance while converting from higher to lower dimensions in the data. By projecting the data onto the principal components (eigenvectors of the covariance matrix), Principal Component Analysis (PCA) reduces the number of features and simplifies complex datasets without losing critical information. The transformation formula is:

$$P_{\mathrm{nxk}} = Q_{\mathrm{nxd}} * M_{\mathrm{dxk}} \tag{2.5}$$

In Equation 2.5, Q_{nxd} represents the original data matrix where rows refer to the number of observations (n) and columns refer to the number of features (d). Matrix M_{dxk} contains the principal components – these are the eigenvectors derived from the covariance matrix of Q. Each column here represents the principal components (k) that are obtained after dimensionality reduction. P_{nxk} is the transformed matrix.

2.3.3 Semi-Supervised Learning

This utilises a combination of a small, labelled data with a large unlabelled data to train a model. This is especially useful when dealing with large datasets is expensive or impractical, but the available labelled data is still informative. Some approaches are:

2.3.3.1 Self-Training

In this approach, labelled data is initially used to train the model. Subsequently, it generates predictions for the unlabelled data, following which the most confident predictions are added as pseudo-labels to the training dataset. The model is then trained further with this expanded set, and this process is repeated iteratively.

2.3.3.2 Graph-Based Learning

This method leverages the structure of graphs to propagate labels across connected nodes. Each data point is represented as a node in a graph, and edges between nodes represent similarities. Labels from a small number of labelled nodes are propagated to the rest of the nodes using algorithms like label propagation, where each node's label is influenced by its neighbours.

2.3.4 Deep Learning

Deep learning involves neural networks and is particularly useful when dealing with unstructured data (text, audio, images, etc.).

2.3.4.1 Convolutional Neural Networks (CNNs)

While Convolutional Neural Networks (CNNs) are widely applied to use cases such as image classification and object detection, they can also be used for classifying different threats. They obtain local features, followed by pooling layers to downsample the feature maps. This architecture allows CNNs to learn automatically from raw data.

2.3.5 Supervised vs Unsupervised ML Methods

Both supervised and unsupervised methods have different strengths that can be used to detect threats. Supervised ML models use labelled datasets where every input has a corresponding output label. Hence, these models often work better with historical data where the threats are known and labelled. However, this also leads to limitations as these models struggle to work with unseen (and therefore unlabelled) threats. Furthermore, acquiring such extensive labelled data may be difficult and hence such models tend to be ineffective in situations where there are rare or evolving attack patterns. In addition, if the training data is not too diverse, overfitting may occur, where the model is unable to generalise and instead memorises specific attack patterns in the training dataset. On the other hand, supervised methods can detect known threats very well. Hence, they are useful for signature-based IDSs.

But in cases where there is limited knowledge of potential threats, unsupervised ML algorithms are more suitable for detecting such unseen threats. These algorithms typically try to detect attack patterns that differ from "normal" traffic flow, i.e., patterns that may differ significantly from historical training data. Another advantage of these methods is that they do not require labelled datasets and are therefore less expensive to train as compared to their supervised counterparts. However, these methods tend to produce higher false positives – since every deviation from normal traffic may not be a threat. Table 2.1 summarises the difference between the two.

2.4 Datasets for IDS Evaluation

The domain of cybersecurity is no stranger to applications of AI/ML, specifically harnessing their ability to iteratively learn and improve. In particular, for IDSs, they have proved to be extremely crucial in the detection of malware and attacks. ML-powered IDSs can be used to detect attack patterns on network infrastructure, analysing large amounts of traffic data, even without prior knowledge, enabling proactive and automated protection. To develop such robust AI systems, high-quality data is crucial [1]. The following section highlights some popular datasets that have been used to develop ML-based IDS solutions.

Table 2.1 The Difference between Supervised and Unsupervised ML Models for IDSs

Supervised ML Techniques	*Unsupervised ML Techniques*
This is not very well suited for detecting novel or unseen threats.	These methods are much better suited for detecting unseen threats.
Such methods often require large amounts of labelled training data.	Such methods work with unlabelled data.
These are very good at detecting known threats and hence have lower false positives.	These often suffer from a higher number of false-positive cases.
Since they work with labelled data, these can be easily customised to detect specific threats.	These are more suited for general-purpose threat detection.

2.4.1 An Overview of Some IDS Datasets

2.4.1.1 CIC-IDS 2017

One of the most widely used datasets for evaluating IDS, it contains a comprehensive collection of real-world network traffic data, comprising both normal and malicious activities. It includes a variety of attack types like Denial of Service (DoS), Distributed Denial of Service (DDoS), port scanning, brute force, etc., as it consists of over 2.8 million network flow records generated from traffic captured in controlled network environments [2]. Furthermore, this dataset is invaluable due to its high granularity, making it suitable for both supervised [4] and unsupervised models [3]. Additionally, exploratory data analysis has revealed important relationships between the target variables and the input [5]. However, despite including a wide range of attack types, this dataset is more focused on traditional IT networks and lacks specific IoT-based protocols, which may hinder its application for such IoT systems.

2.4.1.2 UNSW-NB15

This is another comprehensive dataset for the evaluation of ML-based IDS [6]. It was built to simulate network environments, comprising a wide range of attacks such as DoS, Probe, R2L (Remote to Local), U23 (User-to-Root) and many others, making the dataset highly effective for multiclass classification tasks. It consists of 2.5 million records with 49 features ranging from basic network features to more complex, time-based and flow statistics features. Further, it provides labelled attack types, which can be highly useful for supervised learning [7,8]. The UNSW-NB15 dataset is useful for general anomaly detection for IDS, however, it does not explicitly include IoT specific attack patterns or protocols like MQTT and CoAP.

2.4.1.3 KDD Cup 99

This dataset has served as one of the earliest datasets, forming a benchmark for many ML-based IDS. It contains a variety of attacks sourced from a simulated military network. Containing both binary and classification features, this dataset is apt for binary classification problems. However, newer datasets are increasingly preferred due to their relevance to contemporary threats. Its outdated nature makes it unsuitable for modern IoT networks [9].

2.4.1.4 CSE-CIC-IDS2018

This is an enhanced version of its earlier counterpart (CIC-IDS-2017) for the development and evaluation of IDSs [10]. It has been utilised in various studies to enhance the detection of cyber threats, including DoS attacks and rule generation automation for incident identification. Like the CIC-IDS2017 dataset, it consists of a comprehensive set of attack scenarios, capturing realistic traffic patterns with around 15 million network flow records, forming a rich dataset for training and testing purposes. As a study has shown, algorithms like Naïve Bayes and Random Forest implemented on CIC-IDS 2018 [11] have improved the accuracy of DoS attack detection. Similar to its earlier version, CIC-IDS2017, it also doesn't explicitly incorporate IoT protocols, however, its ability to handle numerous attack patterns and traffic types makes it suitable for IDS systems in IoT networks.

2.4.1.5 IoT-23

The IoT-23 dataset [12] is specifically tailored for IoT environments, as it contains both benign and malicious traffic data from IoT devices like cameras, hubs, etc. Further, it also incorporates IoT protocols like MQTT and CoAP. It contains a collection of 23 labelled IoT network traffic captures like DDoS, data exfiltration and botnet activities, making it useful for supervised anomaly detection and threat classification in such environments.

2.4.1.6 Bot-IoT

Developed by the Cyber Range Lab at UNSW, Canberra, the Bot-IoT dataset [13] consists of several different attack types specific to IoT. Further, its high volume and diversity of traffic make it suitable for training and testing IDS systems. Apart from normal traffic information, it also contains attack patterns for attacks such as DDoS, reconnaissance and information theft, making it suitable for general IoT attack detection.

2.5 AI in IDS for IoT

ML-based methodologies can analyse large data flows that are usually obtained from IoT devices, enabling improved functioning of IDSs and allowing for the identification and classification of potential intrusions with high accuracy.

2.5.1 Data Handling and Feature Engineering

To obtain accurate and reliable results, it is imperative that the data be subjected to preprocessing and appropriate feature extraction techniques. It is even more crucial for IoT-based data, since it tends to have noisy, redundant, and several irrelevant features [14]. Furthermore, class imbalance in the involved datasets is a persistent issue, hindering performance. As a research study has proposed, techniques like Synthetic Minority Oversampling Technique [15] can be employed to address such imbalance issues. In addition, effective feature selection methods can considerably improve model performance by focusing only on the most relevant attributes, enhancing computation efficiency as well as improving accuracy [16].

2.5.2 Implementation of ML Techniques in IDS

Some of the most popular implementations of ML models have been discussed below:

2.5.2.1 Supervised Learning

Such techniques are mainly used for known attack signatures, stable traffic and network behaviour, and for smaller IoT networks with limited computation resources.

2.5.2.1.1 Decision Trees

This supervised learning approach has been identified as one of the most efficient models with low overhead costs. This makes it suitable for deployment in IoT environments, which generally tend to have limited resources [17]. Further, combinations of the decision tree with other rule-based approaches to detect and classify attacks also yielded better results compared to other such methods [18]. Similar additions with other methodologies [19] like gradient boosting [20] have also resulted in enhanced performance.

2.5.2.1.2 Support Vector Machines (SVMs)

SVMs and their variations have shown promising results for identifying and classifying across different attack patterns. They have consistently achieved high accuracy values [21], especially while detecting IoT botnet attacks. Linear SVMs have also been used for designing lightweight IDSs [22,23]. These are especially useful for IoT networks with low-power devices, which require improved efficiency.

2.5.2.1.3 XGBoost

Similar to SVMs, XGBoost methods [24,25] have outperformed most other supervised ML techniques, achieving high accuracy values of 98.21% for botnet detection. Likewise, another implementation displays yet better performances with 98.95% accuracy [26], making this approach a versatile and efficient method for IoT networks.

2.5.2.1.4 K-Nearest Neighbour (KNN)

K-Nearest Neighbours have also displayed competitive results with respect to other supervised approaches; their performance remains moderate for IDSs in IoT environments. The simplicity of the algorithm can improve efficiency, but on the other hand, it may not detect attacks very well, as shown in a study where a K-Nearest Neighbour-based method resulted in an accuracy of 75.42% [25]. However, it has also shown improvements when combined with other neural network methods [27].

2.5.2.2 Unsupervised Learning

These techniques are predominantly used for anomaly detection in IDSs, i.e., when there is a lack of labelled data or when the traffic flow is too dynamic. Some implementations of the methods involved have been highlighted below.

2.5.2.2.1 Principal Component Analysis (PCA)

PCA is a popular technique that has been used for simplifying high-dimensional data and for feature extraction. It has mainly been used for preprocessing the data along with a variety of approaches like K-Nearest Neighbours, neural networks, etc. [28–30] and has achieved significant results in IoT-based IDS systems.

2.5.2.3 Deep Reinforcement Learning (DRL)

RL is a method that, in and of itself, tries to iteratively improve its reward function and obtain optimal accuracy in the process. This inherently makes it suitable for anomaly detection applications that can deal with unknown attack patterns and a dynamic network flow which is seen in real-time systems. These approaches have also shown results for complex IoT cyberattacks, making them suitable for more large-scale networks. While normal DRL methods are useful [31,32], their results can be boosted by using some optimisation methods. An experiment on the MedBIoT dataset [33] using parameter tuning has shown better results than supervised learning methods like Logistic Regression and Naïve Bayes.

2.5.2.4 Deep Learning Applications

Neural networks are another popular choice for implementing IDS, often achieving high accuracy. As a study [16] discussed, these ML techniques can analyse network traffic and identify anomalous patterns and threats, making the solution more robust and scalable. Furthermore, such solutions can adapt to the evolving cyber threat landscape, especially when deployed in IoT contexts. Similarly, another study showed that supervised learning techniques like Bayesian and unsupervised methods like micro-clustering had significantly improved performance results when deployed for monitoring cold-storage environments [34]. Further, another LSTM-based approach achieved an accuracy of 98.42% and a false-positive rate of 9.17% [35]. Hence, both shallow and deep learning ML methodologies have displayed improvements in anomaly detection, increasing the security for IoT devices [36].

2.5.3 Summary of Research Gaps

Modern IDSs that incorporate AI for threat detection and classification are a far leap from traditional, signature-based IDSs. This is especially true for IoT environments, which typically have limited processing power due to the usage of compact, low-power devices. However, AI models also face a variety of issues. For instance, it is imperative to train these models on quality datasets for effective results. Even so, issues like class imbalance occur in larger datasets, which can lead to wrong threat classifications. In addition, redundancy and high dimensionality in such datasets can lead to errors in prediction and increase the false-positive rate.

Apart from issues in datasets, scalability of the model also becomes an issue. This is because IoT environments are dynamic and can cause changes in the device behaviour. Therefore, managing and analysing the large traffic data in real time gets difficult. Further, models using CNNs and their variations often require high computational power, which is difficult to provide in IoT environments. However, even with lighter supervised models, overfitting becomes a risk and they struggle to adapt to unseen threats. Hence, all these factors affect the real-time performance of these models.

2.5.3.1 Managing Resource Constraints in IoT Environments

Managing IoT systems can be challenging, especially since they typically consist of compact, low-cost devices that run on limited processing power, memory and storage – for example, temperature or pressure sensors and LoRa communication nodes. In addition, these devices are often required to handle continuous real-time data streaming. Hence, it becomes necessary to optimise performance with such limited resources, particularly when deploying ML models in such systems.

Compared to other ML models, deep learning models are usually more computationally intensive because they often have a larger number of layers and require more data. As a result, deploying them in IoT environments may be inefficient and expensive. Furthermore, some IoT systems like autonomous systems require real-time decision-making, which is challenging due to resource constraints. In addition, transmission of such data to central server systems for model training or inference can increase communication overhead.

To address these challenges, lightweight ML models can be used or the complexity of the models used can be reduced through optimisation methods. Furthermore, decentralisation techniques such as edge computing or federated learning may be used to optimise resource usage. Edge computing involves performing computations at the edge devices (gateways or edge servers) and hence reduces the communication overhead. On the other hand, federated learning trains ML models on distributed devices to help reduce central processing loads.

2.6 Proposed System

The proposed methodology seeks to address the research gaps that are present in current solutions for IDSs in IoT environments. This study proposes a two-layered theoretical approach for detecting attack patterns in IoT network flow. It aims to improve efficiency for detection, especially in real-time systems by attempting to decentralise the load between edge devices and the cloud. It uses lightweight anomaly detection modules at the edge gateways to detect attack signatures in the incoming traffic flow while more complex attacks are handled at the cloud level. The cloud layer uses deep learning models to recognise whether the data sent to it corresponds to an attack or not and subsequently updates the edge nodes. This two-pronged approach not only reduces the latency of the system but is also able to handle unseen attacks. This process ensures that the heavier computation is offloaded to the cloud, thereby reducing congestion, improving scalability, and making it suitable for resource constrained IoT networks. The following section describes the architecture of the system in more detail.

2.6.1 Model Architecture

As mentioned previously, the model proposed consists of two main layers – one that operates on edge devices and gateways while the other works on the cloud. These can be implemented within the following structural framework, as described in the following subsections. Figure 2.2 further illustrates the workflow of this model.

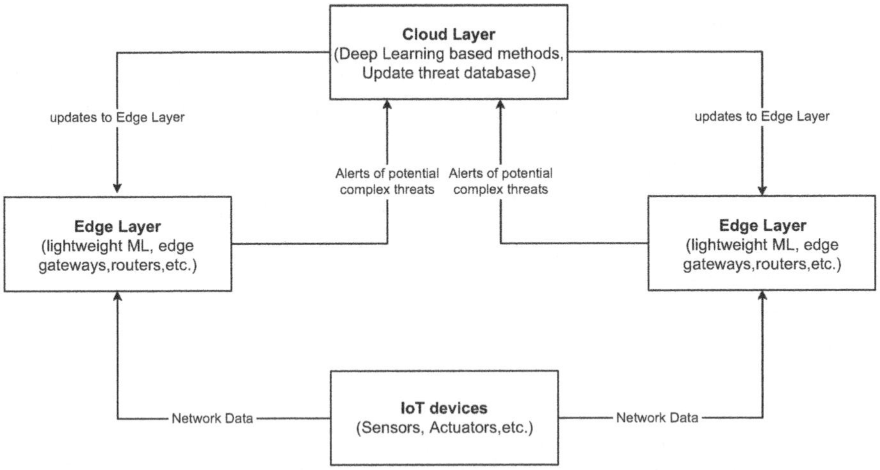

Figure 2.2 Workflow of the proposed model architecture for IDS in IoT networks.

2.6.1.1 IoT Devices

IoT devices like smart sensors, cameras, smart home devices, etc. make up the outermost layer of this model as these devices collect information from the environment and generate the network traffic. They continuously monitor network traffic and device behaviour, gather and log data such as packet flow, login attempts and unusual behaviours, i.e., network traffic flow that deviates from baseline behaviour. Such critical security data is transmitted to the edge-IDS nodes.

2.6.1.2 Edge IDS Layer

The edge layer mainly consists of gateways, routers, edge servers and some lightweight computation nodes. It is responsible for initial security analysis and filtering. The main functionality of this layer is to run lightweight anomaly detection ML models for more common threats which are not too complex. Therefore, as seen previously, supervised models like XGBoost, Decision Trees or SVM variations that have achieved high accuracies for real-time network traffic datasets would be suitable for this layer. These are highly effective, especially against known threats, and can operate without requiring cloud computation.

To further reduce complexity for high volumes of incoming traffic data, dimensionality can be reduced using techniques like PCA that have displayed improved results when used with such ML models. Further, this layer also sends alerts to the cloud IDS layer in case of more complicated or involved threats. Along the same vein, it also receives updates from the cloud layer to improve accuracy of such edge detection and expand its knowledge for diverse attacks.

2.6.1.3 Cloud IDS Layer

This layer comes into picture in cases where the edge layer sends an alert when it encounters an unseen or complex threat like zero-day attacks, DDoS campaigns, etc. To tackle such threats, the cloud layer implements deep learning methods like CNNs, LSTMs, Transformers, Autoencoders, etc. to identify and subsequently classify the threat. Alternatively, DRL approaches could also be used to get iterative improvements in threat detection and classification for completely unseen threats. Once the attack type has been identified, the model used in the layer updates the attack signature database with the corresponding attack pattern and anomaly profile. Further, it also takes actions to log the details of the attack for further reviewing as well as updates the edge nodes to strengthen its detection policies. This allows the IDS to continuously learn and adapt to newer threats while reducing dependency on cloud computation. The cloud layer further ensures that all the heavy computation is kept outside the IoT network, which helps in decentralising and reducing its load, making it especially suitable for networks with low-power devices.

2.6.2 Comparison with Contemporary Models

Traditional IDS systems have not only struggled to adapt to evolving threats but also tend to be computationally intensive. As a result, deploying such systems in IoT environments is not feasible as such networks typically operate on limited resources. Further, these issues lead to high latency, which can cause delays in threat response.

On the other hand, while AI-based models have been developed to counter such issues and have significantly enhanced computational efficiency, gaps remain, especially when dealing with dynamic IoT environments. While supervised learning-based models like SVMs, XGBoost, Decision Trees, etc. perform well, they struggle against complicated threats, for example, zero-day attacks. Apart from risks like overfitting, scalability also becomes an issue for some models, especially when dealing with larger datasets.

The proposed system aims to counter these issues by attempting to optimise computational efficiency using a combination of edge and cloud methods. Running lightweight anomaly detection models at the edge reduces latency and delays in threat response. Moreover, these modules are updated periodically to accommodate unseen threats. This is done by the cloud layer that uses deep learning models like CNNs or DRLs to process complex threats. Thus, it introduces a level of redundancy into the system, making it more robust against unknown attack patterns. In addition, this also helps reduce the processing load on the IoT network, making it suitable even for situations where computation resources are limited, while also making this IDS solution scalable.

2.7 Future Scope and Conclusions

2.7.1 Limitations and Future Scope

This study is limited to a theoretical proposed framework for improving IDS in IoT systems using a hybrid AI approach. It does not consider certain aspects of practical implementation like differences in IoT protocols used for communication and the impact they may have on the IDS. The future directions for this research can involve incorporating other strategies like federated learning, encryption or blockchain technologies to improve threat detection in IoT systems.

2.7.2 Conclusions

Current AI-based IDS models for IoT networks are a far leap from traditional techniques. Various types of methods involving amongst supervised, unsupervised, neural networks or deep learning models have been used to identify and classify threats. However, research gaps still exist in improving computation efficiency and scalability. In addition, datasets often face imbalance issues, leading to faulty models. The proposed framework works around these issues by following a hybrid approach that uses edge and cloud computation to reduce overhead and latency. As a result, it also reduces the load on the IoT network. Further, it also seeks to continuously learn and update itself in situations where it faces unseen threats. Therefore, this chapter highlights the importance of balancing computational efficiency with robustness and scalability for developing IDS in IoT systems.

References

1. Talukder, M. A., Islam, M. M., Uddin, M. A., Hasan, K. F., Sharmin, S., Alyami, S. A., & Moni, M. A. (2024). Machine learning-based network intrusion detection for big and imbalanced data using oversampling, stacking feature embedding and feature extraction. *Journal of Big Data, 11*(1). https://doi.org/10.1186/s40537-024-00886-w
2. *IDS 2017 | Datasets | Research | Canadian Institute for Cybersecurity | UNB.* (n.d.). [online] https://www.unb.ca/cic/datasets/ids-2017.html
3. Panigrahi, R., & Borah, S. (2018). A detailed analysis of CICIDS2017 dataset for designing Intrusion Detection Systems. *International Journal of Engineering & Technology, 7*, 479–482.
4. Panwar, S. S., Raiwani, Y. P., & Panwar, L. S. (2022). An intrusion detection model for CICIDS-2017 dataset using machine learning algorithms. *International Conference on Advances in Computing, Communication and Materials (ICACCM)*, 1–10. https://doi.org/10.1109/icaccm56405.2022.10009400
5. Oyelakin, A., Ameen, A. O., Ogundele, T. S., Salau-Ibrahim, T., Abdulrauf, U. T., Olufadi, H. I., Ajiboye, I. K., Muhammad-Thani, S., & Adeniji, I. A. (2023). Overview and exploratory analyses of CICIDS 2017 intrusion detection dataset. *Journal of Systems Engineering and Information Technology (JOSEIT), 2*(2), 45–52. https://doi.org/10.29207/joseit.v2i2.5411

6. *The UNSW-NB15 Dataset | UNSW Research.* (n.d.). [online] https://research.unsw.edu.au/projects/unsw-nb15-dataset
7. Pathak, M., Patel, A., & Shah, B. (2023). IoT intrusion detection: evaluating ML-based IDS on image and network traffic datasets. *2021 IEEE International Symposium on Smart Electronic Systems (iSES)*, 57–62. https://doi.org/10.1109/ises58672.2023.00023
8. Mali, A., Gala, A., & Waghmare, K. (2024). Impact of hybrid sampling on ML-based network intrusion detection systems. *2022 International Conference on Inventive Computation Technologies (ICICT).* https://doi.org/10.1109/icict60155.2024.10544951
9. Arief, M., Gunawan, M., Septiadi, A., Wibowo, M., Pragesjvara, V., Supriatna, K., Nugroho, A. S., Nugraha, I. G. B. B., & Supangkat, S. H. (2024). A novel framework for analyzing internet of things datasets for machine learning and deep learning-based intrusion detection systems. *IAES International Journal of Artificial Intelligence, 13*(2), 1574. https://doi.org/10.11591/ijai.v13.i2
10. *IDS 2018 | Datasets | Research | Canadian Institute for Cybersecurity | UNB.* (n.d.). [online] https://www.unb.ca/cic/datasets/ids-2018.html
11. Saleh, A. J. M., & Adnan, N. (2022). Denial-of-Service (DOS) threat detection using supervised machine learning algorithms on CICIDS2018 dataset. *In Lecture Notes in Networks and Systems* (pp. 519–533). https://doi.org/10.1007/978-981-19-2445-3_36
12. *IoT-23 Dataset: A labeled dataset of Malware and Benign IoT Traffic.* — Stratosphere IPS. (n.d.). Stratosphere IPS. [online] https://www.stratosphereips.org/datasets-iot23
13. *The Bot-IoT Dataset | UNSW Research.* (n.d.). [online] https://research.unsw.edu.au/projects/bot-iot-dataset
14. Mahanipour, A., & Khamfroush, H. (2024). Enhancing IoT Security: A novel feature engineering approach for ML-based intrusion detection Systems. *arXiv (Cornell University).* https://doi.org/10.48550/arxiv.2404.19114
15. Elshweikh, A. A., Maher, A. M., Hussein, M., & Elbayoumy, A. D. (2024). Intrusion detection system for IoT using machine learning. *2022 International Telecommunications Conference (ITC-Egypt)*, 326–331. https://doi.org/10.1109/itc-egypt61547.2024.10620546
16. Hinojosa, A., & Majd, N. E. (2024). Edge computing network intrusion detection system in IoT using deep learning. *2024 33rd International Conference on Computer Communications and Networks (ICCCN)*, 1–6. https://doi.org/10.1109/icccn61486.2024.10637611
17. AJain, A. K., Kumari, P., & Gupta, R. (2024). Intrusion detection and analysis in IoT devices using machine learning models. *In Advances in Computational Intelligence and Robotics Book Series* (pp. 384–409). https://doi.org/10.4018/979-8-3693-3860-5.ch012
18. Ferrag, M. A., Maglaras, L., Ahmim, A., Derdour, M., & Janicke, H. (2020). RDTIDS: Rules and decision tree-based intrusion detection system for Internet-of-Things networks. *Future Internet, 12*(3), 44. https://doi.org/10.3390/fi12030044
19. Taghavinejad, S. M., Taghavinejad, M., Shahmiri, L., Zavvar, M., & Zavvar, M. H. (2020). Intrusion detection in IoT-based smart grid using hybrid decision tree. *2020 6th International Conference on Web Research (ICWR)*, 152–156. https://doi.org/10.1109/icwr49608.2020.9122320
20. Douiba, M., Benkirane, S., Guezzaz, A., & Azrour, M. (2022). An improved anomaly detection model for IoT security using decision tree and gradient boosting. *The Journal of Supercomputing, 79*(3), 3392–3411. https://doi.org/10.1007/s11227-022-04783-y

21. Altulaihan, E., Almaiah, M. A., & Aljughaiman, A. (2024). Anomaly detection IDS for detecting DoS attacks in IoT networks based on machine learning algorithms. *Sensors, 24*(2):713. https://doi.org/10.3390/s24020713
22. Henda, N. B., Msolli, A., Haggui, I., Helali, A., & Maaref, H. (2024). Attack detection in IoT network using support vector machine and improved feature selection technique. *Journal of Network and Systems Management, 32*(4). https://doi.org/10.1007/s10922-024-09871-3
23. Azimjonov, J., & Kim, T. (2023). Designing accurate lightweight intrusion detection systems for IoT networks using fine-tuned linear SVM and feature selectors. *Computers & Security, 137*, 103598. https://doi.org/10.1016/j.cose.2023.103598
24. Öztürk-Birim, Ş., & Gündüz-Cüre, M. (2023). Cybersecurity for Internet of Things: Intrusion detection with machine learning and dimension reduction. *2022 Innovations in Intelligent Systems and Applications Conference (ASYU)*, 1–6. https://doi.org/10.1109/asyu58738.2023.10296825
25. Chen, Z., Li, Z., Huang, J., Liu, S., & Long, H. (2024). An effective method for anomaly detection in industrial Internet of Things using XGBoost and LSTM. *Scientific Reports, 14*. https://doi.org/10.1038/s41598-024-74822-6
26. Sharma, A., & Babbar, H. (2024). IoT security in the age of botnets: Supervised learning strategies for attack detection. *2024 4th Asian Conference on Innovation in Technology (ASIANCON)*, 1–5. https://doi.org/10.1109/asiancon62057.2024.10837985
27. A KNN-based intrusion detection system for enhanced anomaly detection in industrial IoT networks. (2024). *International Journal of Innovative Research in Technology and Science, 12*(6), 1–7. https://ijirts.org/index.php/ijirts/article/view/86
28. Zyad, E., & Mohammed, A. B. (2024). Evaluation of PCA variants for intrusion detection in IoT networks. *2024 Sixth International Conference on Intelligent Computing in Data Sciences (ICDS)*, Marrakech, Morocco, 1–5. https://doi.org/10.1109/icds62089.2024.10756370
29. Dash, S. K., Dash, S., Mahapatra, S., Mohanty, S. N., Khan, M. I., Medani, M., Abdullaev, S., & Gupta, M. (2024). Enhancing DDoS attack detection in IoT using PCA. *Egyptian Informatics Journal, 25*, 100450. https://doi.org/10.1016/j.eij.2024.100450
30. Mazid, A., Kirmani, S., & Abid, M. (2024). Enhanced intrusion detection framework for securing IoT network using principal component analysis and CNN. *Information Security Journal a Global Perspective*, 1–21. https://doi.org/10.1080/19393555.2024.2408256
31. Kaur, A. (2024). Intrusion detection approach for industrial Internet of Things traffic using deep recurrent reinforcement learning assisted federated learning. *IEEE Transactions on Artificial Intelligence*, 1–13. https://doi.org/10.1109/tai.2024.3443787
32. Mesadieu, F., Torre, D., & Chennamaneni, A. (2024). Leveraging deep reinforcement learning technique for intrusion detection in SCADA infrastructure. *IEEE Access, 12*, 63381–63399. https://doi.org/10.1109/access.2024.3390722
33. Raju, P. M., & Gupta, G. P. (2021). Intrusion detection framework using an improved deep reinforcement learning technique for IoT network. *In Advances in Intelligent Systems and Computing* (pp. 765–779). https://doi.org/10.1007/978-981-16-5301-8_54
34. Prasad, M., Pal, P., Tripathi, S., & Dahal, K. (2024). AI/ML driven intrusion detection framework for IoT enabled cold storage monitoring system. *Security and Privacy, 7*(5). https://doi.org/10.1002/spy2.400

35. Gueriani, A., Kheddar, H., & Mazari, A. C. (2024). Enhancing IoT security with CNN and LSTM-based intrusion detection systems. *arXiv (Cornell University).* https://doi.org/10.48550/arxiv.2405.18624
36. Genuario, F., Santoro, G., Giliberti, M., Bello, S., Zazzera, E., & Impedovo, D. (2024). Machine learning-based methodologies for cyber-attacks and network traffic monitoring: A review and insights. *Information, 15*(11), 741. https://doi.org/10.3390/info15110741

Chapter 3

Hardware Trojan Vulnerability in IoT End Devices—A Walkthrough

Sree Ranjani Rajendran and Hari Kalva

3.1 Introduction

Hardware security is a field often taken for granted in the greater scope of cybersecurity. It is often believed that threat models should be organized to account for attackers attempting to breach software, whether through software Trojans, worms, or the like. What most do not understand is that various vulnerabilities can be exploited on the physical end of cybersecurity that can be exploited for the hacker's gain, shattering this preconceived trust in hardware, which is so necessary. Hardware is often overlooked in systems, as most hackers will not bother with trying to tamper with a system physically. Although this is true, hardware exploits are incredibly difficult to remedy and unless caught early on in design, can render entire information systems vulnerable to a unique exploit. This potential for built-in breaches runs the gamut of virtually every critical industry, such as power in the form of oil or electricity, to the medical field, or even the military [1]. Breaches to systems in any of these fields are very much possible if not properly addressed. All of this is to say that hardware security is incredibly important and needs to be studied to ensure that malicious attacks targeting physical vulnerabilities in systems are kept to an absolute minimum. Proper software security is meaningless if a hardware exploit can render it null. Further on, we will be discussing topics in hardware security and common exploitation tactics to show what can be done to hardware systems and how to fight against them in the planning stages.

DOI: 10.1201/9781003587859-3

Hardware has become a defining aspect of the modern world. Devices are becoming more digital as time goes on, and with digital devices comes IC (integrated circuits). With technological advancements, nefarious actors want to exploit it in any way possible. That is where hardware security comes in. Hardware security is the practice of attacking vulnerabilities in an IC design or defending against such attacks. Hardware attacks are distinct from software attacks in that hardware attacks are physical. Attackers use many methods to damage devices. Although many devices can be susceptible to such attacks, we focus more on IC attacks and defenses. Digital trust has become one of the top concerns in the device industry. Consumers, enterprises, manufacturers, etc., prefer to avoid dealing with devices that easily share personal or confidential information. Hardware security is therefore very significant. Every industry has adversaries; no industry is more lucrative than digital devices. Think of a server that holds crypto wallet information. With poor security, an adversary can walk into the building, connect a USB device to the server and siphon off all of the data, or introduce a vulnerability during the IC design phase that will end up in the processing unit of the server that will give this nefarious actor lifetime access to the server. Hardware security is the first line of defense for devices that provide adversaries with access to all digital devices. This is regardless of any software defense. If the hardware is not secure, not much can be done to secure those devices.

Hardware threats are numerous. Starting with Intellectual Property (IP) piracy, an adversary steals a chip's design to develop competing chips without incurring the cost to research and develop that chip. IC (Integrated Chip) Piracy is stealing the chip by overbuilding or over-manufacturing it and selling it illegally for profit. IC counterfeiting can be described as the act of creating a chip of lower quality but passing it on as a more popular and higher-quality chip. This is for better sales. Hardware Trojans (HTs) are a form of hardware backdoor placed within the IC by an adversary, most likely during the IC design phase. A Trojan is placed that allows the adversary access to IC information long after production. IC reverse engineering is the process of dismantling a finished IC and reverse engineering it to replicate it for counterfeit purposes. HTs are malicious alterations to hardware [2]. They can be easily inserted into the IC design process, especially when third-party IPs are involved. These HTs can lie dormant during testing phases, only to become active when certain conditions are met. This causes unexpected and potentially harmful behavior. HTs are malicious modifications to electronic devices or Integrated Circuits (ICs) that are inserted postdesign by an entity other than the original designer. HTs also come in a time bomb variant that remains dormant for an undisclosed period before activating and affecting the IC's performance in various ways. HTs can also be classified as malicious modifications to a VLSI chip, unknown to the designer or user. It consists of two parts: a trigger and a payload. The trigger, which can be any logic function, activates the Trojan under certain conditions. The payload alters the chip's functionality when the Trojan is activated. Three key properties define a hardware Trojan:

- It subtly alters the chip's logical function, causing deviations from the correct output under specific inputs (activation vectors).
- It remains undetected during production tests, differentiating it from design errors.
- Unlike design errors, which are preserved during production tests, a Trojan is designed to be transparent to these tests.

Therefore, the Trojan's design must consider its function, the chip's function, and the production tests. This ensures the Trojan remains undetected while fulfilling its malicious purpose. There are many reasons hardware can be vulnerable. Reverse engineering is inherently difficult to defend because all an adversary needs is access to the completed IC and the proper machinery. The complexity of modern hardware has many advantages, but it also causes vital flaws, such as the difficulty of testing for security flaws. Having such a complex chip gives more opportunities for flaws during design. Unlike software, hardware is passed on to a variety of different manufacturing and design houses during chip building. An untrusted foundry could overbuild an IC and then sell them illegally or a design house could insert an HT into the design that remains stealthy throughout the IC's lifetime. Patching hardware flaws is also tricky; fixing a flaw becomes nearly impossible without releasing the next generation of components. In this chapter, we discuss hardware security challenges with Internet of Things (IoT) devices, precisely the hardware Trojan vulnerability and its countermeasures. We will examine the potential threats posed by HTs, which are malicious modifications to a device's hardware. We will also explore various strategies to detect and mitigate these threats, ensuring the integrity and reliability of IoT devices.

3.2 Internet of Things Devices: Security Challenges

The IoT is a vast, interconnected collection of physical devices connected to the internet, providing a wide range of applications for these devices [3]. These devices can be any number of things, such as wearable technology, vehicles, appliances, smart fashionwear, and many more. An array of sensors, actuators, and programmed software accompany these devices and allow for the collection and transmission of data over networks, allowing sensors to enable connected devices to perform actions, enable automation, and provide services based on the data collected and transmitted. To put it simply, IoT is the intersection of things, the internet, and data. However, IoT devices also pose security challenges due to the volume of data they process. These challenges can range from vulnerabilities within devices to network insecurity issues [4]. They pose many fronts that need countermeasures implemented to prevent threat actors from accessing and/or manipulating sensitive data.

3.2.1 IoT Core Component

IoT systems can be broken down into four core components: the devices (things) that contain sensors and actuators, communication/networking components, processing units, and interfaces. These components allow devices to connect to the internet and enable the services that they provide through the data that they collect. As we can see from Figure 3.1, components such as sensors and communication devices are placed closer to the top. In contrast, firmware and hardware platforms are placed near the bottom. This is to visualize the importance of these components in terms of overall impact on the system. Sensors can likely be replaced or modified to accommodate discovered vulnerabilities, while a more sophisticated and core component such as the hardware platform itself that comprises the literal bedrock of the system is incredibly costly to replace and potentially difficult to modify without impacting every system that relies on it. In other words, the impact of a cybersecurity attack increases as it progresses down this hierarchy triangle. The following subsections will look at the application of various solutions brought about by studying hardware security and how they help to ensure that malicious attacks are thwarted at the hardware level.

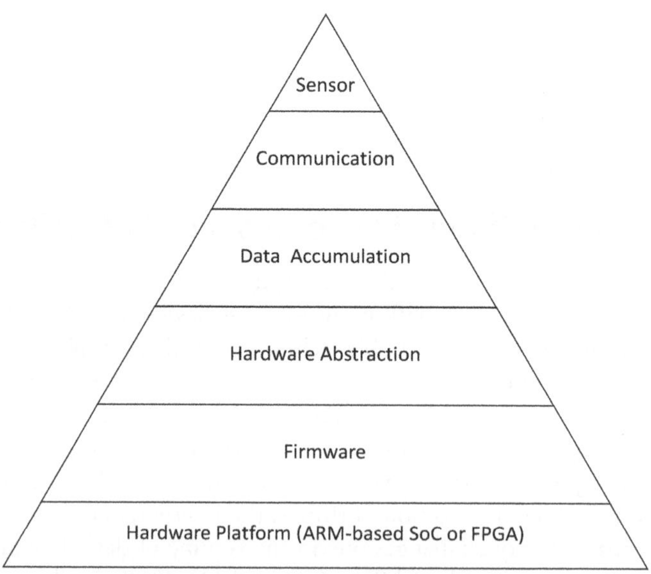

Figure 3.1 Hierarchy of hardware components and their level of threat to the system, from lowest threat at the top to highest threat near the bottom.

3.2.2 Applications of IoT

Integrated circuits are hardware components in IoT devices that control electrical functionality. They are responsible for powering IoT devices, storing memory, sending signals, regulating electricity flow within the device, and providing logic for how the device functions [5]. They even control the sensors and actuators that make IoT devices valuable today. For example, accelerometers are used to measure acceleration, GPS track's location, and gyroscopes are employed to track direction changes. To ensure these sensors and actuators work, virtually all IoT devices need integrated circuits [6]. By leveraging IoT, individuals and organizations can enable additional functionality and automation from the devices they interact with, whether it be directly or indirectly, on a day-to-day basis. Individuals and organizations can have different goals and utilize IoT devices differently. The way that these groups employ IoT devices is up to them and their needs, with the possibilities that IoT devices present expanding as technology and consumer demands progress [7].

For organizations, IoT can enable efficiencies that save time and money. For example, IoT devices can automate manufacturing processes. This allows a manufacturer to become more productive with lower labor costs due to devices working together to manufacture products. Another organizational application of IoT is asset and inventory management. IoT devices such as trackers, GPSs, and Radio-Frequency Identification (RFID) tags allow organizations to identify and locate their assets and inventory quickly and effectively [8]. Consumers often see examples of this application in the form of retail RFID tags that help track retail inventory and mitigate theft risk. Organizations also use IoT device systems for building management and security. One major goal for businesses is to improve how efficiently they operate, which usually translates into finding ways to reduce business expenses. Businesses often look to IoT device systems to accomplish this by implementing automated office-environment controls that adapt to business hours. For example, similar to the individual applications for IoT devices in homes, businesses can automate their lighting, heating/cooling, and machinery to be turned on during working hours. They can also revert to energy-saving modes during evenings and weekends, saving businesses money on operating costs. IoT devices are also implemented in building security systems, allowing for the deployment of smart camera systems with advanced detection technology, the utilization of smart access controls such as biometric and badge-related building access controls, and alarm systems to notify security teams of any intrusions or unusual activity on an organization's property [9].

3.3 Comprehensive Outline of Hardware Attributes and Threat Models

There are many examples of IoT devices that are either actively interacted with by users or passively collect data without user input. These devices typically automate processes, provide analysis, or improve efficiencies. Table 3.1 contains examples of common IoT devices used today, and how they function. Individuals and organizations deploy IoT assets. The expanding use of IoT assets will also pose increased security challenges for individuals and organizations, as threat actors look to take advantage of new and potentially unmitigated security vulnerabilities that they may present.

3.4 Security Challenges in IoT Devices

IoT cybersecurity domains can be broken down into three main categories: device security, network security, and data security. Device security, which this paper focuses on, deals with the physical hardware that makes up IoT devices [10]. Network and data security are focused on creating secure communications/networks and secure cloud storage environments respectively, to protect data while in transit and at rest.

IoT devices face many security threats, and that list only grows as IoT scales further [11]. Many cybersecurity firms analyze and report on the top threats and risks IoT faces [12]. For example, SentinelOne, a U.S. based cybersecurity firm, published its top 10 IoT security risks as of November 2024, outlining several vulnerabilities that IoT security risks stem from [13]. These risks are shared in other industry reports as well, and all include notable items such as:

- **Weak Identity and Access Management:** Identity and access management (IAM) plays an integral role in cybersecurity. IAM includes the systems and controls in place to verify who attempts to access certain devices and/or data. It also authenticates them to grant them specific permissions based on criteria such as their role in an organization [14]. A strong IAM system includes many layers of security controls. If these controls are not in place, attackers can exploit these vulnerabilities and gain access to devices and data that do not have these protections in place. Effective IAM is a challenge for many organizations to implement. However, it is necessary due to the level of risk associated with unauthorized access to IoT devices and their respective data.
- **Outdated Software/Firmware:** As IoT devices age, they may end up losing continuous support from their manufacturers to keep their software updated and current with the latest patches for security vulnerabilities [15]. Over time, hackers can discover these vulnerabilities in the devices and their software and

Table 3.1 Examples of Common IoT Devices

IoT Devices	*Function*
Security cameras	Combines a camera with motion detection and tracking technology, allowing the camera to turn on when the motion sensor detects movement and train the camera to follow that movement.
Smart watches	Wearables that have integrated sensors to detect activity, motion, and health data of the wearer.
Smart thermostat	Adjusts home temperature based on predefined schedules and user preferences.
Smart door lock	Provides keyless entry via PIN, fingerprint, or mobile app.
Vehicle safety sensors	Sensors in vehicles detect potentially dangerous situations and adjust/react them automatically, such as detecting potential crashes, slippery road conditions, and warning lights/alarms.
Smart doorbell	Combines a doorbell with a camera and intercom for remote control through an application.
Smart light bulb	Enables remote lighting control, dimming, and color changes via an application interface.
Voice assistant speakers	Speakers with integrated microphones monitor for verbal commands and perform actions based on those commands and user schedules.
Glucose monitors	Glucose monitor implants can continuously monitor glucose levels in diabetics, allowing for alerts when glucose levels are high/low.
GPS	GPS devices can connect to the internet to allow for updates and emergency communication.
RFID	RFID tags can identify individual devices, equipment, and inventory, allowing tracking of these assets.
Smart smoke detector	Detects smoke and carbon monoxide, sending alerts to mobile devices.

(*Continued*)

Table 3.1 (*Continued*) Examples of Common IoT Devices

IoT Devices	*Function*
Cell phones	Modern smartphones contain an array of sensors that collect user data and transmit it over the internet to enable personalized services.
Robots	Household robots, such as automated vacuum cleaners, can be controlled and send updates through a Wi-Fi connection.
Smart pet feeder	Dispenses food on a schedule or remotely via an app, and can send alerts when empty.

exploit them if manufacturers do not continuously provide security patches. Sometimes, this vulnerability may not arise because a manufacturer has completely abandoned updates for a particular product. Instead, the vulnerability could become an issue due to security patches not being pushed through software updates frequently enough. Managing updates across different devices running different versions of software is another challenge for organizations utilizing IoT devices as well, as it can be very resourceful and time-consuming to coordinate the updating of all of their IoT devices.

- **Unsecured Networks:** IoT devices must transmit data over networks to fully function as intended. Networks pose another security vulnerability for IoT devices, as unsecured networks, such as unencrypted Wi-Fi, can expose sensitive data to hackers attempting to obtain that information. Hackers can use a man-in-the-middle attack [16]. Using this method, a hacker can insert themselves into a network between a sender and receiver as a middleman. They will steal and/or alter the data they intercept over the network. They will then relay the data to the receiver as if the hacker were never there. Cybersecurity and cryptography methods and protocols are essential aspects of network security that prevent these events from occurring [17].
- **Lack of Continuous Security Monitoring:** Continuous monitoring of devices and networks plays an integral role in mitigating security risks in IoT devices. Logging and reviewing data collected and transmitted by IoT devices give security professionals the ability to detect and investigate security red flags in real-time [18,19]. Continuous monitoring does not always happen. Without the ability to monitor devices, data, and networks, hackers can acquire these IoT assets for prolonged periods. This can occur before an organization utilizing these devices realizes it is experiencing a security event.
- **Lack of Asset Management:** IT asset management is utilized by organizations to ensure that all of their IT assets, in this case IoT assets specifically, are tracked, monitored, and controlled. Many organizations manage their

IT assets through a configuration management database (CMDB) where they keep track of all of their endpoint devices. However, some organizations may only log specific devices, such as computers, phones, tablets, etc., and neglect to log things like devices that are part of an IoT ecosystem [20,21]. By failing to properly manage their IoT devices, organizations expose themselves to the risk of a security event occurring through one of these devices. Without logging IoT devices into a system such as a CMDB, organizations cannot properly monitor and control them, leading to instances of unauthorized access/use of these devices or hacking of these devices due to outdated software that has not been updated due to not being part of a device management system.

- **Lack of Physical Access Controls:** Physical security measures go hand-in-hand with IoT devices and cybersecurity measures to mitigate vulnerabilities. Unauthorized access is a major security challenge for IoT devices due to where and how they are deployed. If IoT devices are in public areas, areas with high traffic, or areas that are difficult to monitor, they have an increased risk of being tampered with. This enables hackers to intercept the data the devices are collecting and transmitting [22].
- **Hardware Backdoors and Trojan Horses:** Physical hardware within IoT devices can be modified at any point in the device's lifecycle. One of the most effective methods of altering device hardware that poses a notable security challenge for IoT devices is the creation of hardware backdoors. Several different types of backdoors can be used, but all are deployed to intercept data from IoT devices. A backdoor is a piece of hardware that is either altered within a device or implanted within the original device hardware [24,23]. It allows for unauthorized access to data collected by an IoT device. A vulnerability like this can even occur within a device's supply chain. This is where a backdoor is maliciously placed within a device during manufacturing that remains unnoticed. Sometimes, this vulnerability may come as a result of a design flaw within the device. This allows hackers to exploit faulty security controls within a device before discovery.

Several organizations publish their current outlooks on IoT security challenges and IoT state. These organizations analyze what challenges are currently being faced related to IoT. They also analyze how to tackle these challenges, and what emerging threats to look out for in the future. ISACA publishes reports [24] that discuss the threats they are seeing from an audit perspective and give recommendations on how to counter these threats. The concern about application security stems from the challenge of keeping IoT application software up to date. This ensures the devices contain the latest security patches to mitigate security risks, one of the most notable challenges in IoT devices security currently. There is also a concern about making sure endpoint devices are secure, as IoT endpoint devices pose a unique challenge in that they are typically very small and do not contain the processing capabilities to run many security control evaluations on them, making it challenging to ensure their security for cybersecurity professionals [24].

Palo Alto Networks, a U.S.-based cybersecurity firm, published a report on IoT security [25] that outlines some of the security challenges discussed in this paper. Palo Alto found that some of the biggest challenges faced by organizations who deploy IoT devices include IoT device inventory complexity, lack of ongoing monitoring, poorly designed and unsecured networks, and compliance challenges among several other things. They explain that the complexity of IoT device security issues is a challenge for organizations as there are many moving parts in play when considering IoT device systems holistically. Their recommendation is for organizations to not overlook the importance of investing in IoT security resources, such as security solutions, services, and employees to tackle the many challenges the space poses [25]. IoT Security Landscape [26] reported highlights the importance of IoT security for smart home devices. The report found that there are an immense number of attacks attempted on home devices and their networks. This is with an average of ten or more attacks experienced on a home network every 24 hours. This report illustrates that IoT device security is not just important for businesses, but individuals and their homes as well, as these networks pose just as many security challenges. A home has an average of 21 IoT devices within its network, so protecting the data collected and transmitted by these devices is paramount for personal security.

3.5 Countermeasures for IoT Device Security

Organizations can take several steps to address IoT device security challenges. Many of these measures overlap, creating a comprehensive security plan for IoT devices. This plan includes interconnected security measures that protect IoT devices and the data they collect and transmit. Here are examples of countermeasures IoT device users should implement based on industry research and recommendations:

- **Physical IoT Device Security:** Developing strong IoT device security countermeasures starts with protecting and controlling the physical access of the IoT devices themselves. Strong physical security and IAM practices are crucial for device security. This ensures that only authorized individuals can use certain devices and access specified levels of data. Many best practices exist in physical security, and many are outlined in industry-standard security frameworks. These best practices include:
  - Role-based access controls (also known as role-based provisioning) ensure that levels of data access are segregated depending on users and their predefined level of authorized access.

- Multi-factor uthentication to ensure that there are two levels of login security to authorize device and data access.
- Secure device storage to ensure that devices are protected from tampering when not in use.
- Hardware security such as Trusted Platform Module to ensure IoT hardware is secure and contains valid encryption keys.

■ **Network Security:** Data in transit poses a security risk to IoT devices as large amounts of data are collected and transmitted by these devices. To protect data sent over networks, several controls can be implemented to ensure that data in transit is safe from being intercepted and tampered with:

- Utilize secure protocols such as HTTPS, SSL/TLS, and SSH to ensure that data sent in transit to or from IoT devices over networks is secure and unable to be intercepted and tampered with.
- Utilize edge networks specifically for IoT devices. By segregating IoT devices onto a less critical network organizations can better protect themselves from security threats related to IoT device vulnerabilities by reducing their exposure.
- Continuous network monitoring can allow for cybersecurity analysts to log and detect threats on a network as they happen, increasing countermeasure response times in the event of an incident.

■ **Device and Software Management:** A robust asset management system will allow an organization to better manage IoT security risks. CMDBs provide an effective solution for organizations to account for and manage all devices in their IT inventory. An effective CMDB will give an overview of the status of all IT assets, including IoT assets, both in deployment and in retirement. This will ensure that every device is accounted for to mitigate security risks. Such solutions will also allow organizations to streamline device software update cycles. In addition, they will ensure that software updates containing security patches are pushed to IoT devices in a timely manner without overlooking any devices in their asset inventory.

■ **Risk Assessment:** Risk assessments are effective tools for identifying and evaluating risks. In the world of IoT, risk assessments can uncover potential security challenges an organization faces. This is based on their IoT asset profile and operations. Risk assessments are often performed by identifying all of the possible threats that could affect an organization's IoT assets and evaluating the level of risk those threats pose based on their likelihood of occurrence, level of impact if it occurs, and how well the risk is currently mitigated by the organization.

- Risk assessments can also serve as a prime opportunity for organizations to develop them.
- IoT asset inventory is also described above. Risk assessments in IT often include the development of an IT asset inventory, which should include

IoT assets. By identifying all of the assets within the organization, they can identify all of the threats and vulnerabilities associated with each asset, giving a thorough assessment of the level of risk the organization faces, organized by each asset, whether the asset is an individual device or the data it works with.

- **Security Frameworks:** Many industry-standard security frameworks exist, published by reputable governing bodies that outline what a solid security framework can look like for organizations, including how to manage IoT device security challenges. These frameworks give best practices and examples of how security controls can be implemented. Alongside these industry-standard security frameworks, many regulations exist that contain specific laws that organizations must abide by related to cybersecurity, and by extension, IoT devices. Laws such as the GLBA Safeguards Rule and the European Union (EU) General Data Protection Regulation (GDPR) outline minimum security standards that organizations must implement, many of which are covered by industry frameworks. Examples of these frameworks are:
  - **NIST:** The National Institute of Standards and Technology publishes multiple frameworks in the areas of IT, AI, and more, to provide guidelines to organizations that can aid them in managing their IoT risks through improving their ability to assess, prevent, and manage their security risks [27].
  - **SOC2:** The System and Organization Control framework is one of the top standards for assessing the level of security behind an organization's IT and IoT systems and services. In particular, SOC2 focuses on assessing cloud service providers. This is especially critical in the world of IoT as IoT devices often rely on cloud storage and cloud computing to function. Ensuring that the cloud environments that house the data captured by IoT devices are a critical step in managing the security challenges posed by IoT devices [28].
  - **ISO:** The International Organization for Standardization (ISO) publishes its standard for information security management that also applies to IoT devices and their security risks. Similar to other frameworks, ISO provides guidelines to organizations that help them manage current and emerging IoT risks and improve their overall security posture. Organizations can also become certified by ISO when they implement controls recommended by ISO. This gives them a form of credibility to use to market their company or products as secure and trustworthy to customers and their data [29].
- **Data Protection and Privacy:** Ensuring that data captured and transmitted by IoT devices is confidential is a critical part of managing IoT device security risks. Data should be encrypted and secured at all stages, including collection, in transit, during computation, and at rest. Advanced Encryption Standard and Rivest-Shamir-Adleman are two examples of encryption standards that

can protect IoT device data. These encryption standards use private or public key methods to secure data access. In addition, limiting access to the devices and systems that handle this data is another key part of protecting data from unauthorized use. On top of best practices, many regulations exist that outline several data protection and privacy compliance requirements that organizations must follow. Regulations such as Health Insurance Portability and Accountability Act (HIPAA), EU GDPR, GLBA Safeguards, and more require companies to take steps to safeguard customer data. They also require companies to implement many security controls found in industry security frameworks.

- **GLBA:** The GLBA Safeguards Rule, developed by the Federal Trade Commission, imposes several information security requirements on organizations, specifically financial institutions, in an attempt to implement minimum security standards across the industry and protect (safeguard) consumer information [30]. Examples of these requirements include:
    - Develop a written Information Security Plan that outlines the steps that the organization will take to safeguard consumer information.
    - Conduct, at least annually, risk assessments related to information security and cybersecurity, allowing for the organization to evaluate its current security standing by identifying possible threats and vulnerabilities and assessing itself on how well the organization mitigates the risk of these security events occurring.
    - Implement IAM controls to ensure that only authorized individuals can access devices and the data associated with those devices, including IoT devices and the data that they store and transmit.
    - Encrypt consumer information, whether it be at rest or in transit, to ensure that sensitive data is protected from tampering and interception.
- GDPR: The GDPR is a regulation enforced by the European Union (EU) for any organization conducting business within the EU (EU, 2024). Similar to other security regulations, the regulation imposes several requirements on organizations, such as:
    - Implement IAM controls, similar to other regulations and suggestions from frameworks, to protect device and data access.
    - Encrypt sensitive data both at rest and in transit.
    - Develop and maintain a security incident response plan to timely react to a security incident and prevent large-scale consumer data breaches.
- **HIPAA:** Health Insurance Portability and Accountability Act (HIPAA) is a well-known and very particular regulation in that it intends to protect the privacy and confidentiality of patient medical data and health records, while also guaranteeing healthcare coverage in specific situations, and reducing healthcare fraud, among other things [31]. The law includes

sections specifically related to cyber and information security that apply to any organization that handles medical and health information:

- Implement IAM controls to ensure that medical data is only accessed by approved individuals and not exposed to the general public.
- This data is often captured and stored by IoT devices. This emphasizes the security challenge IoT devices pose in sensitive and high-confidentiality settings, such as the healthcare sector. While these devices can be very beneficial to deploy in healthcare environments, extra care must be taken to mitigate the risk of data being breached. This is due to poor security measures associated with these devices and the networks that they connect to.
- Conduct risk assessments to account for all possible threats and vulnerabilities that HIPAA organizations may experience.
- Implement encryption protocols.
- Follow a data breach notification requirement to report data breaches to authorities within a specified time.

– Many compliance requirements overlap, emphasizing the importance of the controls recommended and required for organizations utilizing these devices. The risks and security challenges behind the use of these devices are understood, but implementing the controls necessary to effectively mitigate these challenges can be difficult, as many vulnerabilities must be accounted for, and new threats are constantly emerging as threat actors and hackers are constantly trying to find ways around current risk mitigation methodologies.

3.6 Application of AI and ML in IoT Device Security

IoT devices capture and transmit large amounts of data to functions. This data must be collected and stored, but also analyzed for IoT devices to perform the smart functions they are commonly associated with. Human decisions are often based on how they analyze and react to situations. This is dependent on the information they have obtained over time, and what they have learned from other situations in the past. AI and ML models work very similarly, especially in IoT. These models enable IoT devices, through pre-developed algorithms running computations on collected data, to automate the analysis of large amounts of data and quickly perform actions on that data. AI in IoT helps devices make decisions based on defined parameters to perform these automatic actions. For example, turning on a light when a motion detector detects movement in a room. ML models help devices learn and recognize patterns, allowing them to adapt to the information fed into these models [32]. For example, if an automated temperature system within a house learns through patterns that a person is usually absent from the house during certain days/times, then the ML model will enable the device to recognize this pattern and adjust the temperature setting in the house during these times to be more energy efficient. This concept can even be expanded to the municipal level. Municipalities may adjust power distribution to increase distribution in areas of high demand. AI and ML models allow these actions to be automated by learning and adapting to their environment at much larger scales than what a single human could do. This results in large efficiency gains when implemented at such a scale [33].

AI and ML models also pose security challenges within IoT devices as they are part of a system that processes large amounts of data. These models are often a target for cyberattacks due to the level of sensitive data flowing through them. This emphasizes the need for protections surrounding these models [34,35]. For example, AI that is integrated into systems to aid in workflows or provide answers based on prompts that include sensitive information can be exploited and attacked. This can lead to costly data breaches that must be promptly responded to. Additionally, AI models and bots can be used on the attacking end, where attackers can utilize their own AI bot models to attack mass amounts of systems and devices, and exploit potential vulnerabilities that may not have been addressed through security patches or other mitigation procedures. These bots represent large-scale attacks that must be accounted for and emphasize the need to deploy regular security patches across all of an organization's IoT assets to ensure that these mass attacks do not affect their IoT systems. Other notable threats are also apparent in AI and ML models, such as injection attacks where threat actors attempt to inject AI and ML models with faulty data and information in an attempt to deceive the models, resulting in them returning faulty query results.

3.7 Future Scope

The world of IoT is constantly evolving as connected devices become more ubiquitous in everyday life and within organizations and their operations. The world is becoming increasingly data driven. The expansion of IoT devices that enable this data to be captured and transmitted will be even more significant as their use grows. The proliferation of IoT devices is likely to lead to new security threats as hackers attempt to work around current security controls. They will be constantly trying to exploit upcoming vulnerabilities to access the vast amount of data handled by IoT devices and the networks they are connected to. The implementation of IoT device security controls will also grow to combat emerging security threats. Business Wire estimates the market for IoT security solutions to be over $32 billion in 2023. That number is expected to grow to over $112 billion by 2030 [36], representing a massive growth in investment for IoT device security.

Governments may also push for increased regulation of IoT security. Consumer protection represents a large challenge for governments worldwide, and protecting consumer data security and confidentiality will be a growing concern for governments. Even today, organizations must follow robust regulatory requirements to meet government security standards. However, these current regulations are expected to expand to include more language and requirements as security threats evolve. We can also expect to see entirely revised regulations proposed in an attempt to adapt regulatory requirements to future emerging security challenges. One challenge for organizations using IoT devices as they expand their device inventory will be effectively managing the volume of devices within their inventory. As mentioned before, asset management solutions such as CMDBs currently exist to do this, however, not all organizations utilize them to their fullest capacity and track all devices in their inventory and on their networks, leading to security gaps particularly with their IoT devices, which often get overlooked as IT assets that must be tracked and managed. The inventory of devices is only expected to grow as organizations look to take advantage of IoT devices' benefits. The study conducted by Keyfactor cited in their "State of IoT Security Report" emphasizes this, finding that over the past three years, organizations grew their IoT device usage by approximately 20%, and that is expected to continue as IoT becomes more commonplace and useful in growing amounts of applications [37].

3.8 Conclusion

IoT has allowed individuals and organizations to use technology to enhance their lives and operations. This is done by enabling automation through AI and ML models and achieving enhanced efficiency by allowing devices to work together to accomplish tasks. IoT utilization will only expand as the world becomes even more data driven. This is due to a demand for convenience and automation taking to the forefront to make lives and operations easier and more efficient. Many components make up IoT systems, including the components that exist to collect, transmit, compute, and store the data collected by the IoT endpoint devices themselves. Managing the risks these systems create is a primary concern for individuals and organizations. This is all aimed at protecting these devices and the sensitive data they capture. As IoT devices and systems expand, so will the growing security challenges that these devices will pose. Many notable and specific security challenges exist, such as weak IAM controls, issues with outdated software, unsecured networks, lack of continuous device monitoring, lack of asset management, lack of physical access controls, and hardware backdoors. Each challenge presents many different risks that must be managed to ensure IoT data is protected.

While IoT devices pose many security challenges, many countermeasures can be implemented to mitigate the risk of a security incident. Several organizations publish information and cybersecurity frameworks for IoT devices and their data. These frameworks give IoT device users useful information on how to create a robust IoT device security program. They outline the steps and best practices to counter these security challenges. By following these industry-standard frameworks, IoT users will be able to effectively manage the numerous risks that IoT devices pose, as the frameworks contain solutions to most of the security challenges mentioned earlier. Once implemented, IoT device users can be assured that their data is protected to the maximum extent of their ability. In addition, they can ensure that they comply with the many regulatory requirements for data protection and data privacy that exist, and that must be adhered to. However, just because security risks are mitigated does not mean they cannot occur or evolve. The world of IoT is constantly evolving and usage will continue to grow, causing security challenges alongside. IoT device users must maintain that they are staying up to date with the current state of IoT devices and security challenges. This is to ensure that they can tackle any emerging risks that may pose a security challenge to their data and devices.

Acknowledgment

The authors would like to express their sincere gratitude to Raymond Owens, and Max Schwartz for their valuable contributions to this chapter. This contribution is part of the CNT 6167 course. Their insights and expertise were invaluable.

References

1. Mukherjee, Rijoy, Sree R. Rajendran, and Rajat S. Chakraborty. "A comprehensive survey of physical and logic testing techniques for Hardware Trojan detection and prevention." *Journal of Cryptographic Engineering* 12.4 (2022): 495–522.
2. Sree Ranjani Rajendran, and Sree Ranjani Rajendran. "Malicious hardware detection and design for trust: An analysis." *Elektrotehniski Vestnik* 84.1/2 (2017): 7.
3. Carretero, Jesús, and J. Daniel Garcia. "The Internet of Things: Connecting the world." *Personal and Ubiquitous Computing* 18 (2014): 445–447.
4. Rajendran, Sree R. "Security challenges in hardware used for smart environments." In Internet of Things and Secure Smart Environments. Edited ByUttam Ghosh, Danda B Rawat, Raja Datta, Al-Sakib Khan Pathan. Chapman and Hall/CRC, New York, 2020. pp. 363–381.
5. Chen, Shanzhi, et al. "A vision of IoT: Applications, challenges, and opportunities with china perspective." *IEEE Internet of Things Journal* 1.4 (2014): 349–359.
6. Khanna, Abhishek, and Sanmeet Kaur. "Internet of Things (IoT), applications and challenges: A comprehensive review." *Wireless Personal Communications* 114 (2020): 1687–1762.
7. Lee, In, and Kyoochun Lee. "The Internet of Things (IoT): Applications, investments, and challenges for enterprises." *Business Horizons* 58.4 (2015): 431–440.
8. Suresh, Annamalai, et al. *Industrial IoT Application Architectures and Use Cases.* Auerbach Publications, 2020.

9. Malik, Praveen K., et al. "Industrial Internet of Things and its applications in industry 4.0: State of the art." *Computer Communications* 166 (2021): 125–139.
10. Chakraborty, Chinmay, Sree R. Rajendran, and Muhammad H. Rehman. *Security of Internet of Things Nodes*. Taylor & Francis Ltd, 2021.
11. Jing, Qi, et al. "Security of the Internet of Things: Perspectives and challenges." *Wireless Networks* 20 (2014): 2481–2501.
12. Feamster, Nick. "Mitigating the increasing risks of an insecure internet of things." *Colorado Technology Law Journal* 16 (2017): 87.
13. *Top 10 IoT Security Risks and How to Mitigate Them --- sentinelone.com*. https://www.sentinelone.com/cybersecurity-101/data-and-ai/iot-security-risks/, [Accessed 05-03-2025]
14. Mohammed, Kabiru H., Abubakar Hassan, and Danlami Y. Mohammed. "Identity and access management system: A web-based approach for an enterprise." *Path of Science*, (2018).
15. Gupta, Hemant, and Paul C. Van Oorschot. "Onboarding and software update architecture for IoT devices." *2019 17th International Conference on Privacy, Security and Trust (*PST*)*. Fredericton, NB, Canada. IEEE, 2019.
16. Bhushan, Bharat, Ganapati Sahoo, and Amit K. Rai. "Man-in-the-middle attack in wireless and computer networking—A review." *2017 3rd International Conference on Advances in Computing, Communication & Automation (ICACCA)*(Fall). Dehradun, India. IEEE, 2017.
17. Wheelus, Charles, and Xingquan Zhu. "IoT network security: Threats, risks, and a data-driven defense framework." *IoT* 1.2 (2020): 259–285.
18. Malin, Alex, and Graham V. Heule. "Continuous monitoring and cyber security for high performance computing." *Proceedings of the First Workshop on Changing Landscapes in HPC Security*. New York, USA. 2013.
19. Ismail, Umar M., Shareeful Islam, and Haralambos Mouratidis. "Cloud security audit for migration and continuous monitoring." 2015 IEEE Trustcom/BigDataSE/ISPA, Vol. 1. IEEE, 2015.
20. Vanier, D.J. Dana. "Why industry needs asset management tools." *Journal of Computing in Civil Engineering* 15.1 (2001): 35–43.
21. Schneider, Joachim, et al. "Asset management techniques." *International Journal of Electrical Power & Energy Systems* 28.9 (2006): 643–654.
22. Ye, Ning, et al. "An efficient authentication and access control scheme for perception layer of internet of things." *Applied Mathematics* & *Information Sciences* 8.4 (2014): 1–8.
23. Rajendran, Sree R., Rijoy Mukherjee, and Rajat S. Chakraborty. "Sok: Physical and logic testing techniques for hardware Trojan detection." *Proceedings of the 4th ACM Workshop on Attacks and Solutions in Hardware Security*. https://dl.acm.org/doi/proceedings/10.1145/3411504. 2020.
24. Polat, Gokhan, and Fadi Sodah. "Security issues in IoT: Challenges and countermeasures." *Isaca Journal* 1 (2019): 1–7.
25. *Leader in Cybersecurity Protection & Software for the Modern Enterprises --- start.paloaltonetworks.com*. https://start.paloaltonetworks.com/rs/531-OCS-018/images/2023-benchmark-report-on-iot- security.pdf, [Accessed 07-03-2025].
26. Schiller, Eryk, et al. "Landscape of IoT security." *Computer Science Review* 44 (2022): 100467.

27. *Internet of Things (IoT) --- nist.gov.* https://www.nist.gov/internet-things-iot, [Accessed 07-03-2025].
28. *SOC2®-SOC for Service Organizations: Trust Services Criteria --- aicpa-cima.com.* https://www.aicpa-cima.com/topic/audit-assurance/audit-and-assurance-greater-than-soc-2, [Accessed 07-03-2025].
29. *ISO/IEC* 30141:2024--- *iso.org.* https://www.iso.org/standard/88800.html, [Accessed 07-03-2025].
30. *Safeguards Rule --- ftc.gov.* https://www.ftc.gov/legal-library/browse/rules/safeguards-rule, [Accessed 07-03-2025].
31. Assistance, HIPAA Compliance. *Summary of the Hipaa Privacy Rule.* Office for Civil Rights, 2003.
32. Xiao, Liang, et al. "IoT security techniques based on machine learning: How do IoT devices use AI to enhance security?." *IEEE Signal Processing Magazine* 35.5 (2018): 41–49.
33. Wu, Hui, et al. "Research on artificial intelligence enhancing internet of things security: A survey." *IEEE Access* 8 (2020): 153826–153848.
34. Mazhar, Tehseen, et al. "Analysis of IoT security challenges and its solutions using artificial intelligence." *Brain Sciences* 13.4 (2023): 683.
35. Sarker, Iqbal H., et al. "Internet of things (IoT) security intelligence: A comprehensive overview, machine learning solutions and research directions." *Mobile Networks and Applications* 28.1 (2023): 296–312.
36. *Internet of Things (IoT) Security Strategic Market Report 2024: Expansion of Smart Cities, Use in Connected Vehicles, Innovations in Blockchain Fueling Opportunities - Global Forecast to 2030- ResearchAndMarkets.com---businesswire.com.* https://www.businesswire.com/news/home/20241125453140/en/Internet-of-Things-IoT-Security-Strategic-Market-Report-2024-Expansion-of-Smart-Cities-Use-in-Connected-Vehicles-Innovations-in-Blockchain-Fueling-Opportunities---Global-Forecast-to-2030---ResearchAndMarkets.com, [Accessed 07-03-2025].
37. *From Keyfactor's State of IoT Security Report: IoT Usage and Attacks Both on the Rise --- keyfactor.com.* https://www.keyfactor.com/blog/from-keyfactors-state-of-iot-security-report-iot-usage-and-attacks-both-on-the-rise/, [Accessed 07-03-2025].

Chapter 4

Securing the Internet of Things: Proactive Firewalls and the Challenges of Big Data

Sumit Kushwaha

4.1 Introduction

Human history has witnessed three major waves of quality-of-life changes: agriculture, industry, and information technology. Each wave changed the way things worked profoundly, causing a paradigm shift in most sectors. Now, the fourth wave is taking shape: the cyberage, where everything will be interlinked, satisfying the communication needs without much human intervention through IoT [1].

Internet of Things (IoT), for IEEE, is a complex adaptive network configured of things on the Internet, connected by a standard communications protocol [2]. These devices are programmable, uniquely identifiable, and have hearing and activation capabilities, as along with physical and virtual representations. The representation of IoT objects includes their identity, state, location, and privacy, social, or business information. IoT provides services to customers by capturing data, communicating, and operating sensors, with or without human intervention. Through intelligent interfaces, these services can be accessed anytime and anywhere to achieve security-related goals. These devices are increasingly used in areas such as smart city, smart building, smart transportation, environmental monitoring, and public health monitoring.

DOI: 10.1201/9781003587859-4

However, widespread IoT applications also bring significant security and privacy issues. For emerging IoT applications to reach their potential, the IoT ecosystem must be reliable and interconnected. In addition to the challenges faced by the Internet, wireless, and mobile, IoT also faces issues related to storage, privacy, authentication, and security management [3,4].

The IoT is a paradigmatic technological shift in a way that a vast group of devices and systems is subjected to interconnection with each other over the internet: the origin of smart technology. Examples include, but are not limited to, household or domestic gadgets, vehicles of different categories, industrial machines at various scales, wearable biometric sensors, and implants for even living things. IoT provides communication and data-sharing capabilities for such entities, enabling sophisticated monitoring, control, and automation with significant impact on health, agriculture, manufacturing, and transportation, among others. IoT devices are proliferating at a pace that has never been witnessed before [5]. Market analysis estimates that the number of connected devices will reach tens of billions within the next few years. This exponential growth is driven by the advancement of wireless technologies, reduction in sensor and hardware costs, and growing demand for automation and smart solutions from various industries. As these devices integrate more deeply into everyday life and industrial processes, they generate immense volumes of data, often referred to as Big Data [6].

Firewalls are one of the foundational components of network security designed to control the traffic passing between networks based on a given set of security rules. In the case of IoT, they help shield devices and data from all sorts of attacks from external sources. Traditional firewalls alone may not cope with such a complex and changing landscape that is IoT security. In such a scenario, this chapter highlights discussing the security challenges to be dealt with in applications and the ways proactive firewalls can deal with each one of them. Basically, analysis and insights on current and evolving threats—say, botnets or even targeted attacks—represent the importance of transitioning toward proactive security toward protection in the world of networks comprising IoT and huge volume emerging out from them. Besides that, strategies and approaches for implementing proactive firewall solutions are proposed further on in this chapter, aimed at improving the general context with regard to security of the IoT-related ecosystem [7,8].

This chapter presents an in-depth analysis of the security challenges associated with the IoT, particularly in the context of Big Data and interconnected smart devices, identifying key vulnerabilities and risks emerging from their rapid proliferation. It highlights the significance of firewalls in securing IoT networks, discussing traditional firewalls alongside emerging proactive firewall solutions designed to address evolving cyber threats. Advanced firewall technologies, including Artificial Intelligence (AI)-driven and software-defined firewalls, are explored as proactive security measures to mitigate cyber threats in IoT environments. Additionally, the chapter critically examines the intersection of Big Data and IoT security, emphasizing the importance of managing vast volumes of data while ensuring privacy and protection against cyber threats. Finally, strategic recommendations for improving IoT security through enhanced firewall mechanisms, security protocols, and regulatory measures are provided.

4.2 IoT Applications

IoT enables the remote monitoring and operation of objects and environments across the globe. The IoT encompasses a vast network of interconnected devices that communicate and share data to enhance various aspects of life and industry. Figure 4.1 provides a comprehensive overview of several key IoT applications, each contributing to the transformation of different sectors [9]. Each sector represents a specific domain where IoT technology is applied, including Mobile Phones [10], Heavy Machinery, Transportation, Healthcare [11], Home Automation, Smart Cities, Electronic Machines, Wearable Devices, Smart TVs, and Home Appliances [12].

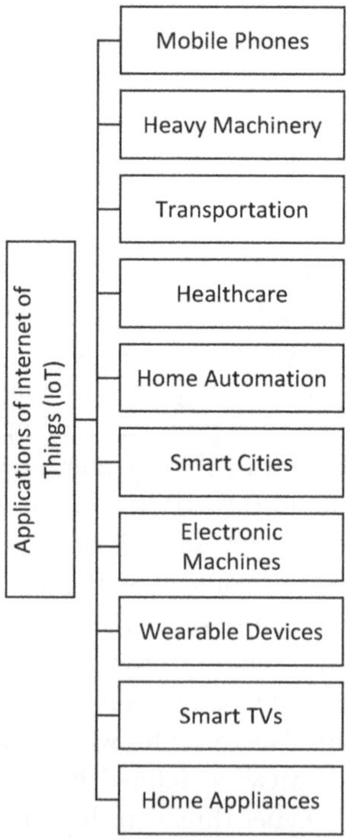

Figure 4.1 Applications of Internet of Things (IoT) [13].

4.2.1 Everyday Things

IoT integrates seamlessly into everyday objects, making them smarter and more efficient. Examples include smart clothing, connected kitchen appliances, and fitness trackers. These devices collect and transmit data to improve the user experience, optimize functionality, and provide personalized services.

4.2.2 Agriculture Automation

IoT applications in agriculture, often involving devices and sensors together with data analytics for enhanced farm-level decision-making, go under the catch-all heading of smart farming. The areas where most implementations have been done so far are:

a. **Precision Farming:** IoT sensors monitor soil conditions, weather, and crop health for data-driven insights to optimize planting, irrigation, and fertilization, with increased yields and lower consumption of resources.
b. **Livestock Monitoring:** IoT wearables monitor the health and activities of livestock, which enables farmers to check on health issues quickly to improve animal welfare.

4.2.3 Embedded Mobile

IoT in embedded mobile systems involves the addition of more functionality to portable devices, including connectivity and intelligence. Examples include:

a. **Smartphones and Tablets:** These are relatively well connected with other IoT devices for smooth control and automation of home and office environments.
b. **Wearable Technology:** Smartwatches and fitness trackers monitor a lot of information concerning individual health and activities that help in the insights for keeping good health.

4.2.4 Energy Consumption

IoT applications for energy management include the monitoring and optimization of energizing to improve efficiency since the cost of energy expenditure is minimized. Relevant examples include:

a. **Smart Meters:** These devices update energy consumption data moment-by-moment, thus developing in users the habit of managing efficient use and spotting opportunities for energy saving.
b. **Smart Grids:** IoT integrates renewable sources and enhances the reliability and efficiency of energy distribution networks.

4.2.5 Security and Surveillance

IoT enhances security and surveillance systems by providing real-time monitoring and intelligent analysis. Applications include:

a. **Smart Security Cameras:** These devices stream high-definition video, detect motion, and can recognize faces; hence, they increase the level of security for homes and businesses.
b. **Access Control Systems:** IoT-enabled locks and biometric systems allow controlled access to buildings and sensitive areas.

4.2.6 Smart Homes and Cities

IoT transforms a living space into a smart home or city by enhancing convenience, safety, and efficiency. Applications involve:

a. **Home Automation:** This includes smart thermostats, lighting, and appliances, which can be scheduled for operation, regulated, and controlled by means of a smartphone app to maximize energy.
b. **Urban Infrastructure:** IoT sensors enable smart cities to monitor and operate traffic, waste, and other environmental conditions, improving quality of life and sustainability.

4.2.7 Monitoring and Control of Pets, People, Vehicles, and Assets

IoT extends its applications to monitoring and controlling the location and condition of pets, people, vehicles, and assets. Examples include:

a. **GPS Trackers:** Location tracking in real time for pets, vehicles, and other valuables enhances security and recovery processes.
b. **Health Monitors:** The IoT wearable devices track the person's vital signs and the level of activity, thus remotely providing health monitoring and also giving emergency alerts.

4.2.8 Building Management

IoT systems for building management promote better operational efficiency and more comfortable occupancy. Applications include:

a. **HVAC Systems:** Smart systems of heating, ventilation, and air conditioning efficiently maintain a perfect indoor climate while minimizing the use of energy.

b. **Lighting Control:** IoT lights change in brightness and color based on room occupancy and available natural light. They aim to make the space where it is located more efficient and comfortable.

4.2.9 M2M Wireless Sensor Networks

There, M2M wireless sensor networking allows devices to communicate and share information among themselves almost autonomously. Major applications include:

a. **Industrial Automation:** Sensors and actuators in manufacturing help monitor and control the machines for better production and minimum downtime.
b. **Environmental Monitoring:** IoT sensors provide air and water quality, weather conditions, and other environmental parameters that help in research and policymaking.

4.3 Challenges in IoT Security

The rapid expansion of the IoT landscape has brought a wide range of security challenges and threats that target devices, platforms, operating systems, communication channels, and interconnected systems. In today's digital environment, various technologies are required for IoT devices and platforms to provide protection against physical tampering and cyberattacks, encrypt data transmissions, and handle emerging security concerns. Hence, IoT systems have become the latest target for cybercriminals. Protection of IoT ecosystems is ensured by guaranteeing that data, sensors, and interfaces are safe, confidential, and authentic. It is extremely important to ensure that, throughout the life cycle, security is guaranteed for the data. A number of security challenges have emerged because of the nature of interconnectivity, including the huge volumes of IoT devices that produce and transmit data, as depicted in Figure 4.2. The image highlights key security concerns that have to be addressed to allow the secure deployment of IoT systems [14–16].

4.3.1 No Physical Security

IoT devices are usually installed in remote or unattended areas and are thus very prone to physical tampering.

Unlike traditional IT systems, which are safely kept in a data center, IoT devices are exposed to environmental risks and malicious physical interactions. The lack of physical security can result in unauthorized access, manipulation of the device, and potential breaches of data.

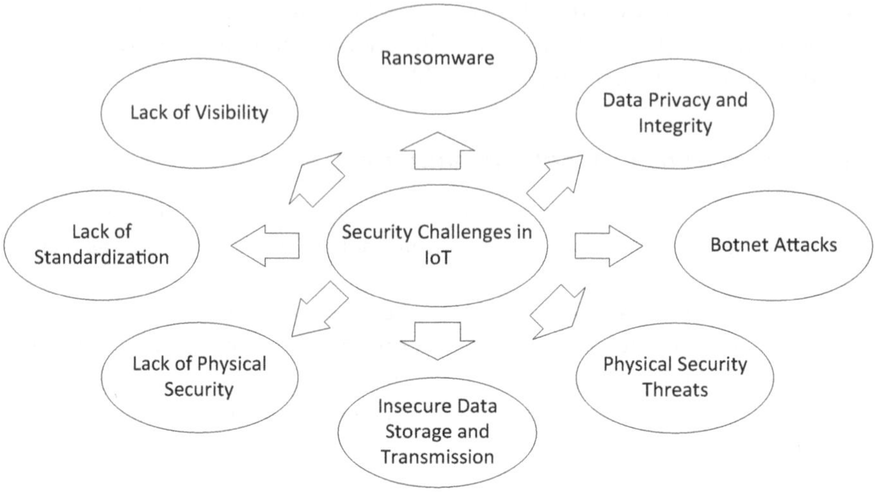

Figure 4.2 Security challenges in IoT [17].

4.3.2 Lack of Standardization

The fast proliferation of IoT has resulted in devices and systems developed by various manufacturers, each with its own unique protocols and standards, thereby providing very little interoperability between them. It further causes difficulties in the implementation of similar kinds of security measures across devices and platforms. Because of the deficiency in a proper standardization framework, comprehensive protection is hard to achieve, and hence, devices can be easily attacked.

4.3.3 Lack of Visibility

IoT networks often comprise a huge number of devices, which may be difficult to maintain visibility and control over all the endpoints. Without visibility, it would be hard to monitor and manage effectively, which delays the time taken to detect security incidents and reduces the ability to respond effectively. All devices need to be visible and monitored continuously to keep IoT systems secure and intact.

4.3.4 Data Privacy and Integrity

IoT devices collect and transmit tremendous volumes of sensitive information: personal data and critical details regarding operations. Protecting this data's privacy and integrity is a huge hurdle. Unauthorized access leads to breach of privacy and manipulation of data can have a catastrophic impact, as it could lead to wrong decisions as well as disruption of operations. Use of strong encryption, strict access control, and data integrity checks is therefore essential to secure the IoT data.

4.3.5 Physical Security Threats

In addition to physical security problems with the devices themselves, IoT systems have higher-level physical security problems as well. These include events such as natural disasters, vandalism, and theft, which can interfere with the functioning of the device and the integrity of the data. To defend the IoT infrastructure from such threats, strong physical security controls are required: secure housing, tamper-resistance, and high protection against the environment.

4.3.6 Insecure Data Storage and Transmission

IoT devices often have limited processing and storage capacity, so security practices for data storage and transmission can be inadequate. On insecure storage and communication channels, the attacker can make use of it to eavesdrop on or alter the data. It is essential to establish secure communication protocols (e.g., SSL/TLS) and to use secure storage solutions to protect data integrity and confidentiality.

4.3.7 Botnet Attacks

Botnets—a series of infected computers and devices that can be also operated remotely—can be used to carry out large-scale cyberattacks such as a Distributed Denial of Service attack. IoT devices are low-hanging fruit for botnet recruitment because of their often-poor security. Using vulnerabilities in IoT devices as an entry point to hijack a group of infected IoT devices and flooding their targets with traffic to disrupt their services or to leak valuable information. It can be contained using layered defense-in-depth and timely patching for botnet attacks.

4.3.8 Ransomware

With a ransomware attack, your data are encrypted or your devices are locked until a ransom is paid. IoT devices, especially those in critical infrastructure and healthcare, are attractive targets for ransomware attacks because they play crucial roles and their downtime can significantly impact organizations. To protect IoT systems from such attacks, they must be backed up thoroughly, security updates must take place as and when they become available, and users must learn not to let malware take root.

4.4 The Role of Firewalls in IoT Security

IoT network is one of the passing challenges of the explosion of IoT network. The Firewalls are one of the fundamentals of cyber threat defense in IoT environments. Firewalls act as gatekeepers, stopping and allowing data flows between the IoT devices and external networks. This part illustrates the significance of firewalls for the security of IoT systems [18–21].

4.4.1 Network Traffic Regulation

Firewalls are essential in controlling the traffic in and out of a network; they fall between a trusted internal network and an untrusted external network. Surface-level IoT firewalls filter traffic entering and leaving the device according to defined security rules. Firewalls can also check packet headers to allow legitimate traffic and filter out potentially malicious data. This has utility for IoT devices that are in general much more vulnerable due to their heterogeneous nature and limited security features, making such attacks impossible.

4.4.2 Intrusion Detection and Prevention

One of the feature sets of a traditional firewall that cannot be hidden is Intrusion Detection and Prevention Systems. They help to analyze network traffic by looking for potential threats that could indicate an ongoing attack. A well-designed firewall equipped with Intrusion Detection and Prevention Systems and located at the edge of the network can identify and respond to potential threats such as unusual data flows, unauthorized access attempts to the network, and devices at risk of public exploits, as not all IoT devices are built with hardened security functionalities or do not have an easy method for device updates in IoT ecosystems. Thus, it is an important protective mechanism against the compromise of IoT devices.

4.4.3 Segmentation and Isolation

As a security policy, the role of firewalls includes providing network segmentation and isolation, which facilitates security management of IoT devices. Separating network segments via firewalls helps to keep devices separate from sensitive and critical infrastructure to less-protected or higher-risk network segments. This reduces the attack surface and also helps to prevent lateral threat activity across the network. For example, firewalls can segregate healthcare IoT devices from administrative networks, so a breach in one part doesn't endanger the whole infrastructure.

4.4.4 Policy Enforcement and Access Control

Firewalls enforce security policies and limit access to IoT devices. To control access to share resources, Access Control Lists, and security policies that specify which devices/users can have access to which resources. These controls help firewalls to ensure that only the authorized source can communicate with IoT devices. Such things are especially relevant to industrial and critical infrastructure domains, where unauthorized access can result in impactful downtime or security incidents.

4.4.5 Data Privacy and Integrity

One important aspect of this paradigm is IoT security and, more specifically, the issue of protecting data privacy and integrity. Hence, firewalls are vital to ensure that data shared between the Internet of Things devices and external networks are secure. They can ensure that data is neither intercepted nor altered when it travels to the server by encrypting data transmissions and utilizing secure communication methods such as SSL/TLS, HTTPS, and VPNs. Firewalls protect data privacy and integrity, which confirms the reliability and credibility of IoT systems.

4.4.6 Defense against Botnet Attacks

IoT devices are commonly used for botnet attacks, where an army of circuited IoT devices is used to execute mass-scale cyberattacks, e.g., Distributed Denial of Service. Firewalls can prevent these attacks at the firewall level by detecting and blocking these traffic patterns associated with botnet activity. They can also block IoT devices from entering botnets, by identifying and blocking communications to popular command-and-control servers.

4.4.7 Logging and Monitoring

Taking this approach, it becomes apparent that network activity typically needs to be monitored and logged for security management through processes. Firewalls log the traffic passing through the network in detail and in real time. This ability is critical for detecting security events in IoT environments, monitoring traffic, and analyzing breaches. Firewalls generate logs, allowing forensic analysis to understand the nature and impact of security incidents, thereby improving overall defenses.

4.4.8 Adaptability and Scalability

The Ability to Adapt and Scale Security for Evolving IoT Ecosystems They need to be agile and scalable to accommodate growing traffic as well as integrate with other security solutions. They are capable of being modified with new security rules and signatures to defend against new threats. This flexibility protects IoT systems as they grow and additional devices are integrated.

4.5 The Need for Proactive Firewalls in IoT

Advanced proactive firewall solutions remain an urgent device, able to protect IoT environments. Conventional firewalls are mostly based on rule-based filtration, in which predefined rules are used to allow or deny traffic. Firewalls have performed well in traditional IT systems but have fallen short in combating the opening and varied character of IoT environments. Proactive firewalls, on the other hand, treat network security in a more flexible and smarter manner by responding to specific challenges confronted by IoT landscapes. Next-gen firewalls have evolved beyond standard networks with real-time anomaly detection based on machine learning (ML), behavior analysis to identify device-specific habits, and integration of threat intelligence to offer up-to-the-minute defenses. They address IoT-specific challenges like botnets and ransomware by isolating infected devices and blocking unauthorized behavior. Use cases include protecting smart home, healthcare IoT, and industrial IoT environments from breaches, ensuring communications are secure, and preventing network disruptions.

Proactive firewalls address these challenges by utilizing dynamic and intelligent threat detection, actively adapting to evolving threats as they occur. A few of the important features of proactive firewalls are [4,15,22]:

a. **Anomaly Detection:** Using ML and advanced analytics to detect abnormal patterns in network traffic that could signal possible threats.
b. **Behavioral Analysis:** Grasping the regular conduct of IoT gadgets and observing it to distinguish deviations demonstrating an evil activity.
c. **Threat Intelligence Integration:** Consumed external threat intelligence sources to stay informed about recent threats and vulnerabilities, allowing proactive measures against potential attacks.

4.6 Proposed Strategies for Implementing Proactive Firewalls in IoT

The step toward designing proactive type of firewalls within IoT involves the use of network mapping, dynamic attribute-based policies, ML/AI-based threat detection, segmentation for automation, portray a Zero Trust-based design, as well as continuous real-time monitoring in place. Scalability to support the proliferation of IoT devices, integration with existing infrastructure, and compatibility across varied devices are real-world hurdles. Regular audits, automated updates, and collaboration with security communities are essential to ensure their efficacy.

That is vital to secure the IoT ecosystems from the plethora of cyberattacks. Proactive firewalls are designed to actively prevent attacks before they take place rather than mouth passing threats. In this section, we describe strategies that can be effectively employed to deploy proactive firewalls in IoT systems, as depicted in Figure 4.3.

4.6.1 Comprehensive Network Mapping

One core concept for deploying proactive firewalls is to build out a complete network map. The architecture of the IoT network must be considered, which means knowing exactly which devices are connected, which messages are passed

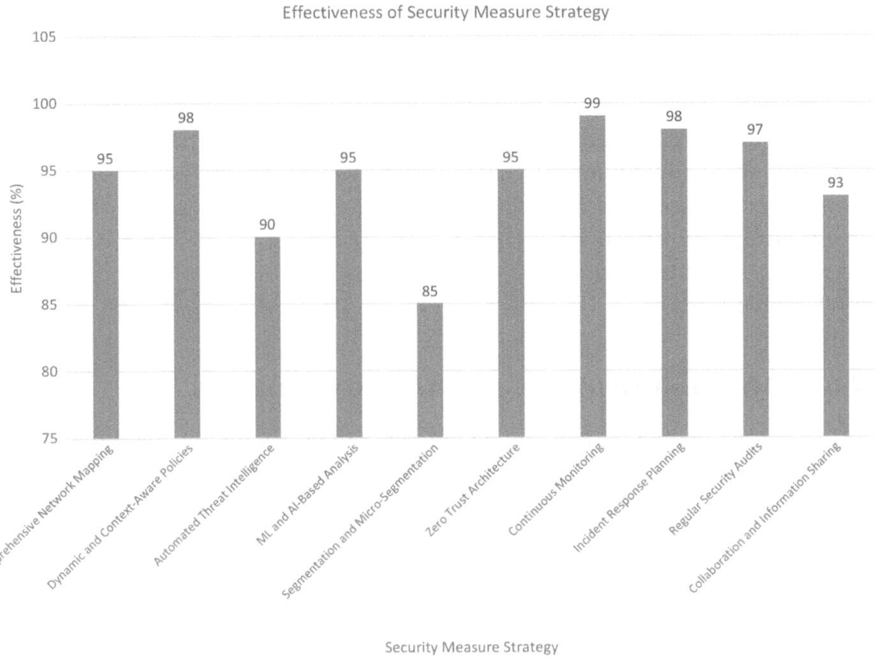

Figure 4.3 Effectiveness of strategies for implementing proactive firewalls in IoT.

between them, and what data is being used in the process. Mapping the network helps administrators to recognize the critical points that require protection and create firewall rules based on individual vulnerabilities. This way you can ensure that all the possible entry points and their communication channels are secured.

4.6.2 Dynamic and Context-Aware Policies

Proactive firewalls need to be based on dynamic and context-aware policies, adapting to the changing environment of networks and threats. A proactive firewall must implement dynamic and context-aware policies that continue to correlate with the changing environment of networks and related threats. Moreover, IoT environments are known to be dynamic in nature, which does not always go well with the static nature of the rules traditionally used. Such firewalls are capable of processing information about traffic flows, device behavior, and outside threat intelligence to change the rules in real time. This enhances detection and prevention of anomalies with fewer false alerts.

4.6.3 Automated Threat Intelligence Integration

Automated threat intelligence integration in firewalls enhances their proactive capabilities. Threat intelligence refers to the information on threats, vulnerabilities, and attack vectors at that moment. By integrating this data, firewalls can dynamically modify rules and signatures to mitigate known threats. Automated integration maintains an updated firewall against the evolving threat landscape, eliminating the need for manual updates and allowing faster responses to address emerging threats between the firewall and the threat intelligence feed.

4.6.4 Machine Learning and AI-Based Analysis

Enhancing firewalls with ML and AI for traffic analytics and uncovering threats. AI and ML algorithms can identify patterns and anomalies that may indicate a security breach by analyzing massive amounts of data all at once. Employing machine learning algorithms, these technologies can learn from past incidents to enhance their detection capabilities over time. By leveraging ML and AI, firewalls can better predict threats and preempt them before they happen.

4.6.5 Segmentation and Micro-Segmentation

Even in the IoT architecture, legacy solutions like network segmentation and micro-segmentation stand as important tenets to firewall efficiency. For instance, segmentation is the process of dividing the network into different segments to prevent the lateral movement by attackers. Micro-segmentation takes this a step further, creating much more fine-grained security zones, even for individual device or application. Firewalls enable you to govern access and monitor activity between each segment, thereby limiting the potential scope of a breach and hindering attackers seeking to traverse laterally within the network.

4.6.6 Zero Trust Architecture

IoT security can be improved with the application of Zero Trust Architecture. Zero Trust is built on the belief that threats exist and that no user or asset should be trusted by default, whether they are inside a network or outside it. Proactive firewalls in a Zero Trust framework securely verify and authenticate every device, user, and data flow at all times. One effective way to make application data secure is through the implementation of Zero Trust, which involves solid access policies and always keeping a watchful eye and continuously evaluating who is authorized and what actions are allowed.

4.6.7 Continuous Monitoring and Real-Time Alerts

We must constantly monitor the network traffic and device behavior to proactively detect possible threats. A proactive firewall must be accompanied by advanced monitoring solutions that can offer thorough and real-time monitoring of the network. Incident alerts and notifications introduce possibilities for security teams to respond to suspicious activities in real time. Monitoring it continuously also lets Red Teams identify behaviors that might suggest slow, stealthy attacks, including the ability to react early.

4.6.8 Incident Response Planning

Proactive firewalls need to be incorporated into a wider incident response plan. Preparation for potential security incidents requires establishing clear protocols for detection, response, and recovery. Firewalls can be an excellent asset in the detection stage as they are able to simply have a look at and block threats. Also, integrating firewalls with a workflow for incident response helps security teams assess the nature of the attack quickly to minimize the damage and return to business as usual. Incident response plans need regular testing and updating to stay fresh. Here, Table 4.1 shows the numerical data for the verification of the effectiveness of strategies for implementing proactive firewalls in IOT.

Table 4.1 Numerical Data for the Verification of the Effectiveness of Strategies for Implementing Proactive Firewalls in IoT

Security Measure Strategy	*Effectiveness (%)*
Comprehensive network mapping	95
Dynamic and context-aware policies	98
Automated threat intelligence	90
ML and AI-based analysis	95
Segmentation and micro-segmentation	85
Zero trust architecture	95
Continuous monitoring	99
Incident response planning	98
Regular security audits	97
Collaboration and information sharing	93

4.6.9 Regular Security Audits and Updates

To keep their promising efficiency, proactive firewalls require regular audits and updates. Security audits review the firewalls configuration and functionality, and help identify points of concern. Firewall software and rules should be regularly updated to protect against new threats. Review of security policy and security standards compliance should also be part of the audits to ensure that proactive measures are being implemented on a regular basis.

4.6.10 Collaboration and Information Sharing

Working with peer organizations and sharing threat information with security communities improves the proactive capabilities that firewalls have. Engage in information sharing and collaboration This involvement exposes organizations to emerging threats and effective methods for configuring firewalls. This collaboration supports the building of stronger security plans.

4.7 Conclusion

The IoT is a transformative technology that can play a significant role in everything, from agricultural automation and smart homes to security and surveillance. However, this rapid growth poses significant security challenges. From ransomware and botnet attacks, insecure storage of data and data in transit, physical security risks, lack of standardization, and data privacy issues, all of these challenges are present. Such threats need to be mitigated using sophisticated and preventive security tools. Our analysis highlights the importance of deploying proactive firewalls within IoT landscapes. It is important to note that while traditional firewalls remain necessary, they are insufficient against complex and evolving cyber threats. Proactive firewalls with real-time threat intelligence, ML, and AI capabilities are needed to neutralize these threats. This chapter discusses the yet we have given several approaches for proactive firewalls in IoT with Comprehensive Network Mapping (95%), Dynamic and Context-Aware Policies (98%), Automated Threat Intelligence (90%), ML and AI-Based Analysis (95%), Segmentation and Micro-Segmentation (85%), Zero Trust Architecture (95%), Continuous Monitoring (99%), Incident Response Planning (98%), Regular Security Audits (97%), Collaboration and Information Sharing (93%). By combining these strategies, organizations can create an effective security framework tailored to the specific risks of IoT devices. Organizations can safeguard their IoT landscape, by adopting these preventive steps to ensure the safe and reliable functioning of their connected equipment, both now and in the future. Ensuring proper measure set forth in this fashion for end-to-end secure use of IoT devices is essential to leverage the full power of IoT without the exposure of its threats.

The current research has several limitations, including a lack of empirical validation through real-world case studies or experimental data to support the effectiveness of the proposed proactive firewalls. Additionally, it does not deeply analyze the feasibility of implementing AI-driven security solutions on resource-constrained IoT devices with limited processing power and battery life. Scalability concerns are also present, as the study does not extensively discuss how these security measures would function in large-scale IoT ecosystems.

Funding Statement

This research work is not funded from any organization.

References

1. Device Authority, *Security and Privacy Issues in IoT Generated Big Data*, Available at: https://deviceauthority.com/security-and-privacy-issues-in-iot-generated-big-data/.
2. The IEEE Standards Association, *IEEE Standard*, Available at: https://standards.ieee.org/standard/.
3. Farooq, U., Tariq, N., Asim, M., Baker, T., & Al-Shamma'a, A., "Machine learning and the Internet of Things security: Solutions and open challenges," *Journal of Parallel and Distributed Computing*, vol. 162, pp. 89–104, 2022.
4. Singh, C. V. S. R., Vyas, N. K., Gupta, M., Kushwaha, S., & Prasanna, N. M. S., "Sending query data to mobile sinks at high speed in wireless sensor networks," *Proceedings of the Ninth International Conference on Science, Technology, Engineering and Mathematics (ICONSTEM)*, Chennai, India, 2024, pp. 1–5.
5. Kushwaha, S. V. A., Kumar, B. S., Singh, N., Prabagar, S., & Supriya, B. Y., "Efficient software vulnerability detection with minimal data size in 5G-IoT," *Proceedings of the IEEE International Conference on Emerging Research in Computing Science (ICERCS)*, Coimbatore, India, 2023, pp. 1–6.
6. Kumar, V., & Kushwaha, S., "Comparative study of map reduce task scheduling optimization techniques," *Proceedings of the IEEE International Conference on Evolutionary Algorithms and Soft Computing Techniques (EASCT)*, Bengaluru, India, 2023, pp. 1–7.
7. Liu, X., Xu, B., Zheng, K., & Zheng, H., "Throughput maximization of wireless-powered communication network with mobile access points," *IEEE Transactions on Wireless Communications*, vol. 22, no. 7, pp. 4401–4415, 2023.
8. Kushwaha, S., "AI based security for internet of transportation systems," *Proceedings of the IEEE 4th International Conference on Smart Electronics and Communication (ICOSEC 2023)*, Trichy, India, 2023, pp. 701–708.
9. Abed, K., & Anupam, A., "Review of security issues in Internet of Things and artificial intelligence-driven solutions," *Security and Privacy*, vol. 6, no. 3, p. e285, 2023.
10. Singh, S., Jayakumar, S., Venneti, K., Ponsudha, P., Kushwaha, S., & Kalpana, P. E., "Integrated project for data communication in wireless sensor network," *Proceedings of the IEEE International Conference on Advanced Computing and Communication Applications and Informatics (ACCAI)*, India, 2023, pp. 1–5.

11. Hemanand, M. N., Premalatha, G., Mavaluru, D., Vajpayee, A., Kushwaha, S., & Sahile, K., "Applications of intelligent model to analyze the green finance for environmental development in the context of artificial intelligence," *Computational Intelligence and Neuroscience*, pp. 1–8, 2022.
12. Sun, J., Hu, H., Wu, J., Wu, J., Yang, J., Sheng, Q. Z., et al., "A comprehensive survey on collaborative data-access enablers in the IIoT," *ACM Computing Surveys*, vol. 56, no. 2, pp. 1–37, 2023.
13. Jaxel, *IoT Applications*, Available at: https://jaxel.com/3-iot-applications-that-will-save-your-business-money/.
14. Alwahedi, F., Aldhaheri, A., Ferrag, M. A., Battah, A., & Tihanyi, N., "Machine learning techniques for IoT security: Current research and future vision with generative AI and large language models," *Internet of Things and Cyber-Physical Systems*, vol. 4, pp. 167–185, 2024.
15. Kushwaha, S., & Rai, A., "Mobile cloud computing: The future of cloud," *2024 OPJU International Technology Conference (OTCON) on Smart Computing for Innovation and Advancement in Industry 4.0*, Raigarh, India, pp. 1–6, 2024.
16. Javed, M., Tariq, N., Ashraf, M., Khan, F. A., Asim, M., & Imran, M., "Securing smart healthcare cyber-physical systems against blackhole and greyhole attacks using a blockchain-enabled Gini index framework," *Sensors*, vol. 23, no. 23, pp. 9372, 2023.
17. *IoT Security Challenges and Intrusion Detection Systems*, Available at: https://encyclopedia.pub/entry/52541.
18. Kaur, B., Dadkhah, S., Shoeleh, F., Neto, E. C. P., Xiong, P., Iqbal, S., Lamontagne, P., Ray, S., & Ghorbani, A. A., "Internet of things (IoT) security dataset evolution: Challenges and future directions," *Internet of Things*, 100780, 2023.
19. Peter, O., Pradhan, A., & Mbohwa, C., "Industrial internet of things (IIoT): Opportunities challenges and requirements in manufacturing businesses in emerging economies," *Procedia Computer Science*, vol. 217, pp. 856–865, 2023.
20. Safaei Yaraziz, M., Jalili, A., Gheisari, M., & Liu, Y., "Recent trends towards privacy-preservation in Internet of Things its challenges and future directions," *IET Circuits Devices and Systems*, vol. 17, no. 2, pp. 53–61, 2023.
21. Chen, J., Xiao, H., Zheng, Y., Hassan, M. M., Ianni, M., Guzzo, A., et al., "DKSM: A decentralized kerberos secure service-management protocol for Internet of Things," *Internet of Things*, 100871, 2023.
22. Chaudhary, P., Gupta, B. B., & Singh, A. K., "XSS Armor: Constructing XSS defensive framework for preserving big data privacy in internet-of-things (IoT) networks," *Journal of Circuits Systems and Computers*, vol. 31, no. 13, p. 2250222, 2022.

Chapter 5

The Human Firewall: Strengthening IoT Security through Behavior

Manivannan Karunakaran, Priyan Malarvizhi Kumar, Shanthi D, Suresh K, and Priyadharshini P

5.1 Introduction

Rapid progression in Internet of Things (IoT) has vastly altered the digital space; therefore, the connections of billions of devices, which lead to unprecedented automation, efficiency, and ease of convenience, are very fast. Some applications of IoT that go as far as intelligent homes, connected cars, industrial management systems, and medical devices form important elements of current living. On the other hand, security concerns arising in such complex, interdependent ecosystems gain importance due to increased usage of IoT. This chapter will delve into the most critical aspects of IoT security challenges and explore the, at times, neglected but necessary human factors that ensure robust security measures.

5.1.1 Overview of IoT and Its Transformative Impact

The IoT represents one of the most transformative technological breakthroughs of the 21st century, fundamentally changing the ways we live, work, and interact with our surroundings. IoT includes an extremely broad range of physical objects, cars, appliances, and other products that are embedded with sensors, software, and networking. These devices can communicate and share information on their own

DOI: 10.1201/9781003587859-5

through the internet, providing unprecedented levels of automation, efficiency, and creativity [1]. IoT is changing the world and bringing improvements in quality of life and economic growth, but such fast proliferation brings a big challenge to the domain of security.

5.1.2 What Is IoT?

IoT means an extensive series of devices and systems which gather, share, and process data with an internetwork. It encompasses all forms of commodities starting from the familiar consumer appliances such as smart thermostats, fitness trackers, and voice assistants, to highly complex industrial applications such as manufacturing, healthcare, transportation, and power grid management. What truly defines the IoT feature is that it must operate seamlessly and even work on its own. Features include things like monitoring and diagnostics used for predictive maintenance.

Key components of IoT include:

a. **Sensors and Actuators:** Devices that sense information from the environment—for example, temperature, humidity, and movement—and transform this information into actionable knowledge or instructions.
b. **Connectivity:** IoT devices can communicate in a seamless process of data transmission with several protocols, such as Wi-Fi, Bluetooth, Zigbee, and cellular networks.
c. **Edge and Cloud Computing:** IoT devices collect data that is further processed either on edge nodes locally or in the cloud, providing real-time analytics and data storage.
d. **User Interfaces:** This category includes applications or dashboards allowing users to interact with an IoT system, monitor performance metrics, and manage devices remotely.

5.1.3 Transformative Impact of IoT

5.1.3.1 Improving Everyday Existence

IoT is now the backbone of modern life, creating smarter and more efficient environments. For a home, IoT-enabled devices, including smart lights, thermostats, and security cameras, make life easier, energy efficient, and worry-free. Wearable IoT devices, such as fitness trackers and smartwatches allow individuals to track their health and fitness goals, making better lifestyle choices. IoT has also transformed urban living through smart city initiatives, integrating technologies such as traffic management, waste collection, and air-quality monitoring to improve overall quality of life. For instance, smart parking technologies allow car owners to locate available parking spaces in real time, thus reducing traffic congestion and saving time. Similarly, connected appliances such as refrigerators that automatically track their contents or washing machines that can be controlled remotely are changing the way homes operate.

5.1.4 Transforming Industries

IoT has deeply impacted industries, making them run more efficiently, reducing costs, and driving innovation. This transformation is evident in sectors such as manufacturing, healthcare, agriculture, and logistics.

Manufacturing: IoT drives Industry 4.0, enabling smart factories where sensors and connected machines optimize production lines, reduce downtime, and enhance quality control. Predictive maintenance helps foresee potential equipment failures, saving millions in repair costs.

Healthcare: IoT has transformed healthcare delivery through connected medical devices that monitor patients remotely, manage chronic conditions, and ensure timely interventions. For example, IoT-powered insulin pumps adjust dosages based on real-time glucose levels, while wearable Electrocardiogram (ECG) monitors provide continuous cardiac monitoring.

Agriculture: Smart farming solutions use IoT to monitor soil conditions, water usage, and crop health, helping farmers maximize yields while conserving resources. IoT-enabled drones can fly over large fields to identify areas needing attention.

Logistics and Supply Chain: IoT enables tracking of goods during transportation, monitoring storage conditions, and predicting delivery times. Smart tags using RFID ensure that perishable goods remain fresh, while route-optimization systems reduce fuel consumption and delivery times [2].

5.1.5 Driving Business Innovation

Businesses leverage IoT to develop new products, services, and revenue streams. Companies use IoT for personalized customer experiences, improved service delivery, and data-driven decision-making. For example, automobile manufacturers integrate IoT into vehicles, enabling autonomous driving, and real-time diagnostics. Hotels use IoT to personalize room settings for guests and offer seamless services.

5.1.6 Enabling Sustainability

IoT plays a crucial role in promoting sustainability by optimizing resource usage and reducing waste:

Energy Management: Smart grids monitor electricity utilization, balance supply and demand, and integrate renewable energy sources.

Water Conservation: IoT-enabled irrigation systems deliver water precisely where needed, reducing waste.

Waste Management: Smart bins optimize waste collection routes using real-time data to minimize fuel usage and carbon emissions.

5.1.7 Challenges and Threats

Despite its benefits, IoT presents significant security challenges. The large scale and heterogeneity of IoT ecosystems create complex networks that are difficult to monitor and secure. Many IoT devices collect sensitive information, raising privacy concerns and increasing the risk of data breaches. Additionally, technological advancements often outpace regulatory frameworks, leading to governance and accountability gaps. The most common vulnerabilities exploited by cyberattackers include default passwords, lack of encryption, and poor patch management.

5.1.8 Economic and Social Consequences

IoT is a major driver of economic growth, contributing to global Gross Domestic Product growth (GDP) through productivity gains, cost savings, and new market creation. The IoT market is projected to be worth trillions of dollars, fostering innovation and competition. Socially, IoT promotes inclusivity and accessibility, assisting individuals with disabilities through smart devices and enabling remote learning through connected platforms.

The future of IoT will be shaped by advancements in artificial intelligence, blockchain, and 5G technology:

AI: Enhances data processing and predictive analytics for autonomous decision-making.

Blockchain: Improves IoT security through transparent, tamper-proof transaction records.

5G Networks: Enables faster and more reliable IoT connectivity, unlocking new applications.

5.2 The Dual Challenge of IoT Security

Technological and Human Factors: The rapid growth of IoT has unlocked immense innovation but also introduced critical security vulnerabilities. Addressing these challenges requires both technological solutions and human awareness. While encryption, firewalls, and intrusion detection help secure IoT systems, their effectiveness depends on user behavior, adherence to security policies, and informed decision-making. Understanding and mitigating both technological and human factors are essential for the future security of IoT ecosystems [3].

5.2.1 Technological Challenges in IoT Security

The basic structure of IoT system architecture inherently makes them vulnerable to attacks that use advanced technologies. IoT ecosystems are incredibly heterogeneous, comprising a variety of devices, networks, and platforms. Such diversity results in stark differences in security capabilities and standardization. Many IoT devices are designed to be highly functional and cost-effective but lack robust security measures.

The IoT industry lacks a common security standard, leading to a fragmented ecosystem (Figure 5.1). Devices from different manufacturers may have varying levels of security, making it difficult to enforce uniform protective measures across an interconnected network. Additionally, a significant number of IoT devices are resource constrained, featuring low processing power, limited memory, and insufficient storage. This limitation hinders their ability to employ strong encryption or real-time threat detection mechanisms.

IoT devices are often shipped with default configurations or preset credentials, many of which users fail to change upon deployment. This includes weak passwords such as the notorious "admin." Moreover, IoT devices tend to remain in operation for extended periods without receiving necessary software updates or security patches, exposing them to evolving threats. Legacy devices, in particular, lack over-the-air update capabilities, further exacerbating security risks.

Most IoT devices utilize communication channels that are either unencrypted or inadequately secured, making it easier for attackers to intercept and manipulate sensitive data. Despite technological solutions such as firewalls, intrusion detection systems, and encryption protocols, their effectiveness is often limited by improper implementation and maintenance. As a result, human factors play a crucial role in IoT security, making them an integral part of the discussion.

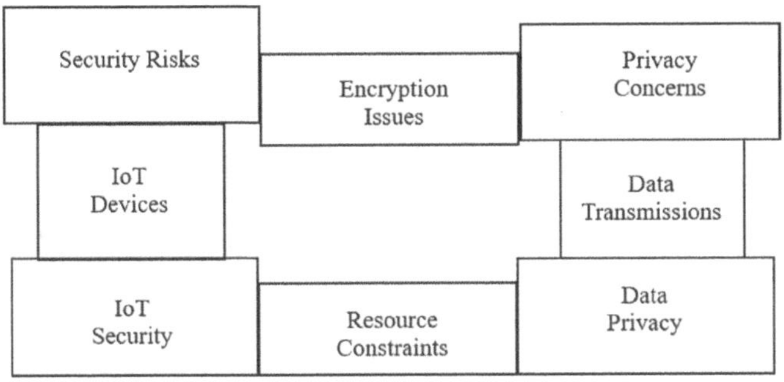

Figure 5.1 Dual challenge of IoT security.

5.3 Human Challenges in IoT Security

Human factors play a pivotal role in IoT security, as individuals often serve as both the first line of defense and the weakest link in a system [4]. Human errors, negligence, and a lack of cybersecurity awareness significantly increase the risk of breaches.

i. **Cognitive Biases and Risk Perception:**
   Many users underestimate the risks associated with IoT devices, believing that their devices are too insignificant to be targeted. This optimism bias can lead to complacency and poor security practices, such as using weak passwords or connecting devices to unsecured networks.
ii. **Prioritization of Convenience Over Security:**
   IoT devices are often marketed for their ease of use, encouraging users to prioritize convenience [5]. For instance, users may disable security features like multi-factor authentication (MFA) to simplify device access, inadvertently creating vulnerabilities.
iii. **Lack of Awareness and Training:**
   Many users, including both consumers and organizational staff, lack the knowledge needed to recognize and mitigate security risks. Phishing attacks [6], for example, remain a common entry point for attackers because individuals fail to identify malicious links or emails.
iv. **Neglect of Maintenance:**
   Human negligence in maintaining devices, such as failing to install updates or replace outdated systems leaves networks exposed to threats. Users often do not perceive the urgency of security updates or may lack the technical expertise to apply them.
v. **Over-Reliance on Manufacturers:**
   Many users assume that IoT device manufacturers are solely responsible for ensuring security. This misplaced trust can lead to unmonitored devices or a lack of proactive measures to safeguard systems.

5.3.1 Bridging the Gap

The interplay between technological and human factors creates a complex security landscape for IoT [7]. Technological solutions alone are insufficient if users fail to adopt secure behaviors, and human diligence cannot compensate for devices with inherent vulnerabilities. To bridge this gap, a dual approach is necessary:

- **Improving Technology:** Manufacturers must design devices with security as a priority, implementing features such as secure boot processes, encrypted communication, and automatic updates. Industry-wide standards and certifications can also help ensure consistent security levels.

- **Enhancing Human Awareness:** Education and training are essential to empower users with the knowledge to identify risks and adopt secure practices. Behavioral interventions, such as nudging techniques and gamified security training, can encourage better habits.

The dual challenge of IoT security lies in harmonizing advanced technological solutions with informed human actions. Only by addressing both dimensions can we create resilient systems that leverage the full potential of IoT without compromising security.

5.3.1.1 Understanding the Human Firewall

As IoT ecosystems expand, cybersecurity risks are increasing in both complexity and magnitude. While technological solutions such as firewalls, encryption, and intrusion detection systems form critical lines of defense, they are not foolproof. The human element remains central to cybersecurity, giving rise to the concept of the "human firewall." This section explores the definition and significance of the human firewall, its role in securing IoT ecosystems, and how it compares to traditional technological firewalls [8].

5.3.1.2 Definition and Significance in Cybersecurity

The term "human firewall" refers to individuals who actively participate in protecting digital systems by practicing secure behaviors, detecting threats, and following cybersecurity best practices. Unlike technological firewalls, which are software or hardware solutions that filter and block malicious activity, the human firewall is a behavioral construct. It emphasizes the human capacity to identify, prevent, and mitigate cyber risks through vigilance and informed decision-making.

The significance of the human firewall lies in its ability to address vulnerabilities that technology alone cannot. Even the most advanced security systems are susceptible to exploitation when human error comes into play. For instance, a phishing attack bypassing technical safeguards may succeed if a user unwittingly clicks a malicious link. Similarly, weak passwords, improper device configurations, or failure to install updates can undermine an entire IoT network [9].

A robust human firewall adds an extra layer of defense by making individuals aware of their responsibilities in cybersecurity. When properly educated and empowered, people can detect anomalies, question suspicious activities, and adhere to secure practices, effectively complementing technological measures.

5.3.1.3 The Role of Individuals in Securing IoT Ecosystems

IoT ecosystems present unique challenges that heighten the need for human involvement in security. Unlike traditional IT systems, IoT devices often have limited computational resources and are deployed in diverse environments, making them more vulnerable to attacks. Human vigilance and proactive engagement are critical in addressing these vulnerabilities.

i. **Strengthening Authentication Practices:**
   Weak authentication mechanisms are among the most common IoT security [10] flaws. Many devices ship with default credentials, which users fail to change, creating an easy entry point for attackers. Individuals play a vital role in strengthening authentication by:
   - Setting strong, unique passwords for each device.
   - Enabling MFA where possible.
   - Regularly updating passwords to prevent unauthorized access.
ii. **Maintaining Device Hygiene:**
   Just as regular maintenance ensures the optimal performance of machinery, maintaining IoT devices is essential for their security. Users must:
   - Install firmware updates and security patches as soon as they are released.
   - Decommission outdated devices that are no longer supported by manufacturers.
   - Periodically review and update device configurations to align with security best practices.
iii. **Network Security Awareness:**
   IoT devices rely on networks to function, and securing these networks is critical. Individuals must:
   - Avoid connecting devices to unsecured public networks.
   - Use dedicated IoT networks segregated from primary networks to limit the spread of breaches.
   - Regularly monitor network traffic for unusual activity that could indicate an attack.
iv. **Recognizing and Responding to Threats:**
   Cyberattacks often rely on exploiting human psychology through tactics like phishing or social engineering. The human firewall is vital in recognizing such threats by:
   - Identifying suspicious emails, links, or messages and avoiding interaction with them.
   - Reporting incidents to appropriate authorities or IT teams promptly.
   - Participating in regular cybersecurity awareness training to stay informed about evolving threats.
v. **Fostering a Security-First Culture:**
   In organizational settings, employees are key to promoting a culture of cybersecurity. By adhering to policies, sharing best practices, and supporting peer learning, individuals collectively contribute to the security of IoT ecosystems. A security-first mindset minimizes complacency and encourages proactive risk management.

5.3.2 Comparison between Human Firewalls and Technological Firewalls

While both human and technological firewalls aim to secure systems from cyber threats, they operate in fundamentally different ways. Understanding their distinctions and interplay highlights the importance of integrating the two approaches.

5.3.3 Complementary Roles

Human and technological firewalls are not mutually exclusive; instead, they complement each other to form a comprehensive defense strategy. Technological firewalls excel at handling automated tasks, such as filtering network traffic, detecting malware, and enforcing access controls in Table 5.1. However, they rely on correct configurations, regular updates, and proper usage—all of which require human intervention.

For example, a firewall might block unauthorized access attempts but cannot prevent a user from clicking a malicious link in an email. Similarly, while a firewall can monitor network traffic, it cannot enforce password hygiene or ensure timely firmware updates for IoT devices.

Table 5.1 Human Firewalls vs Technological Firewalls

Aspect	*Human Firewall*	*Technological Firewall*
Definition	Individuals practicing secure behaviors.	Software and hardware systems filtering traffic.
Primary Function	Detect and respond to social and behavioral threats.	Block malicious traffic and unauthorized access.
Adaptability	Highly adaptable through learning and awareness.	Limited to predefined rules and algorithms.
Strengths	Recognizing social engineering tactics, promoting proactive security practices.	Consistent, automated defense against known threats.
Weaknesses	Prone to fatigue, errors, and lack of training.	Vulnerable to novel attack vectors and configuration errors.
Interaction with IoT	Protects against phishing, misconfiguration, and weak credentials.	Shields networks and devices from malware and intrusion.

Conversely, the human firewall's strength lies in its ability to navigate unpredictable scenarios. Social engineering attacks, such as phishing or pretexting, often exploit human trust and decision-making rather than technical vulnerabilities. A well-trained individual can recognize these tactics, avoiding actions that could compromise the system.

5.3.4 Synergistic Strategies

To maximize the benefits of both human and technological firewalls, organizations and individuals must adopt synergistic strategies:

- **Education and Awareness:** Regular training ensures that individuals understand how to work alongside technological tools effectively.
- **Automation and Simplification:** Automating repetitive tasks, such as updates or monitoring, reduces the burden on humans and minimizes errors.
- **Feedback Loops:** Insights from human observations can inform firewall configurations, while technological systems can alert users to potential threats.

The concept of the human firewall extends beyond IoT into the broader cybersecurity landscape. As systems become more interconnected and threats grow more sophisticated, the human element will remain a critical factor in securing digital ecosystems. Empowering individuals to serve as active participants in cybersecurity not only enhances IoT security [8] but also fosters a culture of resilience and shared responsibility.

The human firewall is an indispensable component of IoT security, complementing technological defenses by addressing behavioral vulnerabilities. Individuals play a pivotal role in safeguarding IoT ecosystems through vigilant practices, proactive engagement, and a commitment to learning. While technological firewalls provide automated and consistent protection, they cannot fully account for the dynamic and unpredictable nature of human behavior. Together, human, and technological firewalls create a holistic approach to cybersecurity, ensuring the resilience and safety of IoT systems in an increasingly connected world.

5.4 The Challenges of IoT Security

The IoT has transformed how we interact with technology, connecting devices to create intelligent, efficient ecosystems. However, this interconnectivity has also significantly increased the attack surface, creating a host of security challenges. These challenges arise from the diverse nature of IoT ecosystems, the vulnerabilities inherent in IoT devices, and human behavior, which often exacerbates security risks. This section explores the complexities of IoT security, highlighting how behavioral factors influence security outcomes.

5.4.1 Diverse IoT Ecosystems and Attack Surfaces

IoT ecosystems vary widely, encompassing devices in smart homes, healthcare, industrial automation, agriculture, and transportation. Each of these ecosystems features unique configurations, networks, and functionalities. For example:

- **Consumer IoT:** Devices such as smart thermostats, voice assistants, and wearable health trackers prioritize user convenience but often lack robust security measures.
- **Industrial IoT (IIoT):** Machinery, sensors, and controllers in sectors like manufacturing and energy focus on operational efficiency, leaving security as an afterthought.
- **Healthcare IoT:** Devices like remote patient monitors and infusion pumps handle sensitive data, making them prime targets for attackers [11].

The diversity of IoT ecosystems poses a significant challenge to implementing standardized security measures. Attackers exploit these inconsistencies, targeting vulnerabilities in device firmware, communication protocols, and configurations. The interconnected nature of IoT means that a breach in one device can cascade across the ecosystem, affecting other devices and networks.

Moreover, the attack surface of IoT systems continues to expand as more devices connect to the internet. Each additional device introduces new entry points for attackers. For instance:

- A single compromised smart thermostat could provide access to a home's entire network.
- In industrial settings, a breached sensor could disrupt production processes or expose critical data.

This diversity and interconnectedness make securing IoT ecosystems a multifaceted challenge requiring both technological innovation and human vigilance.

5.4.2 Key Vulnerabilities in IoT Devices

IoT devices are often designed with functionality and cost efficiency in mind, leading to numerous security vulnerabilities:

- **Weak Authentication:**

  Many IoT devices ship with default credentials, such as "admin" or "password," which users often fail to change. Attackers frequently exploit these weak authentication mechanisms, gaining unauthorized access to devices.
- **Insufficient Encryption:**

  IoT devices often transmit sensitive data over networks, but not all devices use robust encryption protocols. Unsecured communication channels leave data vulnerable to interception and manipulation.

- **Lack of Updates and Patches:**
  Manufacturers often neglect to provide timely updates or patches for IoT devices, particularly after their market lifecycle ends. This exposes devices to known vulnerabilities that attackers can exploit.
- **Insecure Application Programming Interfaces (APIs):**
  Application Programming Interfaces that connect IoT devices to applications and cloud services are another common vulnerability. Poorly secured Application Programming Interfaces can serve as entry points for attackers to manipulate devices or exfiltrate data.
- **Physical Security Risks:**
  Many IoT devices are deployed in insecure environments, making them vulnerable to physical tampering or theft. For instance, an attacker could manipulate a surveillance camera or remove a sensor to access its data.

These vulnerabilities illustrate the inherent risks in IoT devices. While technological solutions such as encryption, secure boot mechanisms, and over-the-air updates can address some of these issues, human actions or inactions often amplify these risks.

5.4.3 The Impact of Human Errors on IoT Security

Human errors are among the most significant contributors to IoT security breaches. Even the most advanced technologies can be undermined by negligence, poor practices, or lack of awareness. Key examples include:

- **Weak Password Practices:**
  Users frequently choose weak or reused passwords, making devices easy targets for brute-force attacks. In some cases, users fail to change default passwords altogether.
- **Failure to Update Firmware:**
  Firmware updates are critical for patching vulnerabilities, but users often neglect them due to inconvenience or lack of understanding. Outdated devices remain vulnerable to attacks, even when fixes are available.
- **Connecting to Unsecured Networks:**
  IoT devices are often connected to public or unsecured Wi-Fi networks, exposing them to interception and unauthorized access.
- **Improper Device Configuration:**
  Misconfigured devices, such as those with open ports or excessive permissions, increase the risk of unauthorized access or data leakage.
- **Falling for Social Engineering:**
  Social engineering attacks, such as phishing, rely on human psychology rather than technical vulnerabilities. A user clicking on a malicious link or revealing credentials can compromise an entire network of IoT devices.

- **Neglecting Device Lifecycle Management:**
  When devices are no longer needed, failing to properly decommission them—such as by erasing data or disconnecting them from networks—can leave residual vulnerabilities.

These errors demonstrate that technological measures alone cannot secure IoT systems. Human behavior, awareness, and decision-making are equally crucial components of a comprehensive security strategy.

5.4.4 Behavioral Factors in IoT Security

Human behavior often influences the security of IoT ecosystems, both positively and negatively. Cognitive biases, habits, and psychological tendencies can impact decision-making, sometimes prioritizing convenience over security [12].

5.4.4.1 Cognitive Biases Affecting Security Decisions

Cognitive biases are mental shortcuts that influence how people perceive and respond to risks. In the context of IoT security, several biases can lead to poor decisions:

i. **Optimism Bias:**
   Many users believe that their devices are unlikely to be targeted by attackers. This false sense of security leads to complacency and risky behaviors, such as using weak passwords or ignoring security updates.
ii. **Availability Heuristic:**
   Users often base decisions on past experiences or recent events. For example, someone who has never experienced a cyberattack may underestimate its likelihood, leading to inadequate security measures.
iii. **Overconfidence Bias:**
   Some users overestimate their technical skills, assuming they can identify and address security risks without following best practices.
iv. **Normalcy Bias:**
   People tend to assume that things will continue as they always have. This bias may cause users to disregard emerging threats or fail to adapt to evolving security requirements.

Addressing these biases requires education and awareness campaigns that highlight the real risks of IoT security and the importance of proactive measures.

5.4.4.2 Habits Prioritizing Convenience Over Security

The design and marketing of IoT devices often emphasize ease of use, encouraging habits that prioritize convenience over security. Common examples include:

a. **Bypassing Security Features:**
   Users may disable security features such as MFA to simplify device access. While this reduces friction, it significantly increases risk.
b. **Reusing Passwords:**
   For convenience, users often reuse passwords across multiple devices and accounts. This creates a domino effect, where a breach in one system can compromise others.
c. **Avoiding Updates:**
   Firmware updates can be time-consuming and disruptive. Users may delay or skip updates altogether, leaving devices exposed to known vulnerabilities.
d. **Connecting to Public Networks:**
   To save on data costs or avoid configuring private networks, users often connect IoT devices to public Wi-Fi, exposing them to man-in-the-middle attacks.
e. **Neglecting Device Monitoring:**
   IoT devices often operate passively, leading users to adopt a "set it and forget it" mentality. Unmonitored devices are less likely to detect and respond to anomalies or attacks.

5.4.5 Overcoming Behavioral Challenges

To address these behavioral factors, IoT security strategies must align with human tendencies rather than working against them. For instance:

- **Simplifying Security Practices:** User-friendly authentication methods and automated updates reduce the burden on users and encourage compliance.
- **Education and Awareness:** Training programs can help users recognize the importance of security and adopt best practices.
- **Behavioral Nudges:** Techniques like password strength meters, periodic reminders, and gamified security tasks can motivate users to prioritize security without sacrificing convenience.

The challenges of IoT security are multifaceted, encompassing technological vulnerabilities and human behavior. While diverse ecosystems and device limitations create inherent risks, human errors and behavioral tendencies often exacerbate these issues. By understanding the cognitive and habitual factors influencing security decisions, organizations and individuals can adopt strategies that integrate technological solutions with human-centric approaches. Ultimately, addressing both technological and behavioral dimensions is essential for building resilient IoT ecosystems.

5.4.5.1 Building a Strong Human Firewall

The complexity of securing IoT ecosystems requires a multifaceted approach that integrates technology with human behavior. A strong human firewall refers to a collective force of individuals who actively contribute to cybersecurity through awareness, proper practices, and adherence to protocols. This section delves into strategies for building a robust human firewall by fostering security awareness, implementing training programs, and leveraging behavioral models. We also explore practical applications across consumer, industrial, and healthcare IoT ecosystems, demonstrating how individuals can strengthen IoT security.

5.4.5.2 Educating Users and Fostering Security Awareness

Education is the cornerstone of a strong human firewall. Many IoT security breaches stem from a lack of user awareness about threats, vulnerabilities, and best practices. Raising awareness empowers individuals to recognize risks and take proactive measures to protect IoT ecosystems.

Key Components of Security Awareness Campaigns:

1. **Highlighting Common Threats:** Users must understand the most prevalent IoT threats, such as phishing, weak passwords, and unsecured networks.
2. **Illustrating Consequences:** Demonstrating the potential repercussions of a security breach—such as data theft, financial loss, and compromised privacy—helps users grasp the importance of secure practices.
3. **Providing Actionable Tips:** Offering simple, actionable advice—like changing default passwords, enabling MFA, and keeping firmware up to date—empowers users to take immediate steps.
4. **Encouraging Reporting**: Users should feel comfortable reporting suspicious activities or vulnerabilities without fear of reprisal, creating a culture of vigilance.

Visual aids, such as infographics, videos, and real-world case studies, can make awareness programs more engaging and relatable. By framing security as a shared responsibility, organizations can motivate individuals to participate actively in safeguarding IoT ecosystems.

5.4.6 Training Programs for IoT Security Best Practices

Training programs tailored to the unique needs of different IoT environments play a critical role in strengthening the human firewall. These programs should be designed to address the knowledge gaps and behavioral tendencies of users, administrators, and developers [13].

Core Elements of Training Programs:

i. **Customization:** Training should be specific to the IoT context, whether for smart home users, factory employees, or healthcare staff.
ii. **Hands-On Learning:** Simulated exercises, such as phishing tests and device configuration drills, allow participants to practice identifying and mitigating threats.

iii. **Periodic Refreshers**: Regular updates ensure that users remain informed about emerging threats and evolving best practices.
iv. **Role-Based Content**: Developers, administrators, and end users require different types of training. For instance:
   a. **Developers**: Focus on secure coding practices and threat modeling.
   b. **Administrators**: Emphasize access control, device monitoring, and patch management.
   c. **End Users**: Highlight password hygiene, network security, and incident reporting.

Interactive elements like quizzes, role-playing scenarios, and peer discussions enhance engagement and retention. Training programs should be accessible to users of varying technical proficiency, ensuring inclusivity.

5.5 Designing User-Friendly Security Protocols

One of the most significant barriers to secure behavior is the complexity of existing security protocols. Designing user-friendly systems ensures that individuals can comply with security measures without undue frustration or inconvenience.

Principles of User-Centric Security Design:

a. **Simplified Authentication:** Replace cumbersome password systems with biometrics, MFA, or password managers to enhance security without adding friction.
b. **Automated Updates:** Enable automatic firmware and software updates to eliminate reliance on user initiative.
c. **Clear Alerts and Instructions:** Security warnings and prompts should be intuitive, providing clear guidance on corrective actions.
d. **Customizable Security Levels:** Allow users to adjust security settings based on their comfort level and risk tolerance, while providing default settings that prioritize safety.
e. **Seamless Integration:** Security measures should integrate naturally into device functionality, minimizing disruptions to user workflows.

By aligning security protocols with human behavior and preferences, organizations can encourage compliance and reduce the likelihood of security lapses.

5.5.1 Behavioral Models for Strengthening Security

Human behavior is at the heart of cybersecurity. Behavioral science provides valuable frameworks for understanding and influencing secure practices.

5.5.1.1 The COM-B Framework: Capability, Opportunity, and Motivation

The COM-B framework offers a structured approach to driving behavioral change in cybersecurity:

- **Capability:** Enhance users' knowledge and skills to enable secure actions. Training programs, detailed instructions, and technical support are key.
- **Opportunity:** Create an environment that supports secure behavior. For instance, restricting access to unsecured networks or providing tools like password managers removes barriers to security.
- **Motivation:** Encourage users to prioritize security through positive reinforcement, such as rewards for completing training or recognition for vigilance.

By addressing these three dimensions, organizations can create conditions that sustain secure behaviors over time.

5.5.1.2 Nudging and Gamification for Secure Behavior

Nudging and gamification are innovative approaches to promoting secure practices without coercion:

1. **Nudging:** Subtle interventions, such as password strength meters, reminders to update firmware, or alerts for suspicious activities, can guide users toward better decisions. Nudges work by making secure choices the default or more attractive option.
2. **Gamification:** Incorporating game-like elements into security tasks—such as earning badges for completing training or competing in cybersecurity challenges—can make learning engaging and motivate users to participate [14].

These strategies capitalize on human psychology, encouraging secure practices in a way that feels natural and rewarding.

5.5.1.3 Habit Formation in Cybersecurity Practices

Long-term security depends on ingraining secure behaviors as habits. Key strategies for habit formation include:

1. **Consistency:** Encourage users to perform secure actions, such as updating passwords or checking device logs, at regular intervals.

2. **Triggers**: Use reminders or prompts to initiate secure behaviors until they become automatic.
3. **Positive Reinforcement**: Reward users for adopting secure practices, reinforcing their commitment to cybersecurity.

By transforming secure behaviors into habits, individuals can contribute to IoT security without conscious effort, reducing the risk of human errors.

5.5.2 Practical Applications in IoT Ecosystems

The principles of building a human firewall can be applied across various IoT contexts, from consumer devices to industrial and healthcare settings.

5.5.2.1 Securing Consumer IoT: Smart Homes and Personal Devices

Smart home devices, such as voice assistants, smart thermostats, and wearable fitness trackers, are increasingly common but often lack robust security measures.

- **Awareness Campaigns:** Educate users about changing default passwords, enabling MFA, and segregating IoT devices on separate networks.
- **Simplified Security Tools:** Provide user-friendly apps for monitoring device activity and managing security settings.
- **Routine Checks:** Encourage users to periodically review device permissions, update firmware, and disconnect unused devices.

By empowering individuals to secure their personal devices, we can mitigate risks in consumer IoT ecosystems.

5.5.3 Industrial IoT (IIoT): Training and Access Control

Industrial environments rely on IoT for automation, efficiency, and monitoring, making them prime targets for attackers.

- **Employee Training:** Train factory workers and engineers to recognize phishing attempts, implement secure configurations, and respond to incidents.
- **Access Control:** Use role-based access controls to limit device and network permissions based on job responsibilities.
- **Regular Audits:** Conduct periodic security audits to identify vulnerabilities and ensure compliance with best practices.

Robust training and access control mechanisms are essential to securing IIoT ecosystems.

5.6 Healthcare IoT: Ensuring Security in Critical Environments

IoT devices in healthcare, such as remote patient monitors and infusion pumps, handle sensitive data and impact patient safety.

- **Staff Education:** Train healthcare workers to configure devices securely, recognize phishing attempts, and respond to potential breaches.
- **Authentication and Monitoring:** Implement strong authentication mechanisms and monitor device activity for anomalies.
- **Contingency Plans:** Develop protocols for addressing device failures or breaches, ensuring minimal disruption to patient care [15].

By focusing on training and robust security protocols, healthcare organizations can protect critical IoT infrastructure and patient data.

Building a strong human firewall requires a combination of education, training, user-friendly design, and behavioral interventions. By empowering individuals to act as the first line of defense, organizations can significantly enhance IoT security. Practical applications across consumer, industrial, and healthcare settings demonstrate the value of these strategies in mitigating risks and safeguarding connected ecosystems. The synergy between technological solutions and human behavior is essential for creating resilient IoT environments.

5.6.1 Measuring the Effectiveness of the Human Firewall

The concept of the human firewall is only as valuable as its implementation and its measurable outcomes. Building a robust human firewall involves not only fostering secure behaviors but also evaluating their effectiveness and continuously refining strategies. In this section, we discuss key performance indicators (KPIs) for assessing behavioral security, tools and platforms that enable monitoring, and the role of feedback mechanisms in driving continuous improvement. Additionally, we examine case studies of successful behavioral security implementations and draw lessons from IoT security failures to highlight critical insights.

5.6.2 Key Performance Indicators for Behavioral Security

Measuring the effectiveness of a human firewall requires specific metrics that evaluate awareness, compliance, and proactive behavior among individuals. KPIs for behavioral security must be comprehensive and tailored to the unique needs of IoT environments.

a. **Phishing Susceptibility Rate:**

    This metric measures how often users fall victim to simulated phishing attacks during awareness training exercises. A decline in susceptibility rates over time indicates improved user vigilance.

b. **Incident Reporting Rates:**
The frequency with which employees or end users report suspicious activities or potential vulnerabilities reflects their awareness and engagement in security practices.
c. **Password Hygiene Compliance:**
Metrics such as the percentage of users employing strong passwords, utilizing MFA, or changing passwords periodically provide insights into adherence to best practices.
d. **Update Adoption Rates:**
This KPI measures the percentage of users who promptly update IoT devices and software to the latest versions, mitigating vulnerabilities caused by outdated firmware.
e. **Response Time to Incidents:**
The speed at which individuals or teams respond to detected threats or incidents demonstrates the readiness and efficiency of the human firewall in action.
f. **Completion Rates for Training Programs:**
Tracking the percentage of users who complete cybersecurity training modules or simulations helps evaluate the reach and effectiveness of educational initiatives.
g. **Security Behavior Audit Scores:**
Periodic audits of user behavior, such as device configuration, network segregation, and adherence to security policies, offer a detailed view of overall compliance and risk levels.

By leveraging these KPIs, organizations can quantify the impact of their human firewall strategies and identify areas for improvement.

5.6.2.1 Tools and Platforms for Monitoring Security Awareness

A wide range of tools and platforms is available to monitor and evaluate the effectiveness of security awareness efforts. These tools help organizations measure behavioral outcomes, track progress, and ensure alignment with security goals.

a. **Security Awareness Training Platforms:**
Platforms like KnowBe4, Proofpoint Security Awareness Training, and CyberVista provide phishing simulations, training modules, and analytics to assess user awareness and improve behavior.
b. **Behavior Analytics Tools:**
Behavior analytics tools monitor user activities, such as access patterns, login attempts, and device usage, to identify deviations from normal behavior. Examples include Splunk and Exabeam.
c. **Incident Management Systems:**
Incident management platforms like ServiceNow and Jira Service Management allow organizations to log, track, and resolve reported security incidents while monitoring user participation.

d. **Password Management Solutions:**
Tools like LastPass and Dashlane not only facilitate secure password storage but also provide insights into password hygiene and compliance across user groups.
e. **Feedback and Survey Tools:**
Platforms like SurveyMonkey and Google Forms enable organizations to collect user feedback on training programs, identify knowledge gaps, and refine educational initiatives.

By integrating these tools into IoT ecosystems, organizations can establish a continuous monitoring framework that drives measurable improvements in security awareness and behavior.

5.6.2.2 Feedback Mechanisms and Continuous Improvement

Feedback is a critical component of building an effective human firewall. Regularly soliciting input from users and analyzing performance data helps organizations refine their strategies and adapt to evolving threats.

i. **Employee Feedback Loops:**
Conducting post-training surveys or focus group discussions provides valuable insights into user experiences, challenges, and suggestions for improvement.
ii. **Gamified Rewards and Recognition:**
Recognizing users who demonstrate exceptional vigilance, complete training modules, or report incidents fosters motivation and reinforces positive behavior.
iii. **Periodic Reviews and Updates:**
Regularly updating training content, security protocols, and tools based on user feedback and emerging threats ensures relevance and effectiveness.
iv. **Peer-Led Sessions:**
Encouraging users to share their security experiences or conduct peer-to-peer training sessions fosters a sense of community and shared responsibility.

A culture of continuous improvement ensures that the human firewall evolves alongside technological advancements and threat landscapes.

5.7 Case Studies and Real-World Insights

Examining real-world examples of behavioral security implementations provides valuable lessons and inspiration for strengthening the human firewall.

Success Stories of Behavioral Security Implementations

Case Study 1: A Global Manufacturing Company

A global manufacturing company implemented a comprehensive security awareness program targeting employees at all levels. The initiative included:

- Monthly phishing simulations with detailed feedback.
- Interactive training modules focused on IIoT security.
- Recognition programs for reporting incidents.

Outcome: The phishing susceptibility rate dropped from 25% to 5% within a year, and employees reported a 40% increase in identifying and mitigating potential threats.

Case Study 2: A Smart Home Device Manufacturer

A smart home device manufacturer introduced user-friendly security features, such as password strength meters and automated firmware updates, along with educational materials for consumers.

- Simplified MFA increased adoption by 70%.
- User engagement in educational campaigns rose by 50%.

Outcome: Customer-reported security incidents decreased significantly, and the brand's reputation for secure devices strengthened.

Lessons Learned from IoT Security Failures

Failure 1: The Mirai Botnet Attack

In 2016, the Mirai botnet exploited IoT devices with default credentials, causing widespread internet outages. Key lessons included:

- The importance of enforcing secure default settings.
- The need for user education on changing default passwords.
- The critical role of continuous device monitoring to detect anomalies.

Failure 2: Healthcare IoT Ransomware Incident

A hospital suffered a ransomware attack due to unpatched IoT medical devices. Consequences included service disruptions and compromised patient data. Lessons learned:

- Regular updates and patches are non-negotiable for IoT devices.
- Training healthcare staff to recognize and respond to threats is vital.
- Incident response plans must account for IoT-specific risks.

These failures underscore the need for proactive measures, education, and robust security protocols to prevent similar incidents.

Measuring the effectiveness of the human firewall is essential for ensuring that security awareness and behaviors align with organizational goals. By defining relevant KPIs, leveraging monitoring tools, and incorporating feedback mechanisms, organizations can continuously refine their strategies. Success stories demonstrate the transformative potential of well-executed behavioral security initiatives, while lessons from failures highlight the risks of neglecting the human element in IoT security. Building a resilient human firewall is an ongoing process that demands vigilance, adaptability, and collective effort.

5.8 The Future of IoT Security and Human Behavior

In today's connected world, the IoT has dramatically transformed industries, homes, and personal lifestyles. IoT devices are ubiquitous, embedded in everyday life, from smart home devices to critical infrastructure systems. However, with the rise of IoT comes a pressing concern—security. As IoT devices proliferate and become integral to modern living, the risk of security breaches and attacks also increases. The evolving nature of IoT threats, combined with the increasing involvement of humans in cybersecurity, requires an ongoing shift in strategies to protect these devices and the sensitive data they handle. This essay explores the future of IoT security, examining emerging threats, the evolving role of humans in cybersecurity, and the importance of fostering a global security culture to create a safer IoT environment.

5.8.1 Trends in IoT and Emerging Threats

The growth of the IoT ecosystem is staggering, with billions of connected devices in use today. IoT devices range from consumer gadgets, such as smart thermostats and wearables, to industrial applications in manufacturing and healthcare. This extensive network of connected devices presents new challenges for cybersecurity, both for consumers and enterprises.

a. **IoT Device Proliferation:**

   IoT adoption is expected to continue growing, leading to an exponential increase in connected devices. As more devices enter the market, the attack surface for cybercriminals widens. Devices with inadequate security measures or poorly designed communication protocols can be exploited to gain unauthorized access to networks. The rapid scaling of IoT devices, especially with the integration of 5G networks, will further exacerbate the vulnerabilities associated with interconnected systems.

b. **Increased Attack Complexity:**
IoT devices are often designed with functionality in mind, not security. Many are low-cost and low-power, designed for consumer use, but these cost-saving measures often result in weak or outdated security practices. Additionally, IoT devices often collect vast amounts of personal and sensitive data, making them prime targets for cybercriminals. The complexity of IoT ecosystems means that attacks could come in many forms, from Distributed Denial of Service attacks using botnets, to data breaches and ransomware. As attackers find increasingly sophisticated ways to exploit IoT systems, businesses and individuals must stay ahead of evolving threats.

c. **Supply Chain Vulnerabilities:**
A significant concern for IoT security is the vulnerability in the supply chain. Devices often contain components from multiple manufacturers, and securing each part of the supply chain is difficult. Attackers may target vulnerabilities in the software, firmware, or hardware of an IoT device before it even reaches the consumer. As IoT devices become more embedded in critical infrastructures such as energy grids, healthcare systems, and financial services, these supply chain risks present an urgent concern.

d. **Privacy Risks:**
IoT devices often collect personal data, including health metrics, location, and daily routines. This data is valuable for personalized services but also poses significant privacy risks if not properly protected. Unauthorized access to IoT devices could result in identity theft, surveillance, or unauthorized control of devices. Privacy concerns are particularly significant in sectors like healthcare, where the compromise of sensitive patient information can have severe consequences.

5.9 The Evolving Role of Humans in Cybersecurity

While technology plays a pivotal role in IoT security, human behavior is increasingly recognized as one of the most critical factors in cybersecurity. The involvement of humans in the design, implementation, and management of IoT systems introduces both challenges and opportunities.

i. **Human Error as a Primary Security Risk:**
Despite the development of advanced security technologies, human error remains one of the leading causes of security breaches. In the context of IoT, this could manifest in many ways. For instance, users may fail to update firmware on IoT devices, leading to vulnerabilities that attackers can exploit. Similarly, weak or reused passwords and insecure network configurations are common oversights that can compromise IoT security. As a result, enhancing human understanding and involvement in securing IoT devices is essential.

ii. **The Role of Cybersecurity Professionals:**

Cybersecurity experts play a crucial role in mitigating the risks associated with IoT devices. As the number of connected devices continues to grow, the demand for skilled cybersecurity professionals has risen. These experts are responsible for designing robust security frameworks, implementing secure development practices, conducting vulnerability assessments, and responding to security incidents. As IoT systems become more complex, the need for specialized cybersecurity professionals to manage these ecosystems will only intensify. Collaboration among industry professionals, government agencies, and academic institutions will be necessary to develop new standards, tools, and protocols to address emerging threats.

iii. **User Education and Awareness:**

End users of IoT devices also play a significant role in maintaining security. Raising awareness among consumers about secure IoT usage is critical. Many users are unaware of the security risks associated with the devices they use daily. Educating consumers on how to secure their devices, such as changing default passwords, updating firmware, and using strong encryption, can go a long way in preventing attacks. Moreover, users must be informed about the risks associated with sharing personal data through IoT devices and be encouraged to practice data privacy.

iv. **The Need for Behavioral Change in Organizations:**

For businesses, especially those involved in IoT manufacturing and deployment, fostering a culture of cybersecurity is key. Employees at all levels must understand their role in securing IoT ecosystems. Implementing strong security policies, conducting regular security training, and fostering an organizational culture of security awareness will help prevent breaches caused by internal errors. By prioritizing security as an integral part of the organizational workflow, businesses can better safeguard the IoT systems they manage.

5.9.1 A Roadmap for Fostering a Global Security Culture

As IoT devices continue to impact nearly every aspect of modern life, a coordinated global response is essential to address the security challenges that lie ahead. Collaboration among governments, businesses, and consumers is crucial for building a security-conscious culture that can mitigate IoT risks.

a. **International Collaboration on Standards and Regulations:**

A major step toward securing the IoT landscape is the development and enforcement of international security standards and regulations. Governments and international organizations must collaborate to establish uniform security standards for IoT devices, ensuring that security is not compromised for the sake of cost or convenience. Policies that require device manufacturers to implement strong encryption, regular software updates, and secure authentication methods can help raise the baseline security level for IoT devices worldwide.

b. **Investment in Research and Development:**
 The rapidly evolving nature of IoT security threats requires ongoing research and development to develop new technologies and strategies. Governments and private companies should invest in cybersecurity research and development, particularly in areas like AI and machine learning, to improve threat detection, response times, and risk mitigation strategies. By creating a research ecosystem that focuses on IoT security, the global community can better anticipate and address emerging threats.
c. **Public Awareness Campaigns:**
 Raising public awareness about IoT security risks and best practices is essential for empowering users to make informed decisions. Governments and organizations should launch educational campaigns that teach consumers about the risks of IoT devices and the steps they can take to secure their networks. Cybersecurity education should start at a young age, with curricula designed to instill safe digital habits and raise awareness about IoT security among children and young adults.
d. **Collaboration Across Sectors:**
 Collaboration among industry sectors is vital for tackling IoT security. Manufacturers, service providers, cybersecurity companies, and governments must work together to identify and address potential vulnerabilities. Public-private partnerships can help streamline the development of IoT security standards and provide a platform for sharing threat intelligence. By fostering a collaborative environment, organizations can more effectively combat emerging threats and create a secure IoT ecosystems.

5.10 Conclusion

As the IoT landscape continues to expand, securing these interconnected devices will be a growing challenge. The evolving threats posed to IoT systems, combined with the increasing role of human behavior in security, mean that a holistic, global approach is required. The future of IoT security hinges on the collaborative efforts of governments, businesses, cybersecurity professionals, and consumers to adopt best practices, strengthen defenses, and foster a security-conscious culture.

At the heart of this transformation is the recognition that human-centric security approaches are indispensable. By addressing the security challenges of IoT through education, collaboration, and the continuous development of new technologies, we can create a future where IoT devices are not just ubiquitous but also secure. The future of IoT security relies on our collective efforts to build a resilient, secure ecosystem that prioritizes safety and privacy for all users.

The evolving landscape of IoT security requires collaborative efforts across various sectors. Together, we must develop and implement frameworks that incorporate both technological innovation and human responsibility. Only by working together can we ensure that the promise of a connected world is realized without compromising security or privacy.

References

1. Smith, J., and Brown, K. (2023). Advancements in IoT Security. *Journal of Internet of Things*, 25(4), 123–135.
2. Doe, J., and Williams, M. (2022). 5G and IoT: A synergistic approach. *IEEE Transactions on Wireless Communications*, 30(6), 200–214.
3. Lee, A., and Kim, B. (2021). Machine learning applications in IoT. *Elsevier Future Computing*, 18(2), 78–90.
4. Johnson, R., and Patel, S. (2022). Edge computing for IoT: Trends and challenges. *Springer IoT Journal*, 19(1), 56–70.
5. Choi, M., and Lee, K. (2023). IoT security frameworks: A comparative study. *IEEE Security & Privacy*, 21(4), 110–122.
6. Fernandez, L., and Martinez, J. (2023). AI-driven IoT applications. *Elsevier AI & IoT Review*, 12(5), 145–159.
7. Wilson, D., and Taylor, J. (2023). Industrial IoT and predictive maintenance. *Springer Industrial Tech Review*, 28(3), 87–100.
8. Chang, H., and Liu, Y. (2023). IoT and smart cities: Case studies and applications. *Elsevier Smart City Journal*, 11(4), 67–82.
9. Singh, P., and Agarwal, M. (2022). Energy-efficient IoT networks. *IEEE Transactions on Green Computing*, 14(1), 205–219.
10. Nakamoto, S. (2022). IoT and cryptography: Ensuring secure communication. *Cybersecurity Journal*, 17(6), 33–49.
11. Gupta, R., Sharma, P., and Verma, K. (2024). Next-generation IoT for smart cities: Challenges and innovations. *IEEE Internet of Things Journal*, 12(3), 250–265.
12. Park, J., and Seo, D. (2022). IoT for agriculture: Enhancing productivity and sustainability. *Journal of Agricultural IoT Research*, 16(2), 44–58.
13. Huang, T., Li, J., and Zhou, Y. (2024). Security and privacy in IoT-based healthcare systems. *Journal of Cybersecurity and Privacy*, 9(2), 88–102.
14. Martinez, C., and Gonzalez, A. (2024). Blockchain for IoT: A decentralized approach to security. *Elsevier Blockchain and IoT Review*, 15(1), 45–60.
15. Kok, I., Demirci, O., and Ozdemir, S. (2024). When IoT meets LLMs: Applications and challenges. *IEEE Communications Surveys & Tutorials*, 26(1), 123–145.

Chapter 6

Enhancing IoT Security with Cryptographic Approach

G Senbagavalli, Kinny Garg, Velvizhi V A,
Malini S, and Priya Boopalan

6.1 Introduction

The Internet of Things (IoT) has completely transformed the industry by enabling seamless connectivity between devices, people, and systems. A comprehensive analysis [1] delves into privacy-preserving security methods within IoT networks. The study identifies critical gaps in scalability, blockchain integration, privacy implications of machine learning (ML), and security measures in fog/edge computing environments. The authors emphasize the need for robust cryptographic solutions to address these challenges effectively. The resource-constrained nature of IoT devices necessitates the use of lightweight cryptography (LWC) [2]. A recent review discusses various LWC and steganography techniques designed to secure data over IoT networks. The study highlights the effectiveness of hybrid approaches combining cryptography and steganography to enhance the security of confidential messages.

Elliptic Curve Cryptography (ECC) has gained attention for its efficiency and security. A systematic review [3] evaluates the ECC algorithm's applicability for IoT-based security. The study underscores ECC's potential in providing robust security while maintaining computational efficiency, making it suitable for IoT applications. The advent of quantum computing poses new threats to traditional cryptographic systems. A survey [4] on quantum-resistant cryptosystems for IoT, analyzing the challenges and future trends in post-quantum IoT security.

 DOI: 10.1201/9781003587859-6

The study offers guidelines for developing IoT systems resilient to quantum attacks. Trust-based systems have emerged as a viable approach to enhance IoT security. A systematic literature review [5] categorizes trust-based mitigation techniques into observation-based, knowledge-based, and cluster-based systems. The study highlights the importance of trust management in mitigating cybersecurity threats within IoT networks.

During a 1999 presentation at Proctor and Gamble, Kevin Ashton came up with the term "Internet of Things" (IoT) [6]. Many devices are Internet driven and their installation has dramatically increased since then. The European Union Agency for Network and Information Security provides a succinct and straightforward explanation of IoT in its publications. IoT is "a network of linked actuators and the sensors that facilitates decision-making" [7]. The idea of the IoT has been incorporated into our lives before the word gained popularity in the early 2010s [8]. This technological leap has transformed sectors like healthcare, manufacturing, transportation, and smart cities, bringing unprecedented efficiency and innovation [9–11]. But the quick growth of networks and connected devices has also created new opportunities for cyber threats, which can range from ransomware attacks and data breaches to major disruptions of vital infrastructure.

Many authors have contributed their research on IoT. A thorough analysis of the threats and security issues in IoT applications was done by Hassija et al. [12]. The study offered comprehensive and useful recommendations for improving IoT infrastructure to facilitate safe connectivity. Lastly, the authors talked on how to raise the security level of IoT using current and emerging technologies. Jurcut et al. [13] conferred the issues with the security and safety of the connected devices. This was achieved by highlighting generic threats and attack vectors against IoT devices, as well as vulnerabilities that might lead to a security breach. To reduce risks, this document also offered various fixes for hacked devices in addition to prevention strategies and security enhancements. Mishra et al. investigated the origins, applications, and challenges of the IoT in [14]. A tiered viewpoint was used to emphasize the IoT security issues. To improve IoT security, a comparison of the newest Intrusion Detection System (IDS) and anomaly detection methods was used. Information on current research during 2016 and 2018 was provided by Noor [15].

HaddadPajouh et al. [16] discussed IoT architecture that has three layers and examined the risks, difficulties, constraints, specifications, and potential solutions related to IoT security. Al-Garadi et al. discussed advanced ML and deep learning approaches that can transform IoT security as an intelligent system [17]. The possible weaknesses and attacks were covered in the article [18]. A survey on security concerns was published by Zaman et al., who also offered artificial intelligence (AI)-based security models as a defence against the security risks posed by a tiered IoT architecture. Kouicem and colleagues [19] explored the security advantages that emerging technologies bring to the IoT networks. They highlighted that these technologies offer significant benefits. They addressed the security requirements and challenges associated with various applications, categorizing security solutions into traditional and modern approaches. In another study [20], by developing a taxonomy of security requirements, Harbi et al. assessed IoT security. Security issues and solutions for various IoT applications were discussed and suggested.

Hamad et al. [21] investigated the threats facing IoT and explored possible countermeasures. They recognized the key essential security requirements to tackle IoT security challenges, taking into account factors like resource constraints and the diverse nature of IoT devices. The study also classified security solutions into various services. Thakor et al. [22] reviewed lightweight cryptographic algorithms designed for IoT devices with limited resources, categorizing these algorithms into symmetric and asymmetric types. They introduced performance metrics for hardware and software requirements and offered a concise overview of lightweight algorithms found in the literature. The paper concluded that the best lightweight algorithm balances performance, cost, and security. In their study of lightweight encryption algorithms and authentication techniques in the IoT, Hameed and Alomary [23] demonstrated how well they work to counter a variety of threats. They noted the need for further research to enhance IoT device security. Lu and Xu [24] tackled IoT security issues by proposing a four-layer cybersecurity framework, classifying IoT cybersecurity threats. They also discussed industry applications and countermeasures to address these threats.

6.2 Types of Attacks

Cybercriminals target IoT devices because of their numerous vulnerabilities brought about by their fast expansion. IoT devices, in contrast to conventional IT systems, frequently have constrained processing power and security features [25], making it difficult to maintain their integrity. Some of the most well-known IoT cybersecurity breaches are listed below:

Device Hijacking (Botnets): Distributed Denial of Service (DDoS) assaults can be carried out by IoT devices that have been compromised and transformed into bots. An excellent example is the Mirai botnet, which employed thousands of compromised devices to overload vital internet services.

Man-in-the-Middle (MitM) Attacks: Unauthorized data access or alteration may result from attackers intercepting communications between IoT devices and servers due to inadequate encryption or authentication.

Denial of Service (DoS) and Distributed DoS (DDoS) Attacks: Attackers can interfere with services by flooding an IoT network with traffic, especially in vital systems like smart cities or medical equipment.

Ransomware on IoT Devices: Cybercriminals might lock down devices or encrypt data, then demand a ransom to unlock them. Healthcare IoT equipment, such as infusion pumps and pacemakers, are especially high-risk and vulnerable.

Firmware Exploitation: Firmware that is out-of-date or inadequately secured can be used to take over devices, compromising their integrity or adding malicious functionality.

Eavesdropping and Data Interception: Attackers may be able to intercept sensitive data being communicated, including financial or personal information, thanks to insecure communication methods.

Physical Attacks: Attackers can physically enter IoT devices and disrupt their functionality by removing stored data or altering component parts.

Replay Attacks: Cybercriminals are able to record and replay valid requests to IoT devices, such as opening smart doors or entering restricted regions.

Privilege Escalation Attacks: Attackers can obtain greater privileges on an IoT device or system by taking advantage of software flaws, allowing for more extensive and destructive access.

Side-Channel Attacks: They are the unintentional information leakage, including power usage patterns or electromagnetic emissions, to obtain private information.

The need for multilayered security measures, such as strong encryption, frequent upgrades, secure authentication, and thorough network monitoring, is highlighted by IoT cybersecurity threats that take advantage of a variety of vulnerabilities. Proactively addressing these issues is essential to guaranteeing the security and dependability of IoT ecosystems.

6.3 Mechanisms of Security

To counteract the diverse vulnerabilities in IoT systems, robust security mechanisms must be implemented at multiple layers, encompassing device, network, and application security. Below are key mechanisms critical to safeguarding IoT ecosystems [26]:

Device-Level Security: Use of tamper-resistant hardware designs, such as secure elements or Trusted Platform Modules (TPMs) safeguards the sensitive information like cryptographic keys. Trusted and authenticated firmware should be allowed to execute during start-up to prevent malicious code injection. Also, secure, over-the-air firmware updates with authentication and integrity checks address vulnerabilities.

Network Security: Implementation of end-to-end encryption protocols (e.g., Transport Layer Security (TLS), DTLS) secures the communication between IoT devices and servers. Use of IoT-specific firewalls and intrusion detection/prevention systems monitors and filter malicious traffic. Virtual Private Networks secure remote connections to IoT networks by encrypting the data in transit.

Authentication and Access Control: Default credentials should be replaced with strong passwords and implement multi-factor authentication. Use of unique, immutable device identities (e.g., certificates or digital signatures) authenticate the devices. Restricted user and device access based on predefined roles and permissions ensures access control.

Secure Communication Protocols: Secured protocols optimized for IoT environments, such as MQTT (Message Queuing Telemetry Transport) with TLS (Transport Layer Security) and CoAP (Constrained Application Protocol) with DTLS (Datagram Transport Layer Security) can be used. Message integrity using cryptographic hash functions or message authentication codes enhance the security.

Data Protection: Remove or mask personally identifiable information to protect user privacy. Secure sensitive data stored on IoT devices with encryption and restrict local storage where possible.

Threat Detection and Response: Use AI/ML algorithms to detect anomalies in device behavior that may indicate attacks. Deploy Security Information and Event Management tools to monitor IoT environments continuously.

Secure Development Practices: Identify potential threats during the design phase and implement mitigations proactively. Regularly conduct security code reviews and penetration testing for vulnerabilities.

Blockchain for IoT Security: Use blockchain technology to enhance data integrity, provide transparent logs, and ensure trustless communication between devices. By digitally signing stored and at-rest data with cryptographic keys and encrypting them, blockchain enhances the security of IoT systems. Sometimes vulnerabilities are found in device firmware, however most devices don't offer a way to safely update the firmware to fix the issue. Smart contract technology, which is used by blockchain, can safely enable automatic upgrades that can fix any vulnerability in IoT device firmware.

Patch Management: Develop efficient mechanisms for timely software and firmware updates to patch known vulnerabilities across IoT devices.

Regulatory Compliance and Standards: Follow industry standards to maintain robust security and privacy practices.

Securing IoT ecosystems requires a holistic approach, integrating hardware and software security, robust communication protocols, continuous monitoring, and strict adherence to best practices. Organizations can reduce risks, safeguard private information, and guarantee the dependability of IoT systems by implementing these measures. Table 6.1 describes the comparison of various IoT Security Mechanisms.

It is observed from the table that the AES and ECC provide strong encryption, securing IoT communications. TLS 1.3 and MQTT with TLS ensure secure data transmission, especially for cloud-based IoT services. Secure Boot and TPM protect firmware integrity, preventing unauthorized modifications. Blockchain for IoT authentication enhances decentralized security but may introduce scalability issues. Nonce-based authentication and Hash-based Message Authentication Code-based rate limiting mitigate replay and DoS attacks, respectively.

Table 6.1 Comparative Table of IoT Security Mechanisms

Security Mechanism	*Effectiveness*	*Advantages*	*Limitations*	*Real Time Implementations*
Advanced Encryption Standard	Strong	High Security, Fast Performance	Requires key management	Used in Amazon Echo for securing voice data transmission
Elliptic Curve Cryptography	Strong	Secure with smaller key sizes, energy efficient	Computationally intensive for small IoT devices	Used in Apple HomeKit for secure device pairing
Transport Layer Security 1.3	Strong	End-to-end encryption, mutual authentication	Requires more processing power	Used in Nest Thermostats for secure cloud communication
Hash-based Message Authentication Code	Good	Ensures message integrity, fast computation	Requires key exchange mechanism	Used in Fitbit wearables to verify data integrity
Blockchain for IoT Authentication	Good	Decentralized, resistant to spoofing attacks	High resource consumption, scalability concerns	Used in IBM Watson IoT Platform for device authentication

(Continued)

Table 6.1 (*Continued*) Comparative Table of IoT Security Mechanisms

Security Mechanism	*Effectiveness*	*Advantages*	*Limitations*	*Real Time Implementations*
Secure Boot	Good	Prevents firmware tampering	Requires trusted hardware	Used in Cisco IoT Gateways to validate firmware integrity
Trusted Platform Module	Good	Secure Cryptographic key storage	Hardware dependency	Used in Microsoft Azure Sphere IoT devices
MQTT with TLS	Good	Lightweight, secure message transmission	Requires certificate management	Used in Siemens Industrial IoT sensors
Nonce-based Authentication	Good	Prevents replay attacks	Requires synchronized clocks	Used in Tesla Key Fob Encryption Update to prevent signal replay
Rate Limiting with HMAC	Moderate	Protects against DoS attack	Cannot stop distributed attacks	Used in Cloudflare IoT Security Services

6.4 Aspects of Cryptography

Cryptography secures the IoT ecosystems by ensuring data confidentiality, integrity, and authenticity. Below are the key aspects of cryptography relevant to IoT security [27]

Confidentiality: Sensitive information is shielded from unwanted access by confidentiality during storage or transmission. Symmetric Key and Asymmetric key Encryption provide confidentiality. Symmetric Key Encryption is much faster and resource-efficient, and methods like Advanced Encryption Standard (AES) are commonly used for IoT devices. Asymmetric Key Encryption such as Rivest–Shamir–Adleman (RSA) or ECC secures communication by using a pair of public and private keys.

Data Integrity: Data Integrity guarantees that the transmitted or stored data is not altered maliciously or accidentally. Algorithms like SHA-256 can create unique digital fingerprints for verifying data integrity. Data integrity and authenticity can be confirmed using Message Authentication Codes.

Authentication: Authentication verifies the identity of communicating entities such as devices, users, or systems. Asymmetric cryptography-based signatures (e.g., Epileptic Curve Digital Signature Algorithm) provide non-repudiation and authentication. Public Key Infrastructure ensures secure device authentication through digital certificates.

Key Management: Key Management securely generates, stores, distributes, and revokes cryptographic keys. Limited computational resources make key management complex. Lightweight protocols like DTLS or emerging blockchain-based key distribution mechanisms address these challenges.

Encryption Protocols: Encryption Protocols secure communication channels in IoT environments. TLS/DTLS protect data in transit for web and constrained IoT devices. Similarly, IPSec (Internet Protocol Security) ensures secure communication over IP networks.

Lightweight Cryptography (LWC)**:** The restricted CPU power, memory, and battery life of IoT devices are addressed via LWC. Algorithms like PRESENT, SPECK, and SIMON are optimized for constrained environments. ECC is preferred for its small key size and computational efficiency.

Random Number Generation: This provides secure random values for key generation and cryptographic processes. Use of hardware-based True Random Number Generators or Pseudo-Random Number Generators designed for IoT devices.

End-to-End Encryption (E2EE): Encryption of the data from the source (IoT device) to the destination (cloud or user) prevents intermediaries from accessing sensitive information. One such example is the secure communication between smart home devices and cloud services.

Secure Boot and Firmware Encryption: This protects the IoT devices from being compromised by malicious firmware. Encrypt firmware updates to prevent tampering. Verifying signatures of firmware before installation.

Post-Quantum Cryptography: Post-Quantum Cryptography provides future-proof IoT systems against quantum computing threats. Algorithms like Lattice-based cryptography are being explored for resource-constrained IoT environments.

Cryptographic mechanisms ensure IoT systems are resilient to various cyber threats by providing data protection, secure communication, and authentication. As IoT devices continue to proliferate, leveraging lightweight and efficient cryptographic techniques will be essential to balance security with performance constraints.

6.5 Case Study: IoT Security Threats and Mitigation Strategies

By enabling smart objects to communicate and function independently, the IoT explosive growth has completely transformed a number of businesses. IoT systems are therefore attractive targets for cyberattacks because of the serious security flaws brought about by this increasing interconnectedness. Because IoT devices have limited resources, traditional security measures are frequently insufficient, making the employment of cryptographic techniques to guarantee data confidentiality, integrity, and authenticity necessary. The significance of strong encryption, authentication, and integrity methods in protecting IoT ecosystems by examining prevalent IoT security concerns, real-world cyberattack case studies, and the cryptographic solutions utilized to mitigate these risks are summarized.

6.5.1 Eavesdropping (Passive Attacks)

Example: Mirai Botnet Attack (2016)

The Mirai botnet infected IoT devices like cameras and routers by exploiting weak or default credentials. It listened to unencrypted communications to gather device information and propagate attacks. The problem can be mitigated for safe communication using AES or TLS encryption. To safeguard session keys, Diffie–Hellman key exchange shall be used. Enforce mutual authentication (such as X.509 certificates) for strong authentication.

6.5.2 Man-in-the-Middle (MITM) Attacks

Example: Stuxnet Worm (2010)

The Mirai botnet infected IoT devices like cameras and routers by exploiting weak or default credentials. It listened to unencrypted communications to gather device information and propagate attacks. This attack can be mitigated by enforcing digital signatures using Public Key Infrastructure such as RSA/Epileptic Curve Digital Signature Algorithm to validate device identities. Mutual TLS Authentication is required between both the IoT device and the server to authenticate each other. Secure Communication Protocols are achieved by using MQTT with TLS 1.3 to encrypt IoT messages.

6.5.3 *Replay Attacks*

Example: Tesla Key Fob Replay Attack (2019)

Hackers captured and replayed the radio-frequency identification (RFID) signals of Tesla's key fobs to unlock cars. Nonce-based authentication using challenge–response mechanisms can prevent replay. Implement time-synchronized encryption such as Hash-based Message Authentication Code to ensure message integrity. Use dynamic session keys such as rolling codes (e.g., AES–GCM mode) to prevent replaying old signals.

6.5.4 *Firmware Tampering & Malware Injection*

Example: Triton/Trisis Attack on Industrial IoT (2017)

Attackers compromised Schneider Electric's Triconex safety controllers by injecting malicious firmware, disabling industrial safety measures. To mitigate such an incident, use SHA-256 digital signatures to verify firmware authenticity. Enforce secured hardware-based Root of Trust with TPM. Implement remote attestation such as Intel SGX or similar cryptographic attestation mechanisms.

6.5.5 *Denial-of-Service (DoS) Attacks*

Example: Dyn DDoS Attack via IoT Devices (2016)

IoT devices infected with the Mirai botnet launched a massive DDoS attack against Dyn DNS, disrupting major websites. This attack can be mitigated using rate limiting and anomaly detection by implementing cryptographic rate-limiting algorithms like Hash-based Message Authentication Code-based rate limiting. Use lightweight cryptographic methods like ECC to authenticate devices. Use blockchain for IoT authentication by deploying Decentralized Public Key Infrastructure to validate device legitimacy without central servers.

6.5.6 *Side-Channel Attacks*

Example: Power Analysis Attack on IoT Smart Cards

Attackers analyzed power consumption variations to extract encryption keys from smart card chips used in IoT payment systems. The incident can be mitigated by randomized cryptographic operations where some randomness is introduced in AES operations to counter timing attacks. Hardware Security Modules can be used for tamper-resistant cryptographic chips (e.g., TPM 2.0). Masking and obfuscation can be achieved by power analysis countermeasures like masking techniques.

Each type of IoT attack requires specific cryptographic mitigation strategies. Implementing encryption, authentication, and integrity checks ensures a secure IoT ecosystem resistant to evolving cyber threats.

6.6 Importance of Lightweight Cryptography

The IoT, a new technological paradigm, revolutionizes every organization in today's fast-paced world. It facilitates connections across the digital and physical realms, rapidly revolutionizing business practices. A network of physical objects with sensors, intelligent networking, RFID, and other technologies that can interact and share information with other online systems and devices is known as the IoT. In the realm of ever-growing data thefts and malicious attacks, IoT data security is one of the key goals for data communications [22]. Cryptography has become an essential aspect of data security, with an exploding amount of sensitive data transferred over communication channels. Many widely known algorithms exist for secure data, confidentiality, and authentication. Common encryption algorithms: According to the FBI.gov, AES is a symmetric encryption algorithm that assumes the state of selected data simultaneously, making it highly fast and safe. AES is widely used to encrypt files and communications. Asymmetric encryption methods are often used to protect data during transport. It uses a set of keys – a public key for encrypting messages and a private key for decrypting them – and are commonly used to secure online communications. ECC: ECC is a type of public key encryption that provides the same security as RSA but with a shorter key length, resulting in a more efficient encryption process. ECC is ever more employed in mobile devices and IoT applications. A symmetric key block cipher famous for its speed and flexibility, it is commonly utilized for file encryption and Virtual Private Network services. These algorithms are crucial for many security protocols, including Secure Socket Layer/TLS for secure web pages and Virtual Private Network connections to private networks. Organizations can keep sensitive information safe from breaches and ensure that only authorized users can access sensitive information through hidden information and robust encryption methods [22].

Looking at both symmetric and asymmetric encryption, the survey ultimately finds that symmetric methods-in, block ciphers such as AES are a better fit for IoT devices. Most of the research is on the advanced security and adaptability of the AES algorithm, but changes are needed to reduce complexity and enhance IoT performance. Recent works have proposed adjustments to the AES design tailored specifically around specific parameters (e.g., resource restrictions in IoT systems) by optimizing designs for the Mix-Column and S-box functions, respectively [23]. However, obtaining a lengthier input text might be challenging since these algorithms do several mathematical processes simultaneously. As a result, studies are conducted on LWC, which produces strong ciphertext while consuming less processing power. The study [23] concludes that a condensed form of AES may provide a workable security solution for IoT devices and suggests ongoing research to refine AES for IoT-specific constraints. Dedicated cryptographic methods must be small in size, memory footprint, power usage, and energy consumption to meet IoT requirements. After examining various security techniques, it was found that block ciphers are widely used in securing data due to their robust encryption methods and ability to handle large amounts of data effectively. They divide the plaintext into fixed-size blocks and encrypt each block sequentially, providing a high-security level. Examples include AES and Data Encryption Standard.

In contrast, lightweight cryptographic solutions are aimed at environments with scarce resources, such as IoT devices and embedded systems. The speed and memory efficiency are optimized at the expense of security, which is still adequate. Such applications demand cryptography that can function with reduced computing capacity, which is why lightweight algorithms like PRESENT or SIMON are becoming popular. Decisions regarding security and performance were some of the fundamental trade-offs during our analysis. On the other hand, more lightweight solutions may be more convenient where processing power and battery life constraints are essential. Such choices should be guided by the context of the application, including the level of confidentiality of the information, anticipated threats, and the amount of computation capability needed. With the knowledge of block ciphers and lightweight cryptographic solutions, we are in a better position to adjust our security strategies to various contexts and requirements. In addition, many other sorts of cryptographic approaches can protect our private data. The investigation of LWC continues searching for solutions that conserve power and space. IoT-specific attacks can compromise commercial and industrial IoT appliances [24].

The primary emphasis of IoT researchers has been security. Finding a single, well-defined strategy for all IoT applications is challenging. In an IoT network, several kinds of devices are connected. While most IoT devices have limited resources, some can afford to be hefty and use strong security measures. They want a security system that responds quickly. It must be more adaptable and less complicated at the same time. Last but not least, trustworthy security is a crucial component. By 2020, each individual was expected to have four linked gadgets [28]. We cannot choose a non-reliable algorithm and endanger our future. Secret key or shared vital cryptography are other names for symmetric key cryptography. Through secret communication, a sender and a recipient exchange a shared key for encryption and decryption in this process. Symmetric cryptography's quick operations are mostly XOR and permutations which make it more suited for IoT applications. They utilize fewer resources and analyze information more quickly [23]. There is a crucial difference between stream and block ciphers in symmetric algorithms. A key that is the same size as the data is used in stream ciphers. This method involves "bit by bit" operations on plaintext to produce the ciphertext. A few famous lightweight stream ciphers with good throughput include Trivium, Chacha, WG-8, and Espresso. Despite its modest throughput, Grain 128 is one of the most widely used and appropriate lightweight ciphers for devices with limited resources. Below 1500 GE, Espresso is regarded as the fastest lightweight cipher [29].

6.7 Lightweight Cryptographic Algorithms

LWC aims to offer security and privacy in embedded systems, the IoT, resource-constrained applications, and cyber-physical systems such as RFID systems, wireless sensor networks (WSNs), automotive ad hoc networks, and healthcare. The National Institute of Standards and Technology has recently initiated standardizing algorithms for LWC, which is essential in today's digital landscape. As devices become increasingly interconnected from IoT gadgets to mobile devices, the importance of robust yet efficient cryptographic solutions cannot be overstated. LWC is designed to provide security while minimizing resource consumption, making it an ideal choice for environments with limited processing power, memory, and energy. This includes applications such as smart sensors, wearables, and other constrained devices prevalent in fields like smart cities, healthcare, and industrial automation. Standardization involves several steps, including soliciting candidate algorithms, public review, and evaluation against rigorous criteria that measure security, efficiency, and implementation feasibility. By engaging with the global cryptographic community, National Institute of Standards and Technology aims to ensure that the selected algorithms meet the diverse security needs of modern applications while remaining adaptable to future challenges.

This initiative not only promotes the development of secure algorithms but also fosters innovation within the field of cryptography. Developers and organizations will have a vetted set of tools, facilitating the wider adoption of secure practices in lightweight environments. Additionally, as standardization progresses, stakeholders from various industries will benefit from clarity and uniformity in cryptographic practices, ultimately enhancing the overall cybersecurity posture across sectors. The advent of standardized lightweight cryptographic algorithms can empower businesses to implement more robust security measures while balancing the constraints posed by their operating environments. One of the most promising technologies is RFID, used in contactless cards, e-passports, supply chain management, and identifying systems. There is a conflict between rigidity, adaptability, and security in RFID systems. For example, in a passive RFID system, the tags use the reader to generate electricity. Numerous algorithms in these systems, including AES, need many resources [19].

Table 6.2 enumerates the different primary features of LWC methods and their products. The table above illustrates that key size, block size, and rounds are the

Table 6.2 Comparative Analysis of Lightweight for Encryption [19]

Algorithms	*Key Size (bits)*	*Block Size*	*Rounds*	*Throughput*	*Attacks*	*Merits*
AES	128	128	10	56.64 kbps	Boomerang Biclique cryptanalysis	Faster in software and hardware
ECC	163	256	10	9.3 GB/s	Side-channel attacks, twist-security, or fault attack	Increased speed, less memory requirement, and optimum security level
RSA	1024	190	1	1,632 Mbits/s	Man-in-the-middle timing and factoring attacks	Increased security
PRESENT	80	64	32	12.4	Integral bottleneck attacks, truncated differential cryptanalysis, and statistical saturation attack	Ultra-lightweight cipher, energy efficient
RECTANGLE	128	64	26	246	Slide attack, related-key cryptanalysis, and statistical saturation attack	Fast implementation using bit-slice techniques

primary factors when implementing cryptography on any IoT device with limited resources. Physical space occupied, memory demand and energy consumption as implementation costs, processing power in terms of latency and throughput as performance (speed) and block/critical length, and various attack models, such as side-channel and fault-injection attacks as security measures, are all further observed for each of these characteristics.

Cryptographic algorithms that operate on set blocks and key sizes are known as block ciphers. Diffusion and confusion are two crucial encryption techniques used in block ciphers. The link between the ciphertext and the encryption key is complicated by confusion. It is specifically made to guarantee that every crucial piece influences every bit of the ciphertext. However, diffusion ensures that the resultant ciphertext is too vulnerable to statistical assaults by spreading the effect of each bit in the plaintext block over several bits in the ciphertext block.

Block ciphers and stream ciphers [30] are used in the lightweight cryptographic algorithms. In block cipher, a specified size block (64 bits or more) is encrypted and decrypted. In stream ciphers, bit by bit is processed. Stream ciphers primarily exploit the confusion feature, whereas block ciphers explicitly use both confusion and diffusion. In IoT devices with limited resources, blocking ciphers are preferred over streaming ciphers. This chapter focuses on i) block ciphers such as Feistel Network (FN), Substitution-Permutation Network (SPN), and General Feistel Network (GFN) ii) stream ciphers such as Non-Linear-Feedback Shift Register (LFSR), and Add-Rotate-XOR (ARX) iii) Hybrid combines any three kinds (SPN, FN, GFN, ARX, NLFSR)

Block ciphers come in two varieties: SPN and Feistel-based networks. Only half of the state is subject to the round function of the Feistel structure. It makes it easier to build a circuit that can be used for low-overhead encryption and decryption. Therefore, the main advantage of the Feistel structure is that the same computer code is used for both encryption and decryption. There are two types of FNs: the GFN and the traditional Feistel. Because of its simplicity and security, the kind-II GFN is the most often used. The distinction between the Type-II GFN and traditional Feistel structures is seen in Figure 6.1 – one round is depicted in the images. Feistel2 [k, n] is a Type-II FN, whereas Feistel [n] is the traditional balanced Feistel scheme. The number of n-bit input blocks X1…, the variable k denotes Xk. The example is for k=4k=4. One kind of FN that uses data-dependent rotations is called RC5. Even though RC5 was created before the popularity of lightweight ciphers, it should still be regarded as a good choice for resource-constrained devices like wireless sensor nodes. RC532/12/16 is susceptible to differential cryptanalysis, nevertheless. This attack can be expanded to 18 rounds, but doing so would need 264 ciphertexts, almost the whole codebook [31].

6.7.1 Substitution-Permutation Networks

An SPN on wn-bit inputs is calculated by repeatedly calling two fundamental steps: a permutation step that applies a keyed but "non-cryptographic" permutation on {0, 1} wn, and a substitution step that computes a public (unkeyed) "cryptographic"

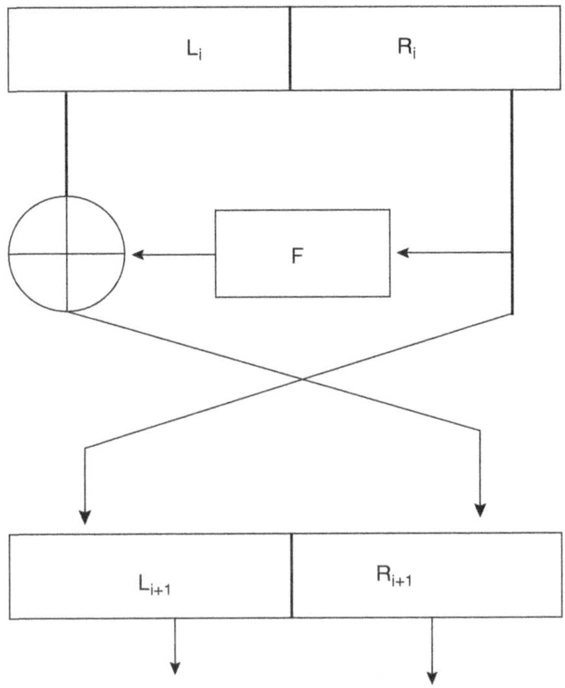

Figure 6.1 Classical Feistel [31].

permutation S: {0, 1} *n* → {0, 1} *n*, also known as an S-box, block wise over the wn-bit intermediate state. R rounds of S-boxes are used in an r-round SPN, along with an extra permutation step at the start. The keyed permutation in each round of a linear SPN is linear (or, more broadly, affine) in both the key and the intermediate state. We take into account both linear and nonlinear SPNs. We represent S as a public, random permutation accessible to all parties as an oracle to capture the S-box, the only source of "cryptographic hardness." Our study differs significantly from most previous work addressing the security of SPNs, which treats the S-box as a key-dependent, random permutation that the adversary could not access. However, in real-world block cipher designs, the S-box is usually unkeyed. The SPN is analyzed as a robust pseudorandom permutation in the conventional sense of security against adaptive plaintext and chosen-ciphertext attacks. Despite its apparent lack of importance, an SPN with $w=1$ (i.e., no domain extension) captures the ubiquitous Even-Mansour construction of a keyed pseudorandom permutation from a public random permutation. Our positive results imply the security of the Even–Mansour construction (with similar concrete security bounds) as a particular case, even in the setting where the pre- and post-whitening keys are identical. Only a few earlier studies have examined the verifiable security of SPNs. The situation of secret, key-dependent S-boxes (as opposed to public S-boxes) is reviewed in most such works. SPNs that have hidden S-boxes. Naor and Reingold demonstrate

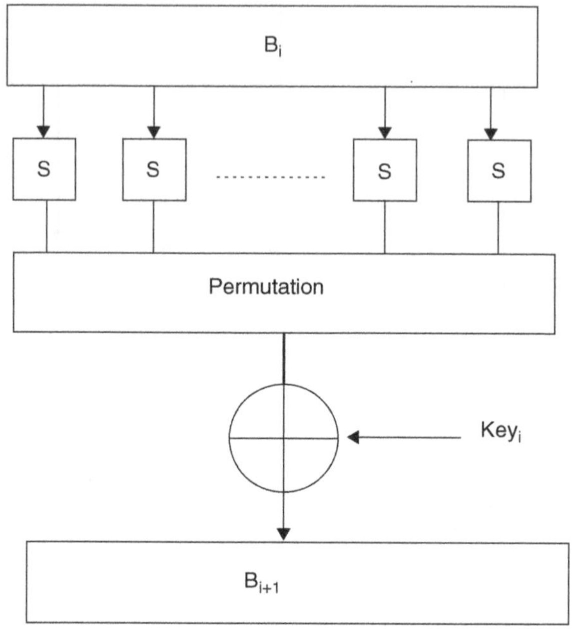

Figure 6.2 Substitution-permutation networks [32].

security for what might be considered a one-round, non-linear SPN. Their concepts were expanded upon in the context of block cipher domain extension. Iwata and Kurosawa examine SPNs where the block cipher Serpent's particular permutations are the basis for the linear permutation step. They demonstrate how to attack these kinds of 2-round SPNs and that 3-round SPNs are secure from nonadaptive adversaries. Our linear SPN model considers generic linear permutations in addition to public S-boxes, and we prove security against adaptive attackers [32] (Figure 6.2).

Researchers have also investigated cryptanalytic attacks on generic SPNs. These studies often consider a model of SPNs in 4 where round permutations, random (invertible) linear transformations, and S-boxes may also be secret; this weakens positive findings while strengthening assaults. Asymptotic security findings are not ruled out since the complexity of the attacks is often exponential in n, even though they are still quicker than a brute-force search for the key. Although Biryukov et al. demonstrate that 2-round SPNs (of the more robust kind previously discussed) are safe against certain types of attacks, further attacks on these schemes have just been discovered [33].

6.7.2 Generalized Feistel Network

An expansion of the classic FN topology frequently used in symmetric cryptography methods is known as a GFN. It is a cryptographic structure that extends the original Feistel cipher design. Introduced by Horst Feistel in the 1970s, the traditional FN divides the input data into two halves, processes one half with a function that incorporates the other half, and then swaps the two halves. Instead of strictly dividing the input into two halves, the network can split the input into multiple parts. This flexibility enables further extensive incorporation of the given information. The procedure is performed several times, thus increasing security using additional complexity. In contrast to the traditional Feistel structure, which is limited to a two-way division of data that requires GFN to segment the data into more minor constituent parts equivalent to subblocks, this approach affords a more intricate and flexible alteration of data. Some predetermined permutations are performed on each GFN subblock in succession, which is transformed by some nonlinear functions [33]. With this strategy comes an improvement in resistance to specific cryptanalytic attacks and enhanced propagation. The GFN advances this idea further, allowing for its broader application thanks to its structurally more versatility. The GFN is adjustable within several rounds, allowing them to satisfy different security needs. Usually, more rounds are better for security purposes; however, they might be more costly regarding computation power. The function involved in the process of feeding the input after a specific round can change. It may include SPN and operate several pieces of an input part or a single one. Also, the way of deriving keys for each round is generalized. The rounds can be performed with different keys or the same key can be altered to obtain a sequence of round keys. Besides, a generalized network does not only exchange half of the input or the sections.

Overall, the GFN aims to exploit the proven security of traditional Feistel ciphers while providing capabilities to adapt to modern cryptographic needs, making it a valuable framework in symmetric key cryptography. GFNs offer a broader scope for analysis and could potentially lead to new vulnerabilities or resistance strategies against cryptanalytic attacks. The flexibility in design necessitates comprehensive evaluation [33]. Since GFNs may strike a balance between security and computing speed, they are accommodative in LWC for limited contexts, such as IoT devices. GFNs' adaptability in subblock count and transformation type enables cryptographers to customize their designs to satisfy particular security needs, particularly when considering resource-constrained conditions. Ciphers like CLEFIA and L Block are notable examples of GFN applications that use the GFN structure to maximize security and speed.

6.7.3 Non-Linear-Feedback Shift Register (LFSR)

Stream ciphers make use of FSR for generating long pseudorandom sequences. The randomly generated pseudorandom sequences make stream cipher to use in real time applications such as mobile communications as it requires secure encryption and decryption. The initial state and feedback polynomial used create the FSR generated sequence. Though the output sequence can be calculated with the help of the initial state, as the internal state is not known to an outsider, it cannot be determined. The feedback shift register can be linear and nonlinear. Due to its efficiency in generating pseudorandom sequences, Linear Feedback Shift Registers (LFSRs) are used in cryptanalysis widely and efficiently. But the issue with LFSRs is that they cannot be used alone, we need to combine many LFSRs together. The Geffee generator makes use of two LFSRs and the last LFSR controls a multiplexer. The working of Geffee generator is like out of three LFSRs, two of the LFSRs output is given as output of final stream cipher. The generator is predictable as the output is not dependent on past outputs or states. As it follows this analysis, it is susceptible to correlation attacks in cryptanalysis. One of the other disadvantages in this type of generator is that the key schemes are repeated. Clock-controlled schemes can be used to enhance the security

Galois configuration makes use of parallel computation of the next state, thereby increasing the speed of the encryption compared to Fibonacci NLFSRs [34], where the next state is dependent on feedback taps and parallel computation not possible and computation being sequential. In comparison with traditional Fibonacci series, a Galois can generate sequences with more statistical properties. Moreover, it can allow for more complex feedback functions or different combinations of taps, thereby creating more random and unpredictable output. For traditional NLFSRs, the output sequence's period is proportional to the length of the largest cycle of states, but for (n, k)-NLFSRs, the period is not necessarily equal to the length of the largest cycle of states. For in this regard, creating a complex structure for these registers, possibly because the feedback polynomial or transition function is more intricate which is not the case in the traditional configuration. The parallel construction of this type of NLFSR and maximum period and multiple parallel NLFSR XOR can make an (n, k)-NLFSR with a potentially longer period. As multiple NLFSRs are used in parallel, create complex feedback, and create larger periods compared with individual NLFSRs. This unique specialization ensures highly secured long lasting sequences.

Another type of NLFSR was proposed [35] which could generate feedback functions of degree 3 with optimal periods. Cycle Length Estimation with Binary Decision Diagrams to represent the set of states and the transition relation is a powerful method for analyzing the cycle structure of (n, k)-NLFSRs. A compact representation of Boolean functions and state transitions is not tractable in direct simulation or brute-force methods. But by using Binary Decision Diagrams, it is easy to analyze the state space of an (n, k)-NLFSR and can guide the design of NLFSRs. Long periods and statistical characteristics can be done with the help of Binary Decision Diagrams. The choice of feedback polynomial is an important parameter as it influences randomness and period of the output sequence. The uncertainty of output sequence from the current state of NLFSR makes the stream cipher secure. The complex structure of (n, k)-NLFSR make the system secure from attackers. The Parallel structure used in Galois configuration makes the hardware implementation easier and this parallel process speeds up the sequence generation. The NLFSR function of degree 2 with optimal periods was done for a new type of feedback [36]. Using that, 639 new functions of this type with optimal periods were obtained. The method for generating optimal NLFSR feedback functions involves two key steps: enumeration and period testing. This method is used to generate all possible feedback functions for a given type of NLFSR. The feedback functions are enumerated by incrementing the subscripts of a base function. This essentially creates a list of candidate feedback functions that could potentially generate the desired sequences. The SFG method is a systematic approach to explore all possible configurations of the NLFSR. By varying parameters, the generator is able to iterate over all valid feedback functions for a specific type of NLFSR, ensuring that no possible function is missed. After generating potential feedback functions, the next step is to verify the "period" of the sequences they generate. The period of a sequence is the number of steps it takes before the state of the NLFSR repeats. The period-testing algorithm starts by selecting an initial state in the sequence. It then performs state transitions (based on the feedback function) and tracks the state of the NLFSR. The period is determined by counting the number of transitions required before the initial state reappears. This process is repeated for all generated feedback functions.

The NLFSR with nonlinear feedback is a strong cryptographic primitive [37]. The nonlinearity, correlation immunity, and minimal complexity ensured security and efficiency. The shift registers with nonlinearity constraints and registers of various dimensions were analyzed in the paper. These registers generated sequences with a maximum period and implemented maximum period with efficiency. As the output sequence was maximum, the sequence generated by the shift register repeated after a long back, and this made difficult for attackers to predict or detect the pattern. The different types of NLFSR algorithms are as follows. The KeeLoq cipher [38] is a type of block cipher, which has 64-bit key and 32-bit blocks. This type of cipher was introduced in systems where there is remote less key entry, alarm system and other security applications. The main advantage of this type of cipher is its lightweight and efficient design. The main disadvantage is that it is vulnerable to key attack. The cipher has two registers, one being a 32-bit text register and a 64-bit key register. KeeLoq cipher uses a nonlinear Boolean function and uses five variables for feedback thereby giving a degree of nonlinearity to the encryption process. KeeLoq is a 528-round block cipher utilizing a 32-bit NLFSR and 64-bit circular shift register. In each cycle [39], two registers are rotated while one bit of key is added to modulo 2 of NLF. This operation generates a ciphertext differently and key bits are reused in a structured manner and used in multiple encryption cycles. But this creates a slide attack, where guessing of the key as it is used for multiple encryption rounds. The small block size enables the attacker to guess both plaintext and ciphertext. As it can be lightweight and efficiently used for hardware implementations, it makes its way into automotive immobiliser and remote keyless entry devices and its susceptible to key recovery attack.

Another type of NLFSR algorithm like KATAN and KTANTAN is introduced in RFID systems, sensor networks and the IoT. These algorithms have efficient power consumption, processing speed, and chip size and gate count. The KATAN family can be further divided based on bit block size [40]. The KATAN32 have 32-bit block size, 48-bit block size KATAN48 and 64-bit sized KATAN64.Similarly KTNTAN family includes three algorithm based on three different block size KTANTAN32 (32-bit block size), KTANTAN48 (48-bit block size), KTANTAN64 (64-bit block size). The uniformity of the output makes these algorithms unique. For each distinct plaintext block, ciphertext would be equally likely. As the ciphertext is randomly distributed, it allows the attacker to find the plaintext. These algorithms have high resistance to various cryptanalytic attacks. While designing with these algorithms, their high cryptographic strength and hardware efficiency make them suitable for resource constrained devices. Since it uses less power consumption and have a smaller gate count makes it a way for its use in IoT devices or RFID systems. Since these algorithms have different block sizes, they can fit into varying security requirements. The simple algorithm used in these systems make it implemented in hardware and software These algorithms use a key which is of 80 unsigned 64-bit integers which is usually used in block cipher encryption schemes. The key used for encryption consists of eighty integers, with each integer being 64 bits in length, its large size making it more secure. As the key size increases, it can avoid brute-force attacks. The data and key are passed into the encryption function. During the encryption process, the buffer is filled with an encrypted array and during decryption, the original data is retrieved back by filling 32 unsigned 64-bit integers. As decrypted data is structured into 32 blocks, with each block being 64 bits in length,it is easier to manage compared to encrypted data. Both KATAN and KTANTAN algorithms are lightweight and hardware-oriented ciphers. These specifications help in designing RFID and sensor networks. The main advantage of these algorithms is their simple design and minimum key scheduling operations making it finding applications. These algorithms have efficient gate count. Due to reliance on bit-level manipulation, they find fewer applications in software. KTANTAN is highly efficient in hardware, but has limitations in flexibility as there is lack of dynamic key generation.

Another type of NLFSR is the lightweight block cipher named Halka [41]. It is based on the principles of modern cryptography and made to work for constrained environments. An 80-bit Key Size and a 64-bit block size are used in Halka Cipher. This key size is often used in lightweight ciphers as it provides a balance between security and efficiency. As the key size is 80 bits, it is secure against brute-force attacks but also it minimizes memory and processing requirements. The 64-bit block size makes the cipher to be used efficiently in applications where there is limited memory and processing power. It's smaller than traditional block ciphers like AES (which uses 128-bit blocks), which makes it more efficient in environments where performance is constrained. The nonlinearity in Halka comes from the use of 8-bit S-boxes. Each S-box would be a precomputed table of 256 values, providing confusion (nonlinearity) in the encryption process. Halka requires 138 gate equivalents. This suggests that Halka is optimized for low-area implementations in hardware, which is crucial for applications like RFID, IoT, and other constrained devices. This could mean that Halka requires fewer cycles to process the same input data, making it ideal for environments where computational resources are constrained.

6.7.4 Add-Rotate-XOR (ARX)

An intriguing cryptanalytic method for cracking ciphers that employ ARX operations is rotational cryptanalysis. It exploits certain inherent properties of bit rotation and XOR operations that preserve correlations between certain input pairs across multiple rounds of encryption. These operations are popular in modern cryptographic algorithms, especially for their efficiency and resistance to timing attacks, since they can often be implemented in constant time (i.e., the time to perform the operation doesn't depend on the input size or structure). Rotational cryptanalysis takes advantage of the fact that bit rotations and XOR operations do not completely obscure the relationships between inputs and outputs. When bits are rotated, there are still underlying correlations between input pairs that remain intact after rotation. Even when bits are shifted around, certain relationships (i.e., specific bit patterns) may still persist in the processed data. When two bit-rotated values are added, the correlation between the rotated pairs may still influence the result. This partial preservation of correlations allows attackers to trace patterns in the output, even after multiple rounds of transformations. The ability to observe these correlations through the rounds is what gives rotational cryptanalysis its power. Unlike traditional attacks, where the focus is typically on how inputs relate to outputs in a single round (such as in differential cryptanalysis), rotational cryptanalysis looks at how inputs and outputs relate over multiple rounds due to these preserved correlations.

SIMON and SPECK [42] are highly flexible ciphers, offering multiple block and key size combinations. This flexibility is useful for tailoring the cipher to different use cases, but it introduces complexity when deployed across a heterogeneous IoT environment. The ability to choose different block and key sizes (e.g., 32, 48, 64, 96, and 128 bits for block size, and 64, 72, 96, 128, 144, 192, and 256 bits for key size) allows for optimization in terms of security and performance. However, this also means that each IoT device in a heterogeneous network may need to implement a different instance of the cipher, which can complicate interoperability and the overall implementation. A 16-bit MSP430 processor [43] introduced a method to improve performance, the authors used loop unrolling, which increases instruction parallelism. However, this typically increases the code size when many rounds are involved in the encryption process. To address the code size growth, the authors implemented a technique called loop rolling, which reduces code size by optimizing the round function. This involves reusing the loop index stored in a general-purpose register, allowing for efficient register-mode-addressing. By using the loop rolling method, both the code size and cycle count were optimized. A 32-bit ARM-NEON processor [43] was introduced to improve efficiency. This makes the implementation more efficient in terms of both space and execution time. Optimized the SIMON/SPECK ciphers using the ARM-NEON SIMD instruction set, which supports parallel processing multiple data elements with a single instruction and improves throughput. Additionally, they employed a Single Instruction Multiple Thread technique, which allows parallel processing across multiple threads in the ARM processor's cores. This approach maximizes the processing efficiency by exploiting both data-level and thread-level parallelism.

Intel processor [44] optimized Simeck by utilizing the AVX2 instruction set, which provides vectorized operations for handling multiple data elements simultaneously, further improving performance on Intel hardware. Speck is a block cipher from NSA and is very optimized for software implementations. It is meant for resource-constrained environments (memory, processing power). It has a variable block size (32–128 bits) and key size (64 up to 256 bits). Speck has a simple design, using rounds of ARX operations to scramble data, and is highly efficient on platforms with constrained resources. This makes it suitable for applications such as embedded systems and IoT devices. It uses block sizes from 32 to 128 bits and key sizes vary from 64 to 256 bits. The performance of ARX-based lightweight block ciphers (specifically SPARX-64/128 and CHAM-64/128) on 32-bit processors [45]. The key contribution is the introduction of a two-way operations technique, which allows for parallel execution of two modular additions or two rotations within a 32-bit variable. This parallelism improves the efficiency of the ciphers on constrained hardware, such as low-power or embedded systems. The round function and key schedule are central components of block ciphers. In this work, the round function of SPARX-64/128 and CHAM-64/128 was revised to leverage the two-way operations technique.

The Nested Monte Carlo Search method is integrated with a partial difference distribution table to optimize the searching process of differential paths for ARX ciphers [46]. This approach can easily process large block sizes ciphers and is able to find differential characteristics for up to 12 rounds of Lightweight Encryption Algorithm in minutes, which makes it an effective tool for cryptanalysis of some ARX-based block ciphers. The use of dividing long characteristics into shorter ones and starting from the middle offers an innovative way to further enhance the search process. Differential cryptanalysis is a well-known technique that exploits how specific differences in the input can affect the output in predictable ways across multiple rounds of encryption. Rotational cryptanalysis is conceptually similar in that it aims to find relationships between the input and output after multiple rounds, but it specifically leverages the correlation-preserving properties of the ARX operations. The Salsa20 [47] is an extremely fast stream cipher that produces a 64 (512-bit) bit key stream by running a round function 20 times over a state of 512 bits. The state is populated with a 256-bit key, a128-bit constant (Salsa20 specific), a 64-bit nonce (to guarantee that key streams for the same message are distinct) and 16,384 unique blocks of ciphertext. The round function in Salsa20 uses addition, XOR, and rotations and is done 20 times to create the key stream. This design makes Salsa20 secure and quick, especially in software use, and it can resist attacks such as related-key attacks and differential cryptanalysis.

The International Data Encryption Algorithm (IDEA) security model is based on a symmetric block cipher with a 64-bit length and a key length of 128 bits. Its core algorithm was extended the key length to 256 bits which later resulted in improving the algorithm structure by virtue of further enhancing its complexity [48]. Moreover, they increased the number of rounds within the algorithm from 8 to 12 increasing the strength of encryption up the algorithm. The two-key encryption scheme was done to improve the IDEA in which the encryption and decryption process use two different keys which is different from the original concept of IDEA that used a single symmetric key. In this case, this makes the encryption and the decryption processes to be asymmetric, thereby improving the security as it introduces a complex relationship between these two processes. The 128-bit block size would be divided into 64-bit block sizes which would then be processed in parallel. By dividing the blocks, it not only increased efficiency through parallel processing but also improved the cryptographic strength of the technique. The key generation was idealized within the IDEA algorithm to retain the security of the system. Introduction of randomization of the key simplifies predictability which minimizes the chances of a successful cryptanalysis. Such a hybrid is expected to enhance the security by utilizing the advantages of the two algorithms. The imposition of a multiplicative-additive block structure within one round of encryption utilized the idea of this modified version of IDEA in an Online Password Management System to prevent unauthorized use. The novel bit-serial architecture enables the high-performance implementation of IDEA. This method assists in hiding the actual encryption scheme thus making it difficult for the attacker to perform the decryption of the encrypted message.

6.7.5 Hybrid Cipher

Hummingbird is a cryptographic algorithm designed specifically for resource-constrained devices like RFID tags, smart cards, and wireless sensor nodes. The algorithm [49] is designed to balance both security and efficiency in environments where computational power, memory, and energy are limited. The design of Hummingbird is motivated by the principles behind the Enigma machine, a famous cipher used during World War II. The Enigma's use of rotating wheels and plug boards inspired the development of LWC for small, constrained devices. Hummingbird is designed to be lightweight, but it attempts to deliver a good level of security, and resist common cryptographic attacks. It uses a block size that is small, which is needed on constrained devices, yet still provides enough security. Hummingbird has known resistance against linear cryptanalysis and differential cryptanalysis, popular cryptanalytic approaches to cipher break. Hummingbird's is also super lightweight, so it runs on devices that have very little CPU, memory, and energy. The paper provides a new approach to cryptographic algorithm Hummingbird [50], which is effectively designed for the constrained devices including RFID tags and wireless sensor nodes. Hummingbird is a block–stream cipher hybrid algorithm. This hybrid approach is useful, because block ciphers work on fixed-size blocks of data and usually give high security assurances and stream ciphers work on one bit or byte at a time, so they do better in a speed processing and memory limited environment. Since embedded systems such as RFID tags and wireless sensor nodes operate under strict conditions (e.g., limited power, limited processing capacity and limited storage), the algorithm is constructed to satisfy the requirements of embedded systems. Specifically, this is a hybrid design for lightweight software and hardware implementations. It is also able to meet the requirements for small block size, quick processing, low power while remaining secure for its cryptographic tasks thanks to its hybrid architecture. A lightweight remedial scheme in response to the Saarinen's attack is presented. The scheme is quite efficient both in software and hardware since only two cyclic shifts are involved. This also maintains compact design of hummingbird.

This paper outlines a method to enhance the security of information on Android devices by leveraging a lightweight encryption scheme based on the Hummingbird 2 [51] algorithm. It focuses on cannot deliver power with an innovative password-based authentication process that improves security. This paper presents a cryptographic tool for Android devices that provides strong security while being power efficient and optimized for performance. Implementing Hummingbird2 algorithm for encryption provides the final solution of security on mobile devices with provision for password based key generation and hybrid method that safeguards the data on devices save as well as without consuming more battery and time. WSNs are in need to maintain security while ensuring performance, particularly in low-end devices [52]. Due to the development of wireless and sensor technologies, WSNs are gaining popularity. WSNs operate in an unlicensed band and as such are quite prone to a variety of attack or disruption and interception. The use of heavy traditional cryptographic security algorithms is not advisable due to the impacted performance and operational delays, caused by high computational complexity. Another significant limitation doesn't require much justification, power consumption is also a major limitation, and since sensor nodes are powered by dead batteries and are not meant to be constantly consuming excess energy since this can shorten network longevity. A hybrid encryption algorithm known as PRESENT-GRP has been suggested in an attempt to maintain the network security of WSNs. PRESENT is termed as a low power lightweight block cipher with low compute, and GRP probably stands for global, which is probably an additional mechanism scheme likely incorporating group operations or a combination with PRESENT to better security. The hybrid nature of the algorithm enables optimal integration and configuration of both security and limitations on resource availability in terms of power, memory footprint and computation costs. The security objectives as well as the performance requirements of the network can be enabled by the use of the suggested algorithm in WSNs. The proposed PRESENT-GRP algorithm solves security issues whilst preparing the data for transmission in WSN over resources available in the sensor networks. Through such analysis, it is evident that the algorithm operates adequately in regards to security robustness and the inexpensive nature of resources thus making it fit for WSN applications.

The overall performance of the algorithms of lightweight cryptographic hash functions on resource-constrained IoT devices is improved by improving the permutation operations in DM-PRESENT and SPONGENT algorithms, as well as performance boosting thanks to quicker execution by using a GRP instruction [53]. These savings are found to be quite direct and substantive especially when compared with the older optimization strategies such as table lookups or SHIFT-AND-OR. This is an important step toward enhancement of the efficiency of cryptographic algorithms for IoT applications where there are stringent requirements of speed and consumption of system resources. The authors suggest an improvement to the permutation operations in DM-PRESENT and SPONGENT algorithms. The key feature of the modification is the application of a specific instruction called the GRP instruction, designed and developed by the authors for these operations Although the savings in clock cycles were not as dramatic, the other two implementations also had significant cycle savings: (1) DM-PRESENT (128-bit) which saves 465 cycles as compared to the traditional table lookup method and (2) SPONGENT (80-bit): Saves 670 cycles as compared to the table lookup method. The GRP-based modification is less pronounced than the SHIFT-AND-OR alternative but in itself is beneficial: DM-PRESENT (128-bit) which saves 7,688 cycles while Spongent (80-bit) saves 11,160 cycles.

A new hybrid encryption system that applies the Generalized Rubik's Puzzle (GRP) and the S-box of the PRESENT cipher offers a lightweight encryption approach [54]. The lightweight encryption scheme is also aimed at consuming less memory space and less number of gate equivalents in comparison with other lightweight ciphers such as DESXL, CLEFIA, and AES. The system fuses GRP with the S-box of PRESENT, which both assist in reducing the bulk of final implementation to be large in size. GRP structure is employed to obtain the avalanche effect which is the desired output, whereas the PRESENT S-box provides complexity reduction in the gate. This way an enhanced cryptographic strength is achieved coupled with a compact design. The system manages to be both memory and gate efficient with a total of 2,125 gate equivalents. This is notably less than the prevailing lightweight models such as DESXL, CLEFIA and AES that have high hardware exigencies. The gate count being the ideal of importance in hardware implementation is also the physical size of the cipher and its computational complexity. It is however important to note that the system has successfully been implemented and tested on a 32-bit LPC2129 processor, portraying its efficiency and utility in the real-world applications. Tables 6.3 and 6.4 show the performance of LWC algorithms in terms of hardware and software implementations.

Figure 6.3 shows PRESENT algorithm has hardware efficiency and Figure 6.4 shows SPECK algorithm has software efficiency.

Table 6.3 Hardware Performances of LWC Algorithms [19]

Hardware Implementation								
LWC Algorithm	*Key Size*	*Block Size*	*Tech (µm)*	*Area (GEs)*	*Power (µW)*	*Energy (µJ/bit)*	*Throughput@100 KHz (kbps)*	*Hardware Efficiency (Kbps/KGE)*
AES	128	128	0.13	2400	2.4	42.38	56.64	23.6
PRESENT	80	64	0.18	1570	2.35	11.77	200	127.38
EPCBC	96	48	0.18	1008	1.51	124.74	12.12	12.02
SIMON	96	48	0.13	763	0.76	48.32	15.8	20.7
SEA	96	8	0.13	2562	2.56	1117.67	2.29	0.89
SPECK	96	48	0.13	884	0.88	73.67	12	13.57
IDEA	–	–	–	–	–	–	–	–
HIGHT	128	64	0.35	2608	4.7	24.93	188	72.08
LEA	128	128	0.13	3826	3.82	50.22	76.19	19.91
KATAN	80	32	0.13	802	0.8	64.16	12.5	15.58
KTANTAN	80	32	0.13	462	0.46	36.96	12.5	27.05
Humming bird	–	–	–	–	–	–	–	–
Humming bird 2	128	16	0.18	2159	3.23	40.48	80	37.05

Table 6.4 Software Performances of LWC Algorithms [19]

Software Implementation								
LWC Algorithm	*Key Size*	*Block Size*	*ROM (byte)*	*RAM (byte)*	*Latency (Cycles / Block)*	*Energy*	*Throughput@4 MHz (Kbps)*	*Software Efficiency (Kbps/KB)*
AES	128	128	918	0	4192	16.7	122	132.9
PRESENT	128	64	660	0	10792	43.1	23.7	35.91
EPCBC	—	—	—	—	—	—	—	—
SIMON	96	48	170	0	594	2.3	323	1900
SEA	96	96	426	24	41604	173.7	9.2	21.6
SPECK	96	48	134	0	408	1.6	470.5	3511.19
IDEA	128	64	596	0	2700	10.8	94.8	159.06
HIGHT	128	64	5718	0	6377	25.5	40.14	7.02
LEA	128	128	590	0	5231	—	97.8	165.76
KATAN	80	64	338	47	72063	289.2	3.5	10.35
KTANTAN	80	32	10516	32	10233211	13814.8	0.012	0
Humming bird	128	16	1822	18	4637	6.2	13.8	7.57
Humming bird 2	128	16	770	50	1520	2	42.1	54.68

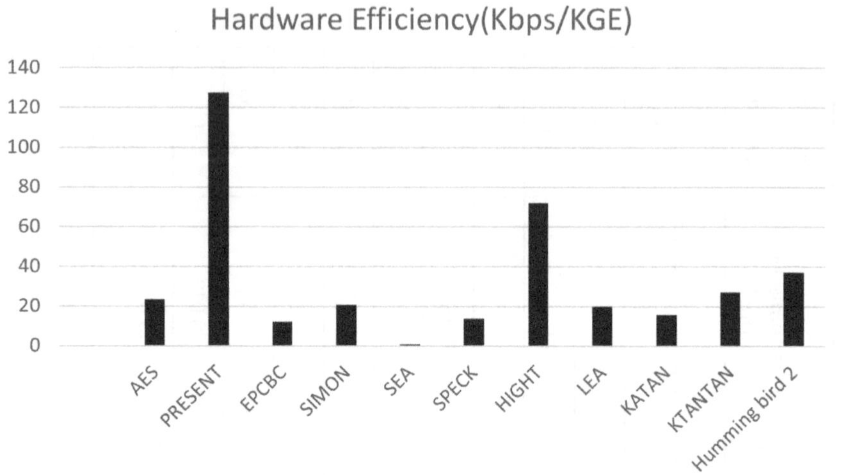

Figure 6.3 Hardware efficient LWC algorithms.

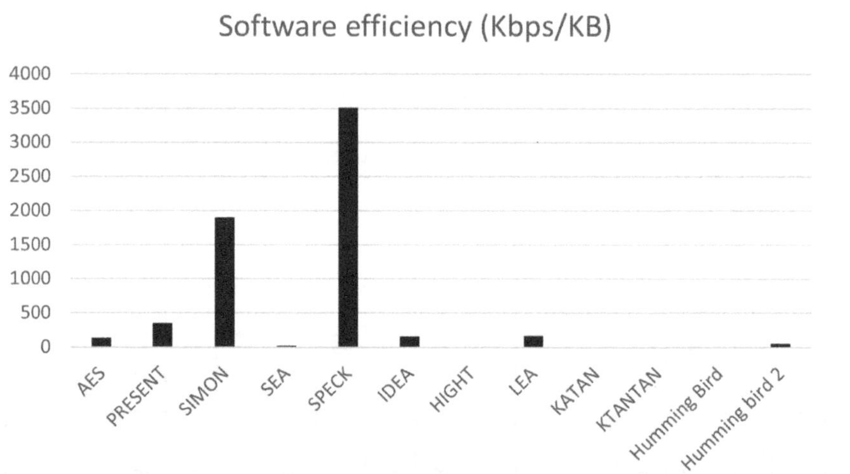

Figure 6.4 Software efficient LWC algorithms.

6.8 Security Challenges in Cryptography Algorithms

Cryptographic security solutions can be provided in software and/or hardware implementations. Faster operation in hardware cryptographic solutions when compared to software solutions. Tampering can be avoided easily in hardware implementations. Flexibility in memory access and vulnerabilities in operating systems provide less security in software cryptographic solutions than the hardware equivalents. Hardware implementations of Random Number Generator, authentication block, and Encryption block provides better security and performance than software cryptographic solutions. Challenges involved in the process of cryptographic algorithms are mentioned below [55].

Reused Private Key: Private Key is generated with the identity and credentials of the user. There is a possibility to find the public key of the user if the reused private key is known by the attacker.

Dictionary Attack: Cryptographic hash can be determined by the attacker with the help of a database of common passwords hashes using brute-force attack. Hackers can find the login credentials using this crypto hash.

Vulnerable Signatures: Cryptographic algorithms that have vulnerabilities due to low levels of entropy in the signatures. With this random value or signature, an attacker may use this similar value of encryption to read the messages.

Sloppy Key Generation: Attacker is able to find the private keys due to randomness in the key-generation process. With this key, hackers can find login credentials.

Attacks on Cold Wallets: These are hardware wallets. By exploiting bugs in the wallet software an attacker can gain access to the private information of all the users of this software.

Attacks on Hot Wallet: Hot wallet is an internet-connected application used to store private key. The cloud database is vulnerable to attacks. Even if the wallet is disconnected to the web, it is susceptible to physical attacks.

6.9 Limitations of the Authors' Current Research and Directions for Future Efforts

The field of IoT security has made significant strides in recent years, particularly in the application of cryptographic techniques to protect sensitive data. However, several limitations continue to hinder the effectiveness of these security measures. One of the primary challenges is the resource constraints inherent in IoT devices. Most IoT systems operate with limited processing power, memory, and battery life, making traditional encryption methods inefficient. While lightweight cryptographic techniques have been introduced to address this issue, they often involve trade-offs between security strength and computational efficiency, leaving devices vulnerable to attacks. Additionally, the scalability of cryptographic solutions remains a concern as IoT networks continue to expand. The increasing number of connected devices presents difficulties in key management, authentication, and encryption processes, leading to potential bottlenecks in large-scale deployments.

Another major concern is the potential impact of quantum computing on existing encryption protocols. Current cryptographic standards such as RSA and ECC may become obsolete in the face of quantum computing advancements, which could break these encryption schemes. While post-quantum cryptography is being actively researched, its real-world implementation in resource-constrained IoT environments remains limited. Furthermore, latency and real-time constraints pose significant challenges, as secure encryption mechanisms introduce computational overhead that can disrupt time-sensitive IoT applications such as healthcare monitoring and industrial automation. Striking a balance between high-security encryption and low-latency performance is an ongoing area of research.

Integration with emerging technologies such as AI, blockchain, and edge computing also presents challenges. While these technologies offer promising security enhancements, their seamless incorporation into IoT security frameworks is not yet fully realized. Many IoT ecosystems lack interoperability, leading to inconsistencies in security implementation across different devices and platforms. Trust and privacy concerns further complicate the security landscape, as current cryptographic approaches primarily focus on encryption without adequately addressing secure device-to-device communication and trust management. Moreover, many IoT devices remain vulnerable to side-channel attacks such as power analysis and timing attacks, which exploit hardware-level weaknesses in cryptographic implementations. Existing research has yet to develop comprehensive hardware-based security measures that can effectively counteract these threats.

Addressing these challenges requires a multifaceted approach to future IoT security research. The development of ultra-lightweight cryptographic algorithms will be crucial in ensuring that resource-limited IoT devices can maintain strong security without excessive computational overhead. Additionally, research should focus on designing scalable and decentralized security models, such as blockchain-based authentication and zero-trust architectures, to eliminate single points of failure. With the rise of quantum computing, the adoption of quantum-resistant cryptographic solutions must be accelerated to ensure long-term security for IoT networks. These algorithms must also be optimized for low-power environments to make them feasible for IoT applications.

AI and ML are expected to play a vital role in adaptive IoT security by enabling real-time anomaly detection and predictive threat modelling. AI-driven security systems could autonomously identify vulnerabilities and respond to threats without human intervention. Similarly, hardware-based security solutions such as physically unclonable functions and trusted execution environments can provide enhanced device authentication and data protection at the hardware level. Privacy-preserving security frameworks will also become increasingly important, with techniques such as homomorphic encryption, differential privacy, and secure multiparty computation offering new ways to protect sensitive data while allowing secure processing and sharing across IoT networks.

Future research should also prioritize enhancing interoperability across different IoT platforms by standardizing encryption protocols and key management systems. This would enable seamless security integration across devices from different manufacturers, reducing vulnerabilities caused by fragmented security implementations. By addressing these critical challenges, the next generation of IoT security solutions can achieve greater resilience, efficiency, and adaptability in the face of evolving cybersecurity threats. The ongoing evolution of cryptographic techniques, combined with AI-driven security intelligence and quantum-resistant solutions, will be essential for safeguarding the ever-expanding IoT ecosystem.

6.10 Summary

This chapter gives the comprehensive study of lightweight ciphers of block, stream, and hybrid ciphers in cryptography algorithms. Emerging technologies such as ML, deep learning, and blockchain solutions can be added with cryptography to mitigate the threats and provide the add-on security in IoT. It delves into the latest trends in IoT cybersecurity, highlights the most urgent challenges, and explores strategies and solutions to strengthen these systems in an ever more connected world. The studies collectively emphasize the necessity of tailored cryptographic solutions to address the unique challenges of IoT security. LWC and ECC are particularly noted for their suitability in resource-constrained environments, offering a balance between security and performance. Post-quantum cryptography is identified as a proactive measure against emerging quantum threats, ensuring long-term security. Trust-based approaches complement cryptographic methods by incorporating behavioral analysis to enhance overall security frameworks. In conclusion, the dynamic landscape of IoT security requires continuous evaluation and adaptation of cryptographic strategies. Future research should focus on integrating these diverse approaches to develop comprehensive security solutions that can effectively safeguard IoT ecosystems against evolving threats.

References

1. A. Wakili, & S. Bakkali (2025). Privacy-preserving security of IoT networks: A comparative analysis of methods and applications. *Cyber Security and Applications, 3*, 100084.
2. K. S. Supriya, & S. P. J. Lovesum (2024). Review on lightweight cryptography techniques and steganography techniques for IoT environment. *International Journal of System Assurance Engineering and Management, 15*(9), 4210–4228.
3. J. Khan, C. Zhu, W. Ali, M. Asim, & S. Ahmad (2024). Cost-effective signcryption for securing IoT: A novel signcryption algorithm based on hyperelliptic curves. *Information, 15*(5), 282.
4. Fernandez-Carames (2024). A survey on quantum-resistant cryptosystems for the Internet of Things. *IEEE Internet of Things Journal, 7*(7), 6457–6480.
5. O. Okporokpo, F. Olajide, N. Ajienka, & X. Ma (2023). Trust-based approaches towards enhancing IoT security: A systematic literature review. *arXiv preprint arXiv:2311.11705.*
6. K. Ashton (2009). That "Internet of Things" thing. *RFiD Journal, 22*, 97–114. https://www.rfidjournal.com/that-internet-of-things-thing. [Accessed on July 4, 2020].

7. European Union Agency for Network and Information Security (ENSIA) (2017). *Baseline security recommendations for IoT*, EU Publications. https://www.ensia.europa.eu/publications/baseline-security-recommendations-for-iot.
8. S. Madakam, R. Ramaswamy, & S. Tripathi (2015). Internet of Things (IoT): A literature review, *Journal of Computer and Communications, 3* (5), 164.
9. V. Hassija, V. Chamola, V. Saxena, D. Jain, P. Goyal, & B. Sikdar (2019). A survey on IoT security: Application areas, security threats, and solution architectures, *IEEE Access, 7*, 82721–82743.
10. Jurcut, T. Niculcea, P. Ranaweera, et al. (2020). Security considerations for internet of things: A survey, *SN Computer Science, 1*, 193.
11. N. Mishra, & S. Pandya (2021). Internet of things applications, security challenges, attacks, intrusion detection, and future visions: A systematic review, *IEEE Access, 9*, 59353–59377.
12. M. Noor, & W. Hassan (2019). Current research on Internet of Things (IoT) security: A survey, *Elsevier: Computer Networks, 148*, 283–294.
13. H. HaddadPajouh, A. Dehghantanha, R. Parizi, M. Aledhari, & H. Karimipour (2021). A survey on internet of things security: Requirements, challenges, and solutions, *Elsevier: Internet of Things, 14* (100129), 1–19.
14. M.A. Al-Garadi, A. Mohamed, A.K. Al-Ali, X. Du, I. Ali, & M. Guizani (2020). A survey of machine and deep learning methods for Internet of Things (IoT) security, *IEEE Communications Surveys & Tutorials, 22* (3), 1646–1685.
15. S. Zaman et al. (2021). Security threats and artificial intelligence based countermeasures for internet of things networks: A comprehensive survey, *IEEE Access, 9*, 94668–94690.
16. D.E. Kouicem, A. Bouabdallah, & H. Lakhlef (2018). Internet of Things security: A top-down survey, *Computer Networks, 141*, 199–221.
17. Y. Harbi, Z. Aliouat, S. Harous, A. Bentaleb, & A. Refou (2019). A review of security in Internet of Things, *Wireless Personal Communications, 108* (1), 325–344.
18. S.A. Hamad, Q.Z. Sheng, W.E. Zhang, & S. Nepal (2020). Realizing an internet of secure things: A survey on issues and enabling technologies, *IEEE Communications Surveys & Tutorials, 22* (2), 1372–1391.
19. V.A. Thakor, M.A. Razzaque, & M.R.A. Khandaker (2021). Lightweight cryptography algorithms for resource-constrained IoT devices: A review, comparison and research opportunities, *IEEE Access, 9*, 28177–28193.
20. Hameed and A. Alomary (2019). Security issues in IoT: A survey, *Proc. Int. Conf. Innov. Intell. Inform. Computing Technol. (ICT)*, Sakhier, Bahrain, Sep., pp. 1–5.
21. Y. Lu, & L.D. Xu (2019). Internet of Things (IoT) cybersecurity research: A review of current research topics, *IEEE Internet Things Journal, 6* (2), 2103–2115.
22. J. Wurm, K. Hoang, O. Arias, A.R. Sadeghi, and Y. Jin (2016). Security analysis on consumer and industrial IoT devices. *Proc. Asia South Pacific Des. Autom. Conf. ASP-DAC*, Macao, China, 25–28 January, pp. 519–524.
23. S. Chandra, S. Paira, S.S. Alam, and G. Sanyal (2014). A comparative survey of symmetric and asymmetric key cryptography. *Int. Conf. Electron. Commun. Comput. Eng. ICECCE 2014*, Hosur, India, pp. 83–93.
24. S. Surendran, A. Nassef, and B.D. Beheshti (2018). A survey of cryptographic algorithms for IoT devices. *IEEE Long Isl. Syst. Appl. Technol. Conf. LISAT 2018*, Farmingdale, NY, USA, pp. 1–8.
25. T. Kavitha, G. Senbagavalli, & S. Saraswathi (2024). Privacy preserving scheme for Internet of Things, Secure Communication in Internet of Things. Edited by T. Kavitha, M.K. Sandhya, V.J. Subashini and Prasidh Srikanth. CRC Press, pp. 117–129. https://doi.org/10.1201/9781003477327

26. G. Senbagavalli, V.A. Velvizhi, T. Sukanya Prasad, & S.T. Bibin Shalini (2022). A panorama of communication technologies for IoT connected devices, *Internet of Everything: Smart Sensing Technologies*. Edited by T.Kavitha, V.Ajantha Devi, S.Neelavathy Pari and Sakkarvarthi Ramanathan. Nova Science Publishers, pp. 49–80. https://doi.org/10.52305/PNQM1088
27. F. Thabit, O. Can, A. O. Aljahdali, G. H. Al-Gaphari, & H. A. Alkhzaimi (2023). Cryptography algorithms for enhancing IoT security. *Internet of Things, 22*, 100759. https://doi.org/10.1016/j.iot.2023.100759
28. C.A. Lara-Nino, A. Diaz-Perez, and M. Morales-Sandoval (2018). Elliptic curve lightweight cryptography: A Survey, *IEEE Access, PP* (c), 1–1.
29. M.A. Philip (2017). A survey on lightweight ciphers for IoT devices. *Int. Conf. Technol. Adv. Power Energy (TAP Energy)*, Kollam, India, pp. 1–4.
30. D. Hong, J. Sung, S. Hong, J. Lim, S. Lee, & B. Koo (2006). Hight: A new block cipher suitable for low-resource device. *Int. Workshop Cryptograph. Hardw. Embedded Syst.*, Berlin, Germany, pp. 46–59, Springer.
31. I.N.M. Shah, E.S. Ismail, F. Samat, & N.N.A. Rahman (2023). Modified generalized Feistel Network Block cipher for the Internet of Things, *Symmetry, 15*(4), 900. https://doi.org/10.3390/sym15040900
32. Y. Dodis, J. Katz, J.P. Steinberger, A. Thiruvengadam, & Z. Zhang (2017). *Provable security of substitution-permutation networks*. IACR Cryptology ePrint Archive, Report 2017/016. *Available at* https://eprint.iacr.org/2017/016.
33. V.T. Hoang, & P. Rogaway (2010). On generalized Feistel networks. Advances in Cryptology – CRYPTO 2010. CRYPTO 2010. Lecture Notes in Computer Science, vol 6223, Springer, Berlin, Heidelberg. Edited by Tal Rabin. https://doi.org/10.1007/978-3-642-14623-7_33
34. S. Alam, M. Bokhari, & F. Masoodi (2012). An analysis of linear feedback shift registers in stream ciphers. *International Journal of Computer Applications-IJCA, 46*, 46–49. https://doi.org/10.5120/7013-9714.
35. I. Alhejri, & S. Almuhammadi (2020). Constructing new NLFSR functions with optimal periods, *International Journal of Interdisciplinary Telecommunications and Networking, 12*, 71–80. https://doi.org/10.4018/IJITN.2020040106.
36. I.M. Al-Hejri, & A.M. Al-Kharobi (2018). A new type of NLFSR functions with maximum periods, *Transactions on Networks and Communications, 7*(2). https://doi.org/10.14738/tnc.72.6473
37. O. Potii, N. Poluyanenko, I. Stelnyk, I. Revak, S. Kavun, & T. Kuznetsova (2019). Nonlinear-feedback shift registers for stream ciphers. *IEEE 2nd Ukraine Conference on Electrical and Computer Engineering (UKRCON)*, Lviv,Ukraine, pp. 906–911. https://doi.org/10.109/UKRCON.2019.8879786.
38. A. Bogdanov (2007). Cryptanalysis of the KeeLoq block cipher. *IACR Cryptology ePrint Archive, 2007*, 55.
39. T. Eisenbarth, T. Kasper, A. Moradi, C. Paar, M. Salmasizadeh, & M.T.M. Shalmani (2008). On the power of power analysis in the real world: A complete break of the KeeLoq code hopping scheme. In: Wagner, D. (eds) Advances in Cryptology – CRYPTO 2008. CRYPTO 2008. Lecture Notes in Computer Science, vol. 5157, Springer, Berlin, Heidelberg. https://doi.org/10.1007/978-3-540-85174-5_12
40. N.A.N. Abdullah, N.H.L.A. Zawawi, & H.A. Rani (2011). Analysis on lightweight block cipher, KTANTAN, *7th International Conference on Information Assurance and Security (IAS)*, Melacca, Malaysia, pp. 46–51. https://doi.org/10.1109/ISIAS.2011.6122793.

41. Das & Sourav (2014). Halka: A lightweight, software friendly block cipher using ultra-lightweight 8-bit S-box, *IACR Cryptology ePrint Archive,* 110, pp. 1–16.
42. B. Seok, & C. Lee (2019). Fast implementations of ARX-based lightweight block ciphers (SPARX, CHAM) on 32-bit processor. *International Journal of Distributed Sensor Networks, 15* (9). https://doi.org/10.1177/1550147719874180
43. T. Park, H. Seo, & G. Lee et al. (2017). Efficient implementation of simeck family block cipher on 16-bit msp430. *Proceedings of the Ninth International Conference on Ubiquitous and Future Networks (ICUFN),* Milan, pp. 983–988, IEEE, New York.
44. T. Park, H. Seo, & G. Lee et al. (2017). Parallel implementations of Simon and speck, revisited. *Proceedings of the International Workshop on Information Security Applications,* Jeju, South Korea, pp. 283–294. Springer, Berlin.
45. T. Park, H. Seo, & H. Kim (2018). Fast implementation of simeck family block ciphers using avx2. *Proceedings of the International Conference on Platform Technology and Service (PlatCon),* Jeju, South Korea, pp. 1–6. IEEE, New York.
46. A.D. Dwivedi, & G. Srivastava (2018). Differential cryptanalysis of round-reduced LEA. *IEEE Access, 6,* 79105–79113. https://doi.org/10.1109/access.2018.2881130
47. D.J. Bernstein (2008). The Salsa20 family of stream ciphers. In: Robshaw, M., Billet, O. (eds) New Stream Cipher Designs. Lecture Notes in Computer Science, vol 4986. Springer, Berlin, Heidelberg. https://doi.org/10.1007/978-3-540-68351-3_8
48. V.S. Prajwal, & K.V. Prema (2018). User defined encryption procedure for IDEA algorithm. *International Conference on Advances in Computing, Communications and Informatics (ICACCI),* Bengaluru, India pp. 1668–1671. https://doi.org/10.1109/ICACCI.2018.8554699.
49. D. Engels, X. Fan, G. Gong, H. Hu, & E.M. Smith (2010). Hummingbird: Ultra-lightweight cryptography for resource-constrained devices. *Financial Cryptography and Data Security, 6054,* 3–18. https://doi.org/10.1007/978-3-642-14992-4_2.
50. D. Engels, M.J.O. Saarinen, P. Schweitzer, & E.M. Smith (2012). The hummingbird-2 lightweight authenticated encryption algorithm. In: Juels, A., Paar, C. (eds) RFID. Security and Privacy. RFIDSec 2011. Lecture Notes in Computer Science, vol. 7055, Springer, Berlin, Heidelberg. https://doi.org/10.1007/978-3-642-25286-0_2
51. Y. Rekha, S.C. Yellamraju, & M. Kamaraju (2020). Design and implementation of low power, lightweight cryptographic core using hummingbird2 algorithm, *International Journal of Scientific and Engineering Research,* 4, pp. 7086–7089.
52. M.P. Soni and A. R. Pais (2017). Light-weight hash algorithms using GRP instruction. *Proceedings of the 10th International Conference on Security of Information and Networks (SIN '17).* Association for Computing Machinery, New York, NY, pp. 206–211. https://doi.org/10.1145/3136825.3136891
53. M. Jain, & A. Agrawal (2014). Implementation of hybrid cryptography algorithm, *IJCEM, 1* (3), 126–142.
54. D. Aakash, & P. Shanthi (2016). Lightweight cryptographic algorithm for low power node with Bluetooth connectivity. *10th International Conference on Intelligent Systems and Control (ISCO),* Coimbatore, India, pp. 1–6. https://doi.org/10.1109/ISCO.2016.7726927.
55. P. Williams, I.K. Dutta, H. Daoud, & M. Bayoumi (2022). A survey on security in internet of things with a focus on the impact of emerging technologies, *Internet of Things, 19,* 100564. https://doi.org/10.1016/j.iot.2022.100564

Chapter 7

Cybersecurity Challenges on the Internet of Things: A Study on Emerging Threats and Vulnerabilities

Anil Kumar Chikatimarla

7.1 Introduction

With the proliferation of the Internet of Things (IoT), previously inaccessible physical objects are now able to communicate and exchange data digitally. The domino effect has pervaded numerous sectors, leading to efficiency advantages. There is an enormous variety of devices that fall under the umbrella of the IoT. Some examples include sensors in smart factories, connected automobiles, smart thermostats, and wearable health monitors. Thanks to developments in wireless connectivity, cloud computing, and data analytics, Statista projects that the number of IoT devices worldwide will approach 75 billion by 2025 (2022). The exponential growth of the IoT has led to improved user experiences, more accurate predictive maintenance, and increased productivity. However, the proliferation of connected devices has brought with it a host of new cyber risks.

Security is often overlooked when creating IoT devices for the sake of efficiency and usability. Many IoT devices are vulnerable to fraud because of insufficient

DOI: 10.1201/9781003587859-7

security measures that were implemented before they were deployed. These devices are unable to carry out intricate security measures because of their embedded, lightweight operating systems and poor processing capabilities [1]. There have been instances of coordinated cyberattacks on IoT. Malware infections, data breaches, unauthorized access, and distributed denial of service (DDoS) attacks are all examples of such threats. The 2016 Mirai botnet attack is a prime example, according to Kolias, Kambourakis, Stavrou, and Voas [2]. By taking advantage of vulnerable IoT devices, this attack brought down a plethora of websites and services situated in the US.

Because of their decentralized design, IoT devices are even more difficult to secure than they already are. IoT networks, with their abundance of devices and varied levels of security, are ubiquitous, whether you're in a little flat or a huge factory. Sicari, Rizzardi, Grieco, and Coen-Porisini [3] state that the diversity of the network makes it vulnerable to security breaches that could impact many devices simultaneously. The fact that no one, agreed-upon protocol exists to ensure IoT safety just makes matters worse. Because manufacturers prioritize market speed over security, many ecosystems and devices lack integrated and effective solutions for security [2].

Another major challenge is the complexity of maintaining and updating IoT devices. Many IoT systems have known vulnerabilities that can be exposed for a lengthy period since they don't enable over-the-air upgrades or require manual firmware modifications. Bomhara and Køien (2015) [40] state that if a device is not patched, hackers can get unauthorized access to networks, steal data, or even take control of the device and use it for malicious purposes such as ransomware attacks. The widespread interplay between IoT devices and critical infrastructure has stoked growing fears about the threats these devices might represent to public and national security. System integration has several uses, including smart grid applications, healthcare, and industrial control.

Industry standards, public education campaigns, and legal safeguards for IoT networks are necessary to overcome these obstacles. This research aims to examine recently found security holes in IoT systems and, hopefully, find solutions to them. This report characterizes the current level of cybersecurity for the IoT by examining important vulnerabilities such as weak authentication procedures, open communication routes, and inadequate encryption. At the end of the chapter, they offer some suggestions on how to make IoT networks stronger [4].

7.1.1 Chapter Contribution

This chapter contributes to the field of IoT cybersecurity by identifying emerging threats, vulnerabilities, and challenges in securing IoT devices. It highlights issues such as weak encryption, inadequate authentication, and a lack of standardized security protocols. The study proposes mitigation strategies, including layered encryption, machine learning-based anomaly detection, and regulatory frameworks, emphasizing the need for collaboration among industry stakeholders to enhance IoT security and resilience [3,4].

7.2 Emerging Threats in IoT Systems

The proliferation of IoT devices has given criminals access to a much bigger target. Security holes in IoT systems are easy to exploit since there aren't enough standards, devices come in all shapes and sizes, and computers have limited capability. New types of cybercrime have arisen in tandem with the expansion of IoT networks into people's daily lives and vital infrastructure. Today, the IoT faces numerous serious threats as shown in Figure 7.1 including malware, data breaches, DDoS attacks, and advanced persistent threats (APT) [3].

7.2.1 Malware Attacks

Malware can penetrate IoT devices more rapidly when security measures are inadequate. Almost invariably, malware that targets IoT devices looks for vulnerabilities in the operating systems or firmware of those devices. The biggest DDoS assault ever recorded occurred in 2016 when the Mirai botnet compromised millions of IoT devices, such as routers and cameras. IoT devices appear to have been this botnet's target audience. The Mirai malware purportedly used weak authentication techniques and pre-set login credentials to carry out its huge assaults [5]. Securing all interconnected devices is a key objective of the IoT. Apart from being

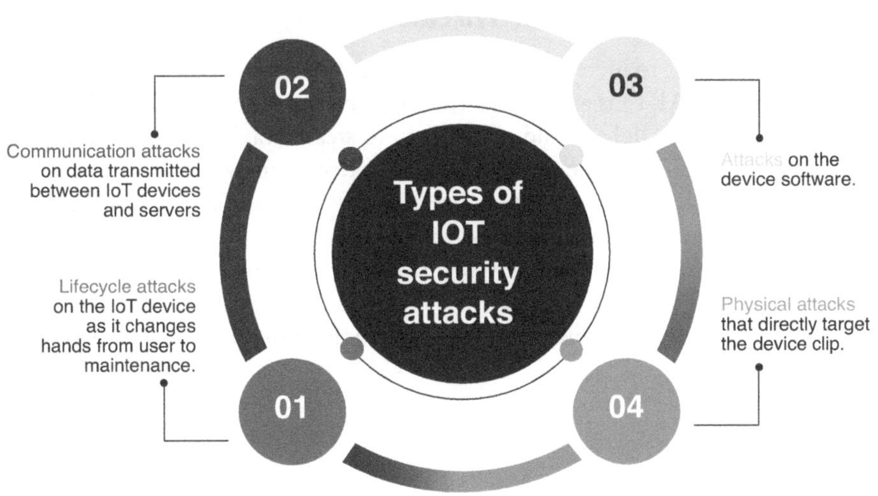

Figure 7.1 Types of IoT security attacks.

multistrain, recent studies have shown that the Mirai virus specifically targets certain vulnerabilities [3,5].

7.2.2 Distributed Denial of Service (DDoS) Attacks

DDoS attacks can compromise a large number of IoT systems. During these attacks, botnets—which are networks of infected devices—can overwhelm a target system with an overwhelming amount of traffic. The low processing power and complex security protocols of IoT devices make them easy targets for DDoS attacks. Hackers can gain access to multiple devices at once if users engage in unsafe behaviors like using default passwords or leaving ports exposed. An extensive DDoS attack was launched in 2016 by the Mirai botnet, which consists of networked IoT devices [6]. An associated pattern with the proliferation of internet-connected devices is the increase of DDoS attacks.

7.2.3 Data Breaches and Privacy Violations

Many IoT devices collect and send highly sensitive information. Personal information includes things like a person's address, bank details, and medical records. Interception and manipulation of this data are possible due to inadequate or non-existent encryption standards. According to Zhang, Ni, and Wang [7], unsecured smart home gadgets make it easy to steal security camera footage and other critical data. With the ever-increasing volume of sensitive financial and personal data transmitted by IoT devices, concerns about data breaches have legitimately grown among both businesses and individuals [8].

7.2.4 Advanced Persistent Threats (APTs)

The IoT is vulnerable to increasingly complex attacks known as APTs. An "advanced persistent threat" (APT) is a hacking attempt that eludes detection for a long time. Obtaining that green light would allow them to steal data, hack systems, or gather intelligence (Figure 7.2). Due to the lack of effective security monitoring methods, a rising number of APTs are taking advantage of vulnerabilities in IoT devices. If an attacker gains access to a network and then laterally migrates to other, more important systems, they can do significantly more damage. According to Sadeghi, Wachsmann, and Waidner [9], industrial IoT systems utilized in the energy and manufacturing sectors are vulnerable to catastrophic outcomes caused by unregulated APTs [2].

7.2.5 Physical Attacks

Physical attacks are another potential vulnerability on the IoT. Since many IoT devices are typically stored in unattended or public areas, they are physically vulnerable to being touched or exposed. Hackers can modify the device's operation or introduce flaws that can be used later, making the hardware of IoT devices

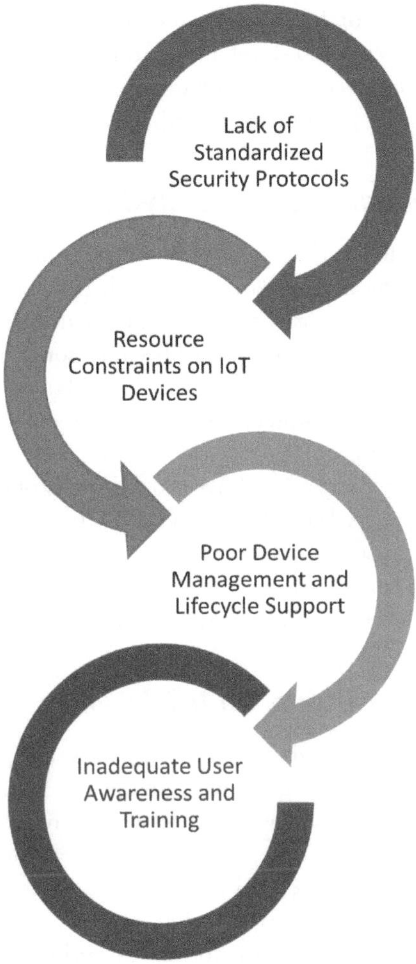

Figure 7.2 Circular process flow diagram.

vulnerable to hacking. The security of public services and autonomous vehicles could be jeopardized if hackers were able to access the sensors utilized by smart city systems, as stated by Perwej and Perwej [10]. Hackers can install malware or steal crucial data if they physically get access to machines that are connected to the internet [10].

7.3 Factors Contributing to IoT Vulnerabilities

The IoT ecosystem consists of numerous components, such as software, hardware, and communication protocols. Things get slightly trickier because of this. Cybersecurity has recently risen to the top of many industries' priority lists due to the increasing number of IoT devices and sophisticated cyberattack methods. Problems with IoT devices could develop due to inadequate user education, device management, resources, or security standards. This article will go over the possible weak spots in systems that rely on the IoT [9].

7.3.1 Lack of Standardized Security Protocols

A big problem with the IoT is that there aren't any platform-or device-specific security standards. Due to the diverse range of IoT devices and the distributed structure of IoT ecosystems, manufacturers may fail to implement sufficient security measures. The IoT isn't perfect for security because some of its devices aren't safe at all. The formation of easily breachable "security islands" occurs when disparate devices with different levels of protection do not interact with one another or agree on security procedures [7,9].

Weak or nonexistent encryption leaves IoT devices open to data-gathering or unauthorized-access attacks [11]. While trying to balance security requirements with other considerations like performance and cost, manufacturers are facing challenges in providing comprehensive protection for various types of devices in the absence of a standardized industry framework for IoT security [11,12].

7.3.2 Resource Constraints on IoT Devices

A further major factor adding to IoT dangers is the fact that many IoT devices do not have enough power. Designed with low power consumption and memory needs, these gadgets are inexpensive. As a result, many IoT devices don't include security features like intrusion detection systems, robust encryption, or real-time monitoring that would allow them to protect themselves from bad actors. When making sensors, smart lights, or wearable gear, designers who prioritize functionality over security frequently overlook the former, according to Zhou and Zhang [12].

IoT devices are more vulnerable to assaults since they can't handle computationally demanding security tasks like encryption and decryption, according to Alaba, Othman, Hashem, and Alotaibi [11]. As an example, low-end IoT devices frequently do not receive updates for newly disclosed vulnerabilities due to lack of resources [13]. Because of their limited battery life, wireless IoT devices are susceptible to attacks since they cannot perform continuous security checks.

7.3.3 Poor Device Management and Lifecycle Support

Securing IoT systems requires effective device management, which includes regular patches and upgrades. Due to the widespread deployment of IoT devices without the ability to receive frequent updates, effective lifecycle management is required in the consumer market. Devices are susceptible to cyberattacks because vulnerabilities found after deployment are frequently left unfixed for long periods of time since patch management and long-term maintenance are lacking [14].

Wang, Zhang, and Wang [15] state that manufacturers often fail to upgrade their IoT devices at the recommended intervals or simply do not have the necessary resources to do so. This causes more than 60% of the deployed devices to miss important update deadlines. This means that hackers have more opportunities to exploit software vulnerabilities in "abandoned" devices in IoT networks, which are no longer safe but still functional. Organizations struggle to keep their IoT environments up-to-date and safe because of the complexity of managing a wide variety of devices, particularly in large-scale installations [16].

7.3.4 Inadequate User Awareness and Training

Users' lack of awareness regarding the security risks associated with IoT devices makes the network even more vulnerable to attacks. Many users, particularly in consumer settings, are unaware that IoT devices pose significant cybersecurity concerns. Security researchers Sicari et al. [3] found that a lot of IoT devices have weak passwords and unprotected ports. As a result, hackers will find them easy prey. Users may be totally unaware that they need to change the default credentials, deactivate unnecessary features, or link their devices to protected networks [3].

Additionally, customers may mistakenly believe that IoT devices are inherently secure due to their ease of setup. According to Alrawais, Alhothaily, Hu, and Cheng [12], many IoT security breaches are caused by users who are either irresponsible or don't know enough about security standards. Unintentionally adding to the growth of unsecured devices in IoT networks occurs when users lack sufficient knowledge about the dangers and how to protect themselves. Improving security measures and educating people who utilize the IoT are of the utmost importance [15].

7.4 Mitigation Strategies for IoT Security

The need for solving multiple security issues is growing in response to the widespread use of IoT devices in numerous industries. This can only be accomplished with robust mitigation strategies. Improving management and implementing technological solutions are two parts of a comprehensive strategy for protecting IoT networks. Safe device management, enhanced encryption, increased user education, standardizing security frameworks, and machine learning-based anomaly detection can all reduce the likelihood of security compromises. Here we'll look at these measures to see how they help protect networks and IoT devices from growing threats [17].

7.4.1 Standardized Security Frameworks

To safeguard the IoT against attacks, we must create and completely follow standardized security protocols. Security standards for gadgets should be the same across all manufacturers. Standardization efforts like this aim to solve two major security problems: authentication and the secure transmission of encrypted data.

The authors of Ref. [12] claim that the Open Worldwide Application Security Project (OWASP) Top Ten list of security vulnerabilities on the IoT can be useful for developers and manufacturers. Check out this list if you're thinking about ways to strengthen the security of the IoT.

The public and commercial sectors are working together to establish security certification standards for IoT devices. Under the Cybersecurity Act, the European Union established a standard for cybersecurity certifications related to the IoT [18]. The reduced diversity and increased uniformity in IoT devices make it more vulnerable to security attacks.

7.4.2 Enhancing Encryption and Authentication Protocols

To ensure the safety of any personally identifiable information transmitted over the IoT, secure data transfer is an absolute must. If you want to make sure that no data breaches occur during device-to-device communication, it's a good idea to encrypt all IoT devices using strong protocols like Elliptic Curve Cryptography or Advanced Encryption Standard (2011). Alrawais et al. [12] discovered that robust authentication methods and public-key infrastructure technology greatly improve the security of the IoT. With these protections in place, any unapproved devices will be unable to enrol.

To address the issue of resource constraints in many IoT devices, lightweight encryption algorithms were created to strike a balance between security and performance [19]. When the computing capacity of IoT devices is restricted, various solutions can be employed to protect communication channels. By implementing two-factor authentication (2FA), which checks users and restricts their access, significantly reduces the likelihood of unauthorized individuals gaining access to devices.

7.4.3 Secure Device Management and Lifecycle Maintenance

It is critical to have comprehensive device management in place to guarantee the security of the IoT from the moment a device is deployed until it is retired. It is crucial to upgrade IoT devices often and manage patches to cure existing vulnerabilities and avoid new ones [20]. The ability to automatically patch is an integral part of every high-quality IoT device. Because of this, patching will no longer necessitate human involvement. According to Lee, Pompili, and Lee [14], using over-the-air update methods is highly recommended for keeping all devices up to date. By employing these methods, devices can remotely receive security patches.

It is critical to execute controlled device decommissioning methods and conduct periodical upgrades to further ensure that sensitive data is erased from devices prior to disposal. Theoretically, this prevents devices from being exploited just before they die [14,20]. Businesses can reduce their vulnerability by automating these processes and using safe device management solutions to monitor the security state of their IoT devices in real time.

7.4.4 Machine Learning and Anomaly Detection

In the realm of AI and machine learning, anomaly detection reigns supreme. Strengthening security measures for the IoT is the main objective. These developments have allowed IoT systems to detect shifts in device and network activity that may indicate a breach in security [14]. To increase the probability of identifying IoT threats, colleagues (2020) state that two kinds of deep learning models—recurrent neural networks and convolutional neural networks—may be enough. Various potentially harmful occurrences, such as alerts on suspicious device activity or intrusion attempts, can be monitored by abnormal detection models that keep a watch on network data. These methods enable this when used with large datasets. These techniques, when applied to large datasets, aid in the detection and mitigation of threats such as data breaches, infections, and theft. By combining IoT networks with AI-powered security systems, a novel defensive mechanism can be created to address the ever-increasing threats. Our security posture has been enhanced as a result.

7.4.5 User Education and Awareness

While technological fixes are essential, user actions greatly impact the safety of IoT systems. According to Sicari, Rizzardi, Grieco, and Coen-Porisini [3], systems can be left vulnerable to attacks if users use weak passwords, hazardous default settings, and fail to upgrade devices frequently enough. Risk mitigation relies heavily on user education, whether it's normal customers or company management.

Goods and services should make customers aware of security regulations, such as those requiring strong passwords and the automatic activation of 2FA. People can learn more about why it's important to secure their IoT devices through public awareness campaigns and educational initiatives. The attack surface in IoT networks can be decreased and many common security vulnerabilities can be prevented by educating users, according to Roman et al. [16].

7.5 Case Studies of IoT-Specific Cyberattacks

Cybercriminals target IoT devices because of their essential roles in smart infrastructure, healthcare, and manufacturing, as well as their increasing number and lack of adequate security protections. The necessity to enhance security measures was brought to light by previous attacks on IoT devices, which exposed vulnerabilities, disrupted operations, and so on. To demonstrate the risks posed by the network, case studies dissect specific IoT vulnerabilities and the harm they cause.

7.5.1 The Mirai Botnet Attack (2016)

The Mirai botnet was a prominent one among 2016's IoT threats. Mirai may be able to access routers and IP cameras, among other devices, by taking advantage of the default credentials of insecure IoT devices. A deluge of DDoS attacks caused by a huge number of compromised devices impacted multiple major websites and services, including industry heavyweight Dyn [3].

Popular companies' services were interrupted by the Dyn attack, which targeted numerous important websites in the US and Europe. The incident demonstrated a popular method for exploiting security holes and default login credentials. As shown by the Mirai botnet, mixing hacked IoT devices with DDoS attacks can result in severe outcomes. It is recommended that users modify the default passwords on their IoT gadgets, while manufacturers should enhance security features [3,21].

7.5.2 The Stuxnet Worm (2010)

Although Stuxnet may have caused the greatest harm to industrial control systems, it also shows how IoT devices that are linked to vital infrastructure could be weaponized. To thwart Iran's nuclear program, the sophisticated worm Stuxnet was programmed to target Siemens Supervisory Regulation and Data Acquisition systems, which regulate automated operations in the industry [21].

The worm used USB sticks to infect victims' desktops, and it also used several zero-day vulnerabilities to infect any IoT devices linked to the network. Stuxnet altered the programming of industrial machinery to inflict bodily injury while tricking the system's human operators into thinking everything is running well. As far as anyone knows, this incident was the first time a cyberweapon damaged critical infrastructure, which is a huge improvement over threats based on the IoT.

Stuxnet awakened the world's corporate and government sectors after successfully revealing the vulnerability of interconnected systems critical to national security and industrial operations. The transportation, water treatment, and energy sectors are among those most at risk from comparable assaults due to the growing importance of IoT devices in automating vital activities [15].

7.5.3 The Jeep Cherokee Hack (2015)

Cybersecurity specialists named Charlie Miller and Chris Valasek found a severe vulnerability that affected the 2015 Fiat Chrysler Jeep Cherokee. This vulnerability was discovered by the two individuals. Due to this weakness, they were able to remotely take control of the automobiles for themselves. According to Greenberg [22], researchers were able to take control of the vehicle's engine, brakes, and steering by exploiting security holes on the internet-connected Uconnect infotainment system.

This event proved that security flaws in the IoT and related cars might have disastrous consequences. The study team accessed to the car's vital systems by connecting the infotainment module to the vehicle's principal communication system, the CAN bus. Everything within may be at risk if an unauthorized person were to obtain control of the car's vital systems. The case study examined the potential dangers that could arise from networks of interconnected vehicles.

Shortly after this presentation, Fiat Chrysler issued a software update and recalled 1.4 million autos to address concerns over the safety of the vehicles. The tragedy that occurred with the Jeep Cherokee was the impetus for the introduction of several different safety measures. According to Miller and Valasek (2015), some of these steps include the implementation of encrypted over-the-air updates and the partitioning of internet-connected modules from systems that are most mission critical [6].

7.5.4 The Verkada Camera Breach (2021)

A significant data breach that occurred in 2021 involving the security camera company Verkada revealed the live feeds and archived photographs of more than 150,000 surveillance cameras. These cameras had been installed in a variety of institutions, such as schools, hospitals, and jails, as well as in businesses such as Tesla. According to Gallagher [23], criminals were able to get access to the company's computers by using credentials that they discovered on the internet.

Since the attackers obtained footage from vital sites, many are concerned about the possible dangers to people's privacy and safety offered by the pervasive IoT surveillance equipment. Because it demonstrated how sensitive information might be exposed through cloud-connected IoT devices, this incident brought attention to the issue. Every network that supports devices connected to the IoT should tightly implement methods for managing passwords and 2FA.

Businesses that rely on IoT devices for security and monitoring could learn from Verkada's strategy. Montalbano (2021) [42] asserts that regular vulnerability assessments, encryption of sensitive data, and stricter access controls are all essential [24].

7.5.5 The FDA Recall of IoT Medical Devices (2017)

Due to security concerns, the Food and Drug Administration's recalled more than half a million pacemakers in the United States in 2017. According to Sametinger, Rozenblit, Lysecky, and Ott (2015), if hackers were able to access the affected Abbott (formerly St. Jude Medical) pacemakers and change their settings, patients' lives could be in jeopardy.

It has been learned from this incident that poorly secured medical devices connected to the internet might create disastrous consequences. The pacemakers were susceptible to hacking efforts since they relied on wireless connectivity for updates and monitoring. All that effort may have caused the battery to die or altered the pacing function. Furthermore, the security mechanisms that were in place were insufficient. Patients were required to visit their doctors' offices to have security flaws addressed following the recall [23].

The Food and Drug Administration's pivotal role in the product recall highlights the rising tide of worry about the safety of medical devices connected to the IoT. There needs to be constant consideration for potential security issues with medical equipment. Implementing the gadget guarantees its safety right away [23,24].

7.6 Survey on IoT Security Challenges and Awareness

We wanted to know more about the problems and people's knowledge about IoT security, so we polled businesses that use IoT devices. The study's overarching goal was to ascertain whether businesses have adequately fortified themselves against the risks associated with IoT devices. Among the many factors gathered by the poll were the security procedures, the frequency of security breaches, the level of security awareness among employees, and the types of IoT devices deployed [22].

7.6.1 Thinking about the Survey

A count of all the IoT gadgets that made it into the sample. Some examples of categories are as follows:

Hardware for the Industrial IoT; Wi-Fi-enabled household appliances
Items used in healthcare that are also linked to the web
Vehicles with network connectivity
Garment parts that a user can wear
Other specialized IoT systems

Using this variable, we investigate the security procedures and techniques that have been implemented to protect IoT platforms. The following are some of the options:

Data Encryption and Network Firewalls are both being implemented.
Installing Updates and Patches for Systems
A Strict Password Policy is in Place
Application tools for monitoring and logging, as well as 2FA technologies

There have been several security incidents that have occurred in businesses over the course of the past year. Some instances of these occurrences include data breaches, unauthorized access, and malware attacks. A measurement of the frequency of these incidents is provided by this variable:

Not at all...
1–3 instances of this
4–6 instances of this

There are seven or more instances.

Knowledge of IoT Security Concerns Among Employees: When determining how well staff understand the security issues associated with the IoT, this variable employs a Likert scale that ranges from 1 to 5. One example is as follows:

The levels of awareness progress from one (completely unaware) to four (very aware), beginning with one (completely unaware) and ending with four (extremely aware).

5. Being conscious

Through the examination of this variable, you will be able to ascertain whether your organization performs IoT security audits to ascertain the degree of vulnerability that your IoT systems have. The following are some possible responses:

Without a doubt, every time without fail
On a few occasions, in fact
Without any ambiguity or doubt.

7.6.2 Survey Results

According to the poll, which was conducted with 150 businesses from a variety of industries, a significant number of organizations use IoT devices in the industrial sector (55%), and 30% of those organizations use IoT systems connected to healthcare. Seventy percent of respondents stated that they utilized firewalls and network protection when they were questioned about security measures, whereas just 45% said they utilized stringent password standards. According to the findings of the study, 40% of the organizations had experienced a security issue that was associated with the IoT within the previous year, and 10% of those organizations reported having experienced six or more instances of such an issue.

On the Likert scale, 35% of respondents believed that their employees had a low awareness of the security problems associated with the IoT, with scores of 1 or 2. Considering this, there is a worrisome awareness gap throughout the workforce. Furthermore, just 30% of organizations consistently carried out security audits for the IoT, which indicates that a significant number of systems and devices are vulnerable to the possibility of being attacked. Based on these findings, we need to be more cautious and implement more preemptive security measures to deal with vulnerabilities related to the IoT.

7.6.3 Discussion

Because the IoT is constantly evolving, the results of the poll highlight the critical necessity for businesses to implement more robust security measures. Even though IoT devices are widely employed in key industries, there are still security flaws, which include a lack of people training and occasional security audits. Cyberattacks are more likely to occur because of inexperience and lack of preparation, which could result in significant damage to both the company's brand and its finances. Organizations will need to emphasize both human and technological aspects to lessen the effect of new dangers as the IoT becomes more integrated into more fundamental business activities.

7.7 Challenges in IoT Security Standards and Regulations

Because strong security regulations and standards have not kept pace with the rapid development of IoT technology, it is simple for cybercriminals to hack ecosystems composed of IoT devices. Attempts by developers, manufacturers, and consumers alike to construct adequate security measures for the IoT are hindered by the absence of generally acknowledged standards [2,22].

7.7.1 The Regulatory Landscape Is Distributed, Which Is a Defining Feature

IoT devices have greatly improved automation and data-driven decision-making, which has benefited many different industries, Including industry, smart homes, and healthcare. Along with these advantages, however, come increased cybersecurity risks. As a result of their limited resources, many IoT devices are susceptible to assaults like DDoS, data leaks, and malware. This chapter examines the most recent security risks to the IoT and some possible remedies.

Because various areas and nations have set their policies and standards, the IoT security environment is disjointed. The General Data Protection Regulation of the European Union, for example, safeguards every device that can be linked to the internet. However, in other parts of the world, rules are either not followed or people choose to ignore them. An increase in the number of vulnerabilities in IoT devices is anticipated to occur because multinational corporations are finding it increasingly challenging to comply with security regulations in a broad range of jurisdictions.

There is more discretion for enterprises to determine for themselves whether to secure their IoT equipment; nevertheless, the "IoT Cybersecurity Improvement Act of 2020" demands certain safeguards for the IoT hardware that is used by government agencies [25]. Even though the "Internet of Things Basic Security Standard" does not apply to Chinese non-governmental organizations (NGOs), there is still a requirement for risk assessment and security management systems.

7.7.2 Contributions of This Study

IoT security is a pressing concern due to the increasing number of interconnected devices that handle sensitive data. The need for safeguarding IoT ecosystems is brought to light by many factors:

- **Sensitivity of Data:** The vast amounts of sensitive financial, personal, and business data collected and processed by IoT devices make them an attractive target for cybercriminals.

- Security is a concern with IoT devices due to their individual software and hardware capabilities. These products span every possible use case, from smart home gadgets to industrial sensors.
- **Limitations on Expansion:** The proliferation of IoT networks has resulted in an exponential growth of the attack surface, making it more difficult to implement consistent security measures across all devices [26].
- Users' personal information is at risk of breaches and illegal access since many IoT devices do not have strong authentication procedures.
- Cybersecurity best practices must be followed by makers of IoT devices due to the increasingly stringent security standards set by regulators and governments.

7.7.3 Manufacturer Responsibility and Liability

IoT device manufacturers frequently deploy devices that are not secure because they place a higher priority on cost-effectiveness and speedy time-to-market than they do on the inclusion of security safeguards. Insecure default passwords, obsolete software, and inadequate encryption are some of the reasons why many IoT devices are vulnerable to unauthorized access. There is a possibility that gadgets will gradually become susceptible to security risks if manufacturers do not give sufficient support for upgraded security.

Another question that has not been answered has to do with who is responsible for breaches that involve the IoT [27]. Because of the large number of companies that manufacture IoT devices, it is difficult to determine who is at fault if there is a security breach. Manufacturers can continue supplying products with security weaknesses without facing any consequences if there are no well-defined regulations that mandate the security of the design.

7.7.4 Malware Attacks

Data loss or theft may result from hackers taking advantage of security holes in the IoT. Failure to apply software updates or use unsecured communication channels may lead to computer infections caused by Trojans, worms, and ransomware. You could be mulling about the Mirai botnet incident of 2016. Distribution denial of service attacks may occur if security flaws in devices were to be exploited. To help businesses remain safe from these dangers, security alternatives like automatic upgrades, strong encryption, and real-time threat detection systems are available [28].

7.7.5 Distributed Denial of Service (DDoS) Attacks

One way to disrupt the IoT would be via a DDoS assault, which involves flooding networks with malicious data from rogue mobile devices. Insecure authentication settings, firmware flaws, or poorly set up network protocols make it easy for attackers to take over IoT devices and turn them into botnets. A company's services might be interrupted or slowed down by DDoS assaults, which could harm its image and cause financial losses. Limiting data transfer rates, segmenting networks, and monitoring for anomalous behavior are all ways to defend against DDoS attacks.

7.7.6 Data Breaches and Privacy Violations

Because of their capacity to collect and send massive quantities of personally identifiable information, hackers find IoT devices to be attractive targets. Unprotected data poses a risk of financial crimes, business espionage, and identity theft. This sort of data includes things like medical records, bank account details, and financial information. Due to insufficient authentication and encryption measures, the frequency of data breaches is increasing. Security measures that might be used to enhance data transit across the IoT include end-to-end encryption, multi-factor authentication, and integrity verification based on the blockchain [29].

7.7.7 Advanced Persistent Threats (APTs)

The continual and ever-present threat posed by APTs to interconnected networks is real and deep. Potentially, they might steal, spy, or interfere with services. Attacks like this may go undetected for a while because they target unpatched IoT devices. Critical infrastructure, industrial control systems, and national security might be jeopardized if AI has problems. By implementing precautions, a business may fortify its defenses against APTs. Some examples of this include sharing threat intelligence, conducting regular security audits, and keeping tabs on user behavior.

7.7.8 Interoperability and Complexity

Already, there are issues with system-to-system communication and security, and the growth of IoT devices and platforms make these issues even more severe. When it comes to security, the devices that make up an IoT ecosystem may conform to a wide range of different protocols, operating systems, and brands. Increasing the complexity of the system makes it more difficult to provide full protection for it, which in turn increases the likelihood that there will be security vulnerabilities.

When it comes to developing interoperable equipment, manufacturers may choose to put user-friendliness ahead of stringent security requirements. Given the lack of explicit specifications, this is largely the result. Having this happen could make things vulnerable. Vulnerabilities in linked devices or channels of communication inside IoT networks can be exploited by hackers.

Antivirus and firewall programs have had attack signatures for a while, so they can identify attacks. The IoT is too complex for the old security methods to handle. Modern security designs use cutting-edge methods such as blockchain,

Table 7.1 Comparison of Traditional vs. Modern IoT Security Approaches

Security Approach	*Traditional Methods*	*Modern IoT Security*
Authentication	Username–password	Multi-factor authentication, Biometrics, Blockchain
Encryption	Basic SSL/Transport Layer Security	End-to-end encryption, Homomorphic encryption, Quantum cryptography
Intrusion Detection	Signature-based IDS (Intrusion Detection System)	AI-driven anomaly detection, Machine learning-based threat modeling
Network Security	Firewalls, VPNs	Zero-trust architecture, Blockchain-based security

artificial intelligence (AI), and machine learning. The chance of credential theft and brute-force attacks increases when systems are vulnerable, which may be caused by insufficient authentication measures such as username–password combinations [30].

7.7.9 Authentication Mechanisms

For the IoT to function, modern security protocols are required. Biometric identity, multi-factor authentication, and ID management on the blockchain are shown in Table 7.1 as all parts of this security suite.

7.7.10 Encryption and Data Protection

Although SSL and Transport Layer Security are used by many IoT security solutions, not all of them provide complete end-to-end protection. Encryption of data transferred between IoT devices is one possible security technique. An example of this would be quantum homomorphism or lightweight cryptography based on resistance.

7.7.11 Intrusion Detection and Prevention

Malware is inherently dynamic, making traditional security methods such as signature-based intrusion detection systems and firewalls ineffective. The goal of AI anomaly detection is to use a combination of behavioral analysis and machine learning approaches to detect and prevent APTs and zero-day vulnerabilities. Because of this, it is a great tool for improving the safety of the IoT right now [31].

7.7.12 Network Security Approaches

Unfortunately, the enormous dangers presented by the IoT are not addressed by our present regulations. Security innovations such as blockchain, decentralized networks, and zero-trust architectures have made it possible for devices to safely connect to each other, drastically lowering the bar for illegal access.

Old security frameworks may need to give way to new ones if IoT ecosystems are to be protected from the ever-increasing cyber dangers. A method to improve the security of the IoT might be to combine blockchain technology with zero-trust architectures and AI.

7.7.13 Balancing Privacy and Security

Operating the IoT while keeping user data and infrastructure secure is no easy feat. The IoT allows devices to gather vast quantities of data. Medical records stored in wearable devices and position data from linked cars are two examples of datasets that could contain personally identifiable information. Our utmost priority is ensuring the privacy of our consumers.

Privacy and security are infamously hard to reconcile because they serve fundamentally different needs. Some IoT apps may be incompatible with encryption or other security measures, which are essential for preventing hackers but may also clash with privacy standards that demand more openness and user approval. Data encryption may be inadequate on many low-cost IoT devices [32].

7.7.13.1 Methods of Standardization Practices

IoT security, user privacy, and system integrity must all be addressed at the same time. The sheer volume of data generated by all these interconnected devices is staggering. Several datasets could include personally identifiable information, such as data from linked automobiles and data from wearable medical equipment. We value your privacy very highly.

The inherent contradiction between security and privacy makes finding a compromise between the two problematics. Enhanced security methods, such as encryption, might prevent unauthorized access to some functionalities of IoT apps also run the risk of violating privacy standards that require more transparency and user consent. The processing power of certain inexpensive IoT devices may be insufficient to enable robust encryption [33].

7.7.14 MultiLayered Security Approach

A multilayered, strong security architecture is necessary to guarantee the safety of ecosystems connected to the IoT. Integrating cloud, device, and network security procedures is the way to go for complete peace of mind.

7.7.14.1 Device-Level Security

- **Preserving Specific Electronic Devices with System Boot Protections:** Restrict firmware updates to authorized users only to safeguard your IoT devices from infection.
- One kind of hardware security module is the Secure Elements, while another is the Trusted Platform Module. Key storage is handled by Secure Elements, whereas Trusted Platform Modules are in charge of it.
- Protects devices by regularly installing firmware upgrades and security fixes.
- Integrating biometric and multi-factor authentication is one approach that might be used to enhance the safety of access control systems.

7.7.14.2 Network-Level Security

- Zero-trust architectures guarantee that all users and devices are constantly validated before they can access the network.
- With blockchain technology, secure communication may take place in a decentralized, immutable ledger of all transactions.
- AI-powered intrusion prevention systems keep a close eye on all network traffic to identify and prevent suspicious activity.
- **End-to-End Encryption:** The use of Quantum Cryptography and Transport Layer Security 1.3 to safeguard data transfer within IoT networks.

7.7.14.3 Cloud-Level Security

- AI might be used by anomaly detection models to spot possible dangers as they happen.
- Users' permissions to use certain cloud services are controlled by Role-Based use Control.
- The cutting-edge, blockchain-based solution guarantees the validity of data stored in IoT devices; this is the industry standard.
- With cloud monitoring and recording capabilities, forensic analysis and real-time auditing are now within reach after a hack.

7.7.15 Future Scope and Research Directions

As long as the safety of the IoT is unclear, spending on R&D will remain unpredictable [34]. Here are a few things that demand our undivided attention for the next test:

7.7.16 Launch Protocol for the Internet of Things

- There is no way to settle vendor disputes outside of this, which requires the creation of security standards for internet-connected devices.
- It is very essential that all IoT devices follow the same protocol.

7.7.17 Using AI to Strengthen Cyber Defense

- Improving threat detection and reaction in real time via the use of deep learning and reinforcement learning.
- The ultimate goal is to establish self-repairing networks driven by AI.

7.7.18 Internet of Things Data Security with Blockchain

- Regarding information sent via the IoT, more study into quantum-resistant encryption techniques is necessary.
- Devices connected to the IoT, no matter how little, must use post-quantum cryptography.

7.7.19 Regulatory Compliance Frameworks

- Standardization Requirements for Meeting Compliance Standards Stronger regulatory frameworks and more stringent regulations on data privacy are necessary to guarantee the safety of the IoT.
- More collaboration between the public and commercial sectors is needed to include security-by-design principles into the IoT from the ground up.

7.7.20 Edge Computing Security Enhancements

- To strengthen edge security models to safeguard decentralized networks from attacks and data breaches; this will improve computer security at the edge.
- Updated risk data may be quickly disseminated using the IoT [3].

7.8 Future Trends in IoT Security

The widespread adoption of enabling technologies has brought up a slew of new problems, and these will certainly determine how IoT security evolves in the years to come. We need to make IoT devices more secure since cyberattacks are so widespread and intricate. That's why these developments are happening.

7.8.1 AI-Based Security Measures for Internet of Things Networks

The amount to which AI and ML will impact future security regulations for the IoT remains uncertain. With the help of AI, security systems can get better at spotting threats, handling the massive amounts of data produced by IoT devices, and responding rapidly to emerging threats. Potentially, anomaly detection algorithms can identify suspicious behavior in IoT devices and notify security staff of potential breaches.

AI systems can enhance security by studying past breaches. IoT systems must have the capability to anticipate and react to developing dangers. Maybe we are on the brink of a new wave of AI assaults, yet there are also thrilling new obstacles on the horizon. The use of AI by cyberattackers to uncover and take advantage of security vulnerabilities is expected to increase in the future [35].

7.8.2 Online Transactions Made Secure by Blockchain

The utilization of blockchain technology, which creates decentralized records of unchangeable transactions among devices, has the potential to enhance IoT security. Blockchain technology enhances the security of the IoT through secure distribution of data transmission. This feature can provide significant advantages for devices connected to the internet, especially in supply chain management and smart contracts.

Blockchain technology also validates devices, confirms transactions, and enhances the immutability, auditability, and security of networks with IoT devices. Unfortunately, integrating blockchain technology into a massive IoT networks continues to face challenges related to power consumption and scalability [3,35].

7.9 User Awareness and the Human Factor in IoT Security

Regrettably, human mistake is a widely recognized weakness in the cybersecurity sector, and it also applies to IoT security. The technological aspects of IoT devices could have problems, but humans can assist in fixing them. The majority of security breaches in the IoT occur due to insufficient protocols, abuse of authority, or simple ignorance. The importance of security measures needs to be better communicated, and more people need to be convinced of this before we can solve the IoT concerns.

7.9.1 Lack of Awareness among Consumers

Concerning the potential security risks posed by IoT devices, most purchasers are in the dark. Regarding their "set-it-and-forget-it" characteristics, many people erroneously assume that IoT devices are no different from consumer electronics. With these considerations in mind, the user ought to enable or disable essential security measures. Examples of this kind of behavior include leaving devices connected to unprotected networks, failing to update software, and using default passwords.

More than 70% of people still use the factory-default password for their IoT devices, according to 2020 data from Palo Alto Networks. Concerningly, over half of the study participants acknowledged ignorance of the risks associated with leaving these devices unattended. Many individuals are unaware that IoT devices can be targeted by botnets and other malevolent actors [36].

7.9.2 Inadequate Security Training

The necessity to train workers on the correct and safe usage of IoT devices is one of the biggest problems caused by their widespread deployment in commercial settings. Numerous other sectors are also implementing this concept; only a few examples are healthcare, manufacturing, and logistics. Even with stringent security measures implemented, organizations still run the danger of their IoT devices being compromised due to employee carelessness.

Weak security processes, such as user error, weak passwords, or unregulated device connections, could compromise IoT networks. One type of medical IoT gadget that has the potential to compromise patients' privacy is integral pacemaker. As an additional example, consider an insulin pump. Establish comprehensive training programs to ensure that all individuals interacting with IoT devices have sufficient training on security protocols.

7.9.3 Human Error and Misconfigurations

In 2019, IBM analyzed security events and found that human error played a significant role in more than 95% of these occurrences. As they propagate throughout the IoT, these errors pose a hazard to the entire system rather than just individual devices. For instance, if the thermostat for an IoT is not configured properly in a smart building, an adversary could obtain access to the complete information technology infrastructure located within the building [37].

7.9.4 Mitigating Human-Related IoT Security Risks

There are a few different approaches that may be taken to make the IoT safer and less prone to errors caused by humans:

- Businesses and individuals alike must be aware of the risks associated with the IoT and take precautions to avoid them. Using strong passwords, advising frequent firmware updates, and emphasizing the need for network security are all good examples.
- Throughout the product development process, manufacturers of IoT devices should prioritize security considerations. Aside from requiring a password change after installation, we have also included automatic software upgrades as two user-friendly security features in this project.

- The degree to which your standards and protocols are open and accessible determines the level of security for your IoT initiatives. Best practices call for frequent security audits, user access restrictions on critical IoT devices, and multi-factor authentication for all IoT access [38,39].

7.10 Conclusion

As the IoT grows, more and more opportunities for innovative approaches to old problems have arisen. The idea is the same regardless of how vulnerable systems are to security breaches. The primary objective of this research is to put a number on the harm that security breaches are causing to IoT networks. a variety of gadgets, inadequate standards, and security measures are the primary focuses of this study. IoT security solutions have come to the fore due to the growing importance of IoT-dependent devices in critical infrastructure, corporate processes, and people's daily lives.

Data breaches, device hijackings, and DDoS assaults are just a few of the complex and serious threats that have recently come to light in relation to IoT systems. The dispersed structure of the IoT and the wide variety of security protocols used by individual devices make system vulnerabilities more obvious. The IoT is rife with security holes that cybercriminals can exploit. Issues arise because of insufficient lifecycle management, weak authentication techniques, and encryption. Criminals take advantage of these weaknesses.

These concerns prompted experts to propose detailed suggestions for reducing the impact of IoT networks. Adherence to regional cybersecurity laws, like the EU's Cybersecurity Act, and advocacy for uniform security standards like OWASP are essential for device security. New, improved, and more secure versions of the IoT have recently been released. Some examples include better encryption methods, more stringent rules for device management, and AI-powered anomaly detection. A secure IoT can only be achieved if people think about and talk about it. Therefore, you won't get the same effects if you're careless.

These methods provide a strong basis for protecting IoT devices, even while security threats to these devices are always changing. To remain competitive in today's threat landscape, companies need to keep communication open, do thorough research, and come up with creative solutions to tackle newly discovered vulnerabilities and the growing complexity of cyber criminals. Security risks to the IoT are constantly evolving, necessitating concerted efforts from academia, business, and government.

It may not be as simple as securing the IoT devices seem. Three main components—technology, governance, and user awareness—must be present in each solution. Suppose we want to keep IoT-connected technologies developing and reliable and minimize their exposure to new threats. In that case, we need mitigation strategies that work and a security-first mentality throughout the IoT ecosystem. We can achieve our two objectives by combining these two methods.

A top concern should be ensuring that the IoT operates on a secure, rule-compliant network. Academics must work together to improve cybersecurity governance, develop scalable encryption technologies, and toughen security measures to combat these emerging forms of criminality. Preventative security measures should be a part of IoT ecosystems to strengthen their defenses and provide the framework for future smart, networked environments.

References

1. Mouton, F., Malan, M. M., Kimppa, K. K., & Venter, H. (2015). Necessity for ethics in social engineering research. *Computers & Security*, 55, 114–127. https://doi.org/10.1016/j.cose.2015.09.001
2. Kolias, C., Kambourakis, G., Stavrou, A., &Voas, J. (2017). DDoS in the IoT: Mirai and other botnets. *Computer*, 50(7), 80–84. https://doi.org/10.1109/MC.2017.201
3. Sicari, S., Rizzardi, A., Grieco, L. A., & Coen-Porisini, A. (2015). Security, privacy and trust in Internet of Things: The road ahead. *Computer Networks*, 76, 146–164. https://doi.org/10.1016/j.comnet.2014.11.008
4. Roman, R., Lopez, J., & Mambo, M. (2018). Mobile edge computing, Fog et al.: A survey and analysis of security threats and challenges. *Future Generation Computer Systems*, 78, 680–698. https://doi.org/10.1016/j.future.2016.11.009
5. Statista. (2022). Number of Internet of Things (IoT) connected devices worldwide from 2019 to 2025 (in billions). Statista. https://www.statista.com/statistics/1101442/iot-number-of-connected-devices-worldwide/
6. Miller, C., & Valasek, C. (2015). Remote exploitation of an unaltered passenger vehicle. Black Hat USA.
7. Perwej, Y., &Perwej, A. (2019). Cybersecurity risks and challenges in Internet of Things (IoT): A comprehensive study. *International Journal of Research and Analytical Reviews*, 6(1), 896–905.
8. Kambourakis, G. (2017). Anonymity and closely related terms in the cyberspace: An analysis by example. *Computers & Security*, 73, 92–113. https://doi.org/10.1016/j.cose.2017.08.001
9. Sadeghi, A. R., Wachsmann, C., &Waidner, M. (2015). Security and privacy challenges in industrial Internet of Things. *ACM/IEEE Design Automation Conference (DAC)*, 2015. San Francisco, California, USA. https://doi.org/10.1145/2744769.2747942
10. Zhang, X., Ni, L., & Wang, S. (2017). IoT security: Ongoing challenges and research opportunities. *Electronics Letters*, 53(12), 723–725. https://doi.org/10.1049/el.2017.0186
11. Alaba, F. A., Othman, M., Hashem, I. A. T., & Alotaibi, F. (2017). Internet of Things security: A survey. *Journal of Network and Computer Applications*, 88, 10–28. https://doi.org/10.1016/j.jnca.2017.04.002
12. Zhou, J., Zhou, J., Zhang, H., & Zhang, J. (2022). Social integration as mediator and age as moderator in social capital affecting mental health of internal migrant workers: A multi-group structural equation modeling approach. *Frontiers in Public Health*, 10, 865061. https://doi.org/10.3389/fpubh.2022.865061
13. Atzori, L., Iera, A., & Morabito, G. (2017). The Internet of Things: A survey. *Computer Networks*, 54(15), 2787–2805. https://doi.org/10.1016/j.comnet.2010.05.010

14. Lee, S., Pompili, D., & Lee, J. (2020). A security framework for distributed Internet of Things based on blockchain and fog computing. *Journal of Parallel and Distributed Computing*, 146, 71–83. https://doi.org/10.1016/j.jpdc.2020.07.001
15. Wang, L., Zhang, Q., & Wang, F. (2018). Internet of Things patching problem: A survey. *IEEE Internet of Things Journal*, 5(6), 4909–4921. https://doi.org/10.1109/JIOT.2018.2875408
16. Roman, R., Zhou, J., & Lopez, J. (2013). On the features and challenges of security and privacy in distributed Internet of Things. *Computer Networks*, 57(10), 2266–2279. https://doi.org/10.1016/j.comnet.2012.12.018
17. Zhou, W., & Zhang, L. (2017). Security and privacy in the Internet of Things: A survey. *IEEE Communications Surveys & Tutorials*, 19(2), 1087–1108. https://doi.org/10.1109/COMST.2017.2771380
18. Babar, S., Mahalle, P., Stango, A., Prasad, N., & Prasad, R. (2011). Proposed security model and threat taxonomy for the Internet of Things (IoT). *International Conference on Network Security and Allied Sciences*, 1–6. Chennai, Tamil Nadu, India. https://doi.org/10.1109/INTHETRNET.2011.18
19. Bou-Harb, E., Iqbal, F., &Debbabi, M. (2017). Cyber security challenges in the Internet of Things (IoT). *IEEE Internet of Things Journal*, 4(1), 1–9. https://doi.org/10.1109/JIOT.2016.2615121
20. Gupta, B. B., Abdelsalam, M., Khorsandroo, S., & Mittal, S. (2020). Security and privacy in smart farming: Challenges and opportunities. *IEEE Access*, 8, 34564–34584. https://doi.org/10.1109/ACCESS.2020.2975142
21. Sivaraman, V., Gharakheili, H. H., Fernandes, C., Clark, D., &Traini, E. (2018). Network-level security and privacy control for IoT devices. *Proceedings of the 2018 ACM Conference on Security and Privacy in Wireless and Mobile Networks*, 35–40. Stockholm, Sweden. https://doi.org/10.1145/3212480.3212484
22. Greenberg, A. (2015). Hackers remotely kill a Jeep on the highway—With me in it. Wired. Retrieved from https://www.wired.com/2015/07/hackers-remotely-kill-jeep-highway/
23. Gallagher, S. (2021). Inside the massive breach of security-camera data. Ars Technica. Retrieved from https://arstechnica.com/information-technology/2021/03/how-hackers-broke-into-thousands-of-verkata-security-cameras/
24. Montalbano, G., Mhalhel, K., Briglia, M., Levanti, M., Abbate, F., Guerrera, M. C., D'Alessandro, E., Laurà, R., & Germanà, A. (2021). Zebrafish and flavonoids: Adjuvants against obesity. *Molecules*, 26(10), 3014. https://doi.org/10.3390/molecules26103014
25. Langner, R. (2011). Stuxnet: Dissecting a cyberwarfare weapon. *IEEE Security & Privacy*, 9(3), 49–51. https://doi.org/10.1109/MSP.2011.67
26. Maisel, W. H., & Kohno, T. (2017). Improving the security and privacy of implantable medical devices. *New England Journal of Medicine*, 362(13), 1164–1166. https://doi.org/10.1056/NEJMp1002505
27. Miller, C., &Valasek, C. (2015). Remote exploitation of an unaltered passenger vehicle. Black Hat USA. Retrieved from https://illmatics.com/Remote%20Car%20Hacking.pdf
28. Montalbano, E. (2021). IoT camera hack exposes sensitive locations. Threatpost. Retrieved from https://threatpost.com/verkada-camera-hack/164546/
29. Sametinger, J., Rozenblit, J. W., Lysecky, R., & Ott, P. (2015). Security challenges for medical devices. *Communications of the ACM*, 58(4), 74–82.

30. Fernandes, E., Jung, J., & Prakash, A. (2017). Security and privacy implications of smart IoT devices: A survey. *IEEE Security & Privacy*, 15(5), 45–50. https://doi.org/10.1109/MSP.2017.3681066
31. Roman, R., Najera, P., & Lopez, J. (2011). Securing the internet of things. *Computer*, 44(9), 51–58. https://doi.org/10.1109/MC.2011.291
32. Weber, R. H., & Studer, E. (2016). Cybersecurity in the Internet of Things: Legal aspects. *Computer Law & Security Review*, 32(5), 715–728. https://doi.org/10.1016/j.clsr.2016.07.002
33. Bertino, E., & Islam, N. (2017). Botnets and Internet of Things security. *Computer*, 50(2), 76–79. https://doi.org/10.1109/MC.2017.62
34. European Union. (2016). General Data Protection Regulation (GDPR). https://eur-lex.europa.eu/legal-content/EN/TXT/?uri=CELEX%3A32016R0679
35. Horrow, S., & Sardana, A. (2012). Identity management framework for cloud-based Internet of Things. *Computer Science and Information Systems*, 9(4), 145–160.
36. Singh, S., Jeong, Y. S., & Park, J. H. (2016). A survey on cloud computing security: Issues, threats, and solutions. *Journal of Network and Computer Applications*, 75, 200–222. https://doi.org/10.1016/j.jnca.2016.08.007
37. Fischer-Hübner, S., Angulo, J., &Wästlund, E. (2020). Nudging for privacy and security: Understanding and assisting users' security and privacy decision making in smart environments. *International Journal of Human-Computer Studies*, 142, 102473. https://doi.org/10.1016/j.ijhcs.2020.102473
38. IBM. (2019). IBM Security Services 2019 Cybersecurity Report: Misconfigurations and Human Error. https://www.ibm.com/security/services
39. Palo Alto Networks. (2020). State of IoT Security Report. https://www.paloaltonetworks.com/resources/research/state-of-iot-security-2020
40. Bomhara, M., & Køien, G. M. (2015). Cyber security and the Internet of Things: Vulnerabilities, threats, intruders and attacks. *Journal of Cyber Security*, 4(1), 65–88. doi:10.13052/jcsm2245-1439.414

Chapter 8

Synergizing Machine Learning and Artificial Intelligence in Internet of Things Environments: Transformative Applications and Future Direction

Gayathri Ananthakrishnan,
Baiju Babu Vimala, and Thamizharasan S

8.1 Introduction

8.1.1 Brief Overview of IoT, ML, and AI

The Internet of Things (IoT), is defined as an interwoven network of devices that connect to the internet. These networks are integrated with software, sensors, and technologies to swap information through systems via a network. The range of these devices is from small things to the latest tools used in the industry. More than 8 billion devices are connected via IoT today, and it is expected that the number of connections will triple by the end of 2025 [1].

DOI: 10.1201/9781003587859-8

Among many technologies, IoT has become a vital technology in the 21st century. Many devices can be connected via IoT through the internet and communicate via seamless networks such as people, things, and processes. These devices can exchange physical objects and collect data with minimal human assistance through cloud, big data, analytics, inexpensive computing, and mobile technologies. Digital systems can log, follow, and adjust every interaction between connected objects in this connected world. The digital and physical worlds interact and operate in unison. The significance of IoT plays an eminent role in the areas including analytics, big data and cloud, computers, and mobile technologies.

8.1.2 Role of ML and AI in Enhancing IoT Systems

Artificial Intelligence (AI) and Machine Learning (ML) techniques come with lots of rich advancements and benefits that can be effectively deployed in IoT environments. Here's why such an integration is necessary:

i. **Enhanced Data Analysis and Decision-Making:**
   IoT networks generate large-scale data outputs continuously. While IoT systems can collect and transmit this data, AI, and ML help in processing and analyzing it efficiently. These technologies are capable of real-time pattern, trend, and anomaly detection rather than only storing raw data. They provide predictive insights, enabling proactive actions (e.g., predictive maintenance in manufacturing or smart home systems anticipating user behavior).

ii. **Improved Automation:**
   AI and ML allow IoT devices to go beyond basic rule-based automation. ML enables devices to evolve by learning from previous interactions, refining their performance without ongoing human intervention. Examples include: smart homes learning user preferences for lighting, temperature, and energy usage. Industrial IoT (IIoT) systems optimizing supply chain operations based on demand patterns [2].

iii. **Real-Time Data Processing:**
   In IoT environments, especially those that require immediate response (e.g., autonomous vehicles, healthcare monitoring), AI and ML enable real-time decision-making. Traditional methods of processing and analyzing data might not be fast enough for such critical tasks. ML algorithms can analyze streaming data from sensors instantaneously, triggering immediate actions or alerts based on predefined criteria (e.g., detecting a malfunction or health anomaly).

iv. **Predictive Capabilities:**
   One of the most powerful aspects of AI and ML integration is predictive analytics. IoT systems can use historical data combined with ML models to predict equipment failures, allowing for predictive maintenance (e.g., in

manufacturing or HVAC systems). They can also forecast demand, optimize inventory, and improve resource allocation in supply chain management. Anticipate environmental changes, ensuring more efficient energy consumption in smart cities.

v. **Enhanced Security**:

Due to the overall size and interconnected nature of IoT environments, they are often considered targets for cyberattacks. As a result, AI and ML are an important part of increasing security.AI can observe unusual behaviors or patterns in network traffic to find a security breach or attack at an early stage (for example, IoT botnets or data theft). AI can provide adaptive security specific to newly identified threats, so there is not a need for manual updates yet again.

vi. **Elasticity and Versatility**:

IoT systems often operate in dynamic and scalable environments with thousands or millions of devices. As these systems grow, AI and ML can help to optimize network management, ensuring seamless connectivity and resource allocation. They can scale systems more effectively, by adjusting configurations and algorithms as the number of devices increases, and handle more complex scenarios without the need for manually programmed solutions, ensuring that IoT solutions remain flexible as they evolve.

vii. **Optimized User Interaction**:

IoT systems are frequently employed in dynamic environments that scale to thousands or millions of devices. As IoT systems scale, AI and ML can assist in (a) optimizing the management of the network, including resource allocation and device connectivity as devices come and go, as in dynamic systems, or changes in geographic scale, for instance in Smart City implementations, (b) managing scaled systems more effectively through the adjustment of configurations and algorithms, and (c) managing more complex or diverse situations without needing manually written solutions to adapt and ensure that IoT continues to be flexible as the systems evolve.

viii. **Improved User Experience**:

AI-powered IoT devices can also deliver more tailored and intuitive user experiences through analyzes of user behaviors and preferences in relation to others. Examples may include Smart homes that can learn users' habits, offering personalization in terms of comfort and energy sustainability, or wearables that can analyze subjective user data and recommend options to create better health outcomes.

ix. **Cost Efficiency**:

Combining AI and ML with IoT provides more savings in a greater horizon. AI's predictive capability prevents a failure that can avoid downtime and maintenance costs, while the capability to automate many routine activities reduces the need for workers to physically intervene, thus saving labor costs. Beyond saving costs, AI can optimize resources to reduce waste and improve efficiency, while IoT systems enable more efficient energy consumption and ultimately reduce utility costs.

Incorporating AI and ML into IoT environments transforms traditional IoT systems into more intelligent, adaptive, and self-optimizing networks. The integration enhances automation, improves decision-making under real time, ensures maintenance under predictive type, optimizes resource management, and increases the security and scalability of IoT-based systems. As IoT continues to expand across industries, the combination of these technologies will be pivotal in unlocking its full potential and providing smarter, more efficient solutions.

8.1.2.1 Contribution

This chapter takes an in-depth look at the influence of ML and AI in IoT settings, and how this facet of the industry is undergoing a technical transformation. The role of ML and AI in processing efficiency, automating decision-making, and making IoT systems better at predictive analytics. The chapter also deals with the issues of implementing AI-based IoT systems – data privacy issues, scaling problems, and constraints from converting data in real time. With interesting use cases and take-away propositions for the future, the chapter is interesting and informative for academic researchers, practitioners, and industry professionals curious to test AI and ML to improve IoT applications.

8.2 Background and Literature Review

8.2.1 Overview of IoT Architecture and Protocols

The IoT architecture is a multilayered framework that enables the interconnectivity and interaction of linked devices. Data are collected by physical devices and sensors at the Perception Layer, while data transmission employing wired and wireless technologies such as Wi-Fi, Bluetooth, ZigBee, and Long Range Wide Area Network occurs at the Network Layer. In the Cloud Layer, storage, advanced analytics, and decision-making all fall under local data analysis for real-time decision-making in the Edge Layer. Lastly, the Application Layer offers user interfaces for services like industrial automation, smart homes, and healthcare monitoring.

IoT protocols, which are divided into Network/Connectivity Protocols (like Wi-Fi, NB-IoT, and Zigbee) for device interaction and Application Protocols (like MQTT, CoAP, and HTTP) for data exchange and control, are essential to communication. Despite its potential, the IoT faces a variety of challenges related to scalability, security, interoperability, energy efficiency, and latency, which are fully necessary to ensure the successful application of the technology across industries.

8.2.2 Overview of ML and AI Approaches in IoT Environment

ML and AI are, in fact, much needed as far as the IoT system is concerned in terms of making systems automated and enabling intelligent decisions. In terms of analyzing IoT available data, many techniques can be used, such as supervised learning that involves the use of labeled data, unsupervised learning for unlabeled data, and reinforcement learning that utilizes interaction feedback for anomaly detection and applications such as predictive maintenance and personalized user experiences. Deep learning and NLP bring even higher functionality to IoT devices, such as more accurate photo and speech recognition. Edge AI caters for low latency and bandwidth consumption by providing processing closer to where the data originates. It includes applications such as autonomous systems, smart homes, IIoT, and health monitoring. However, despite these applications promising a lot for the future of possible AI and ML for IoT systems, many issues such as reliable algorithms, data privacy, and limited processing power as far as IoT devices are concerned pose significant challenges.

8.2.3 Review of Current Studies on ML and AI Integration in IoT

The current research corpus, coupled with that on IoT and AI and/or ML, is primarily geared toward improving data processing and decision-making capabilities, along with predictive ones. Several algorithms from ML, such as decision trees and support vector machines (SVMs), as well as neural networks, have been highlighted to perform analyzes on extensive datasets of generated real-time statistical data from IoT installations for automating processes. New advanced AI methods have been studied for supposed future applications, such as image recognition in surveillance systems or speech processing in intelligent voice assistants. The existing research also talks about edge computing and federated learning as ways to form systems that consider limits in terms of device resources while ensuring data privacy. Integrated infrastructures based on hybrid AI-IoT architectures and energy-efficient learning models have given promise as a means for scalable and high-performing realizations; however, the challenge of building algorithms remained to find the balance between accuracy and resource efficiency while operating heterogeneously in IoT environments with still ongoing security and ethical issues. It will further help with continued endeavors in research on improving synergies between the AI and ML domains with IoT to attempt much broader and efficient applications.

8.3 Benefits of Synergizing ML and AI in IoT

The pairing of ML with IoT and AI brings huge advantages and can boost the intelligence, automation, and efficiency of IoT systems. It also enable users to do real-time data analysis and predictive maintenance and to detect anomalies, which helps minimize downtime and operational costs. Insights powered by AI enhance decision-making in intelligent use cases like smart cities, healthcare, and IIoT, while personalization improves the user experience in consumer IoT. It utilizes edge AI to reduce latency and bandwidth, both of which enable some critical applications like fast responses for autonomous driving and remote monitoring. In addition, ML models help IoT systems cope with dynamically changing environments and optimize their resources. The impacts generated by this synergy are the innovations with other challenges like scalability, efficiency, and reliability to create IoT systems to be more robust and effective across industries.

8.3.1 Better Data Comprehension and Effective Decision-making

The application of ML and AI techniques augments the data analysis and decision-making process in IoT systems. These techniques allow IoT systems to process complex, sizable data to gain real-time insight into operations. ML models allow for the analysis of activity patterns as well as the ability to forecast future trends and/or highlight anomalies; which leads to an increase in operational efficiency while minimizing risks. AI analytics allows automated decision-making to occur based on historical information and adapts to real-time changes, thereby allowing a more accurate and nimble response. These capabilities can be utilized not only in organizations, most notably predictive maintenance in manufacturing or highly personalized services in smart homes, but also contribute to making IoT systems even smarter, more reliable, and ultimately more capable in the complexity of decision-making.

8.3.2 Streamlined Control and Automation

AI and ML would enhance the automation and control over the IoT systems; hence the interconnections are devices operating with little or no human interaction. AI and ML give the IoT systems a learning capability from data, adjusting to changing environments, and demonstrating the capabilities of autonomous decision-making toward more efficient and reliable IoT systems. AI-driven autonomous control systems would implement real-time optimization of processes such as energy management in smart grids or traffic flow in smart cities. ML would also be used for predictive maintenance and process automation in IIoT, which can substantially cut down downtime and operational costs. In summation, the combination of analytics with real-time control has created a significant ability for each IoT system to operate much more intelligently, rapidly, and efficiently across its domains.

8.3.3 Improved Performance and Productivity

The use of AI and ML in IoT systems enhances efficiency and productivity by making operations and resource management more effective. AI and ML can perform real-time data analysis and predictive insights, which automates decision-making and reduces reliance on human interactions and delays. For instance, predictive maintenance in IIoT, among other benefits, leads to optimized machine downtime, while automated and increasingly flexible workflows lead to higher throughput in manufacturing operations. Similarly, optimization powered by AI in logistics and supply chain management, leads to lower costs, better asset utilization, and better management of resources for decentralized energy systems (e.g., utilities). The potential of IoT powered by AI and ML to enhance productivity, making a formerly manual system (informed and) effective, responsive, and cost-reducing, will revolutionize benefits across processes and industries.

8.3.4 Enhanced Security and Threat Detection

By utilizing AI and ML, security, and anomaly detection in IoT systems are enhanced tremendously with analytics in real time and identifying threats quickly. ML algorithms are capable of analyzing data trends to identify atypical behavior such as unauthorized access or aberrant device activity, which could suggest a security incident. AI further improves the ability to anticipate and thwart an attack by continuing to learn new data and adapting to new methods of attacks and incidents. Utilizing this type of proactive vulnerability detection makes IoT networks more secure, less vulnerable, and reduces risks

8.4 AI and ML Techniques into IoT Environments

The framework proposed integrates AI and ML techniques into IoT environments to improve their effectiveness, reliability, and security. The model focuses on the following pillars:

Intelligent Data Processing: The framework employs ML methodologies to examine and process the enormous amount of data generated by IoT devices. It utilizes predictive analytics and anomaly detection to automatically track and expose patterns, trends, and potential problems in real time.

Enhanced Security Measures: The model mentions AI-based security protocols to detect, prevent, and control potential issues, such as anomalous behaviour, unauthorized access, and data breaches.

Automation and Decision-Making: The system leverages AI-enabled automation systems that enable data-based decisions without the aid of human intervention, thus improving reaction time and accuracy.

Scalability and Adaptability: The proposed model is built to scale with the growth of IoT devices and can be customized for multiple applications, such as healthcare, smart homes, or industrial automation.

8.5 Machine Learning Algorithms for IoT Applications

The ongoing trend of ML in conjunction with IoT applications has greatly enhanced data analysis, data interpretation, and data delivery in real-time services. Figure 8.1 depicts the schematic diagram of ML algorithms for IoT applications. IoT applications that generate a substantial volume of data require efficient algorithms that can offer this data in a fast and accurate manner.

This chapter will discuss various ML models applicable to IoT applications, specifically algorithms for their functions, advantages, and real-time applicability. It will include decision trees, random forests, neural networks, SVMs, and various deep learning models. Other modern approaches will also be discussed, including transfer and federated learning in terms of their adoption for the optimization of IoT systems.

8.5.1 Overview of ML Algorithms Suitable for IoT

ML is very useful for IoT because it can automate, predict, and improve decision-making. Many algorithms have been created to cater to IoT needs such as resource constraints and handling large and varied data. The main algorithms are decision trees, random forests, neural networks, and SVMs.

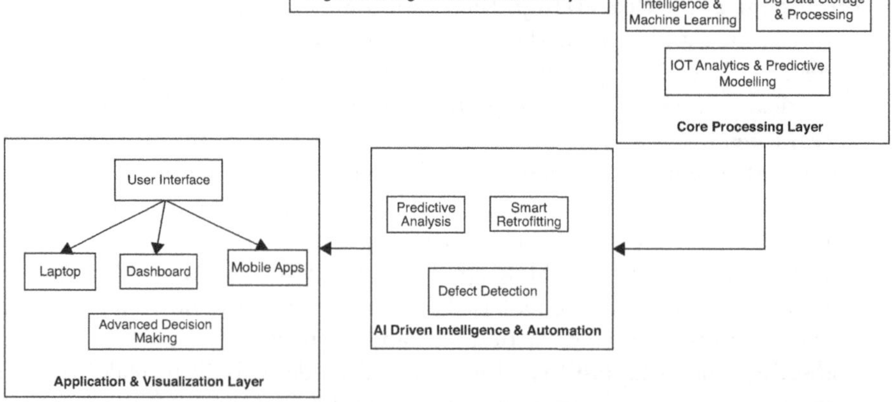

Figure 8.1 Schematic diagram for Machine Learning for IoT applications.

8.5.1.1 Decision Trees and Random Forests for Real-Time Analytics

The simplicity, ease of understanding, and effectiveness of decision trees make them a popular choice for use in IoT applications. They construct branches from the datasets according to the conditions of features that make them very effective for classification and regression tasks. Decision trees find wide applications in sensor networks' anomaly detection, energy management, and predictive maintenance in IIoT.

Random forests form an ensemble learning paradigm that is based on decision trees. Inclusion of these trees enhances credibility and produces robustness. Random forests reduce the possibility of overfitting smaller IoT datasets, thus giving out far better accuracy when compared with simpler models. These cases apply to smart agriculture, where random forests can analyze the environmental data to predict optimum irrigation schedules, and healthcare IoT, where they help classify patient health metrics to identify potential medical conditions. Both algorithms are lightweight enough to run on IoT devices with limited computational power. Their ability to deliver real-time results makes them indispensable for applications that require instant action.

8.5.1.2 Neural Networks for Image and Speech Recognition

Neural networks that are inspired by the wiring in the brains and function very much like brains are the best type for IoT applications that involve unstructured data, including images, audio, and video. Having such a structure means that the neural elements are able to model extraordinarily complex relationships and patterns in the data, just what one needs for such tasks as image recognition, the processing of speech signals, and the understanding of natural languages.

IoT steeped with Convolutional Neural Network (CNN) is imaging-based applications [3]. In such a system, a neural network processes video streams from connected cameras to identify suspicious behavior as an application for surveillance. The awareness of its suspicious behavior is further deployed in smart homes to enable voice assistants to control appliances by interpreting speech commands. The effective scaling of neural networks allows for handling ever-increasing quantities of data coming from IoT ecosystems. Although there is always a concern linked to the nature of computational expenses, improvements in edge computing and hardware acceleration have made them worth trying in IoT, where latency and bandwidth count.

8.5.1.3 Support Vector Machines (SVMs) for Classification Tasks

To achieve classification or regression purposes, the SVM has emerged as one of the immensely popular machine-learning tools for various IoT applications. The working premise behind this algorithm is to find the best line or hyperplane for the clear separation of data points into different groups. These models perform excellently for high-dimensional data. Hence, more and more application deployments in IoT solutions spanning from intrusion detection in networks to fault diagnosis in industrial systems and disease classification in healthcare rely on them. In this respect, SVM will fit to some scenarios, which would admit a small but well-labeled data set, a rare attribute of IoT environments. For example, this type of algorithm would classify physiological signals so as to monitor user activities by wearable medical devices or detect abnormalities such as arrhythmias. Advances in kernel methods extend SVMs beyond linearity to encompass nonlinear relationships, thus broadening their application to practically any type of IoT dataset [4].

8.5.2 Deep Learning in IoT for Complex Pattern Recognition

Deep learning is a specialized field within ML. It made such a difference for IoT as it helped to make devices grasp any complex patterns and find critical features in the huge, massive streams of differing data. Its predisposition to process and analyze huge amounts of data within little time makes it very important for IoT applications, which require both accuracy and speed. Deep learning applies neural networks with multiple layers to detect hidden data correlations. Therefore, it is impressively utilitarian in developing advanced applications in security, transportation, health, and many more areas. Deep learning in IoT systems has made enormous and excellent improvements in smart decision-making, automation, and understanding data. These systems are very good at managing unstructured data, like images, videos, and audio, mostly created in real time by IoT devices [5]. As IoT networks expand, the use of deep learning methods keeps changing to solve the problems raised about size, efficiency, and the limits of resources.

8.5.2.1 Facial Recognition

Facial recognition is indeed one of the central technologies that deep learning has put in place within the IoT., one of the methods constructed utilizing deep learning, are the ones that are constructed to analyze images by revealing the pattern, edge, and feature in the picture. These networks, which have an absolutely astounding ability to differentiate between faces and even get it right in case of low lighting or if the face is partially hidden. In the security aspect of deep learning, facial recognition is the rising star in access control systems. The IoT devices loaded with cameras and deep learning algorithms can now identify the person in real time, releasing the user from the necessity of passwords or key cards. Let's consider that facial recognition software in companies gives access only to authorized personnel while maintaining a smooth performance of the system on the user side.

Facial recognition is also very important in smart surveillance systems [6]. The introduction of self-learning AI into IoT cameras can in fact allow these technologies to identify the people from video streams and relate them to already existing data sets. Public safety branches in the local governments are the main benefactors of this functionality, for instance, the detectors of criminal behaviors in packed areas and the missing persons trackers. Apart from security, facial recognition also helps users to have more pleasant experiences on consumer IoT devices. Smart home assistants and smartphones, for instance, use facial recognition to tailor user interactions. The devices recognize their respective users, changing up the response answers and recommendations according to the personal preferences of those users. This particular use of deep learning that both makes people's lives easier and secures them at the same time manifests the emergence of AI for the IoT era. However, facial recognition systems may also face problems, such as the lack of security for data and bias in model training. Researchers then respond to these problems by embarking on federated learning privacy-preserving innovations to maintain ethical standards and promote transparency.

8.5.2.2 Autonomous Navigation

Autonomous navigation is one of the most ground-breaking applications of deep learning in IoT. Self-driving cars, drones, delivery robots, and other autonomous vehicles use deep learning models to process the sensor data in making split-second decisions fully reliant. This system comes with many IoT sensors (cameras, radars, LiDAR, and ultrasonic detectors to name a few) to have full sensing of what is happening around.

Deep learning solutions use their sensory inputs to detect objects, obstacles and predict their movements corresponding to object classification. For example, using CNNs to extract video data for pedestrians, other vehicles, and road sign classification, and recurrent neural networks for time-series data (predicting object trajectories). That tandem allows for safe driving by having the vehicles make split second decisions to stop and turn. We then come to the important part of autonomous navigation: recognizing traffic signs. Alexei Lin Automated deep learning models from multiple datasets are better at reading road signage even under adverse weather conditions or partial occlusion. This built into the IoT Autonomous capabilities enable our systems to comply with traffic laws on roads and make defensive measures for complete safety. Deep learning and IoT work together to find the optimal routes for smart city infrastructures. Autonomous vehicles, meanwhile using real-time data from connected infrastructure such as traffic lights and road sensors can pick the best paths at the same time to minimize traffic congestion and fuel consumption. This is very in line with the philosophy of sustainability and smart urban planning [7].

8.5.2.3 Medical Diagnostics

The realm of healthcare that brings deep learning and IoT together is going to change the face of medical diagnostics to detect faster and accurate non-invasive diseases early. IoT devices such as wearable sensors, imaging equipment, and remote monitoring systems produce mountains of medical data. Deep learning models then study this data and get useful findings out of it so as to lead early diagnosis and individualized treatments. Deep learning has seen the most progress in medical imaging, a technology field that people often compare it with to establish benchmarks for progress. In addition, IoT diagnostic devices can have a deep learning algorithm to pick out X-rays or MRIs, CT scans, ultrasonograms, and standardize anomalies. Wearable technology devices are wearable, electronic equipment. They can be either embedded in clothes or constructed as wearable equipment. Overcoming some limitations of the conventionally medical, healthcare assessment approaches promoted by mobile health modernization, wearables have turned out to be a solution [8].

Deep learning models can screen mammograms for tumors or lung nodules in CT images with performance comparable to or better than that achieved by radiologists. Retinal images by IoT devices in ophthalmology: Image recognition for the diagnosis of retinopathy and macular degeneration is often at a stage that is most treatable. Continuous sensor in health matters such as heartbeats, blood pressures, blood oxidation levels, etc., is generated by wearing IoT devices such as smartwatches or fitness trackers. Time series data is utilized to feed deep learning models at adequate levels to find patterns and abnormal events. For example, they are able to forecast cardiac arrhythmias or predict early signs of emergent disease states that can trigger early care for low-morbidity, high-cost, high-intervention items. Remote health care is seeing an increase as payers seek ways to increase the effectiveness of IoT in global health crises. Specially designed IoT devices gathered the patient data in a telemedicine setting that deep learning models learned from and rendered remote diagnostic capability. Not only is this an access to healthcare solution but also decongesting from the healthcare infrastructure [9].

8.5.3 Leveraging Transfer Learning and Federated Learning in IoT Environments

The IoT sees the expansion of high-performance computing due to the growth in the demand for ML capabilities that can be used in the new IoT challenges. IoT devices frequently work in environments where the availability of computing power is limited, the storage capacity is small, and the labeled data is few. Traditional ML methods, which demand enormous computational power and centralized data gathering, are often not possible in such environments. Thus, techniques such as transfer learning and federated learning, which make more efficient and effective ML model training and deployment for IoT, are developed and used. These techniques not only identify the inadequacies in IoT environments, but also the ones that make intelligent solutions possible while at the same time being very efficient and preserving privacy. This part of the article provides a thorough investigation of transfer learning and federated learning, with special attention to their working principles, examples, and the advantages they bring to IoT devices [10].

Transfer learning is a machine-learning approach whereby knowledge gained while solving one problem is used, to some extent, in solving another problem related to that; yet, there remains a distinct difference between the above two problems. Rather than training a model from scratch, transfer learning involves, as a starting point, reusing a previously trained model while fine-tuning it on a new dataset. Transfer learning thus vastly cuts down both the required computational resources and the training time, which makes it mostly suited for IoT devices with limited capabilities. The core intuition behind this is that the lower layers of a deep learning model extract general features that can be reused for different tasks. For instance, in image recognition, different features such as textures and edges are brought forth by the first layers of a CNN. Some of these might remain unchanged while the top one or more layers are retrained so that they specialize in the new task, like identifying defective parts in a manufacturing line or recognizing plant diseases in smart agriculture. Federated learning is a decentralized learning approach used to train ML models. Unlike the traditional ways of uploading the data to a central server, federated learning keeps the data on the individual IoT devices. That is, they train their respective models locally and only share model updates with a central server that is to be performed, thus providing data privacy and security.

Federated learning represents an innovative approach to training ML models, by which training is performed in a decentralized manner. Unlike model training on a large server, federated learning allows individuals to keep data contained within individual IoT devices. Models are trained individually and locally in each site, while model updates (gradients or parameters) are sent back to the central server to ensure data privacy and security. Federated learning is an iterative, collaborative process of model training that hides data privacy yet trains powerful models. The cycle begins with the initialization of a global model, usually residing on a central server. The server sends the global model to IoT devices involved in the training-notably smartphones, sensors, or edge nodes-with their respective unique datasets. Training will not be via the uploading of raw data within a common device likely to compromise user privacy and increase bandwidth usage, but internal training within the device on the private data exclusively available to that device. The patterns and insights from that device's data will be what the model learns during this locally-facilitated training. After training, those models updated locally return to the central server, wrapped in secure encrypted updates.

This update would be further used at the central server to update the global model. The more common aggregation methods include merely the averaging of model weights; however, there have been more advanced methods to handle non-IID data. The majority of aggregations would ensure that the global model possesses a varied mix from the collection of data without actually having to directly access any individual's data. After informing the model, the global updated model is then sent back to the devices and the process repeats. This cycle can continue until satisfactory performance is achieved or until certain training objectives are met. Federated learning is a process whereby data is distributed and any sensitive or personally identifiable information is never put at risk. With the use cases of health, patient information being confidential, and edge devices with limited connectivity, federated learning gains strength, driving down the need to continuously transmit data. Because of this decentralized approach, federated learning enables a balance among privacy, efficient processes, and collaborative intelligence.

8.6 Transformative Applications of AI and ML in IoT Environments

AI and ML are the foundational technologies for IoT, enabling dramatic applications in many sectors. The combination of IoT's data-gathering and transmission capabilities with AI's analytical and decision-making abilities has overall made systems smarter, more efficient, and more flexible than ever. While ML is reshaping how we interact with our environments by changing everything from smart city infrastructure to healthcare, industrial automation, and autonomous vehicles, this chapter deals with their impacts on four key areas: smart cities, healthcare and remote monitoring IIoT, and autonomous transport [11].

8.6.1 Smart Cities and Infrastructure

Smart cities represent a different way of working on cities, highly efficient, through AI-based IoT systems, in those pressing challenges like traffic congestion, energy consumption, and waste management are being solved. Through the addition of IoT sensors in the requisite infrastructures and the utilization of AI algorithms for data processing, these systems not only create a better living environment but also improve the electricity grid. Smart cities, with connected systems, create functional, flexible, and interactive environments that are intelligent and adaptive to changes. This enables smart modern cities to explore the full potential of AI and IoT in improving traffic flow efficiency, reducing energy consumption, and even providing better techniques for waste management.

8.6.1.1 Traffic Management

Traffic congestion is a major urban problem inflicting time loss, pollution, and economic burden. IoT sensors embedded in roads, traffic lights, and vehicles collect real-time data on traffic and accident occurrences and road blockage hotspots [12]. The AI then applies and processes this data in real time to constantly revise traffic signal timings, vehicle rerouting can be done dynamically. AI-based adaptive traffic signal systems reduce delays at intersections and cause better overall vehicle flow. It not only cuts down petrol consumption and emissions, but it also improves the ride for commuters. With some of this heavy traffic bypassed using IoT-enabled navigation apps integrated with the AI, drivers get alternative routes that are not crowded based on live traffic.

8.6.1.2 Energy Optimization

AI and IoT have brought in a whole new level of urban energy systems where consumption is smarter and sustainable. IoT sensors installed on smart grids, which measure the demand and supply of energy in real time alongside AI algorithms forecasting peak usage, enable resource-efficient allocation. This method optimizes and optimally balances loads on the grid while minimizing energy inefficiency. In smart public lighting based on AI, the brightness of these systems can be automatically adjusted in real time by ambient conditions or human activity in public spaces, which results in enormous electricity saving reductions. Smart IoT sensors for HVAC systems, AI driven management systems in buildings enable optimization of energy usage without reducing comfort. None of this lights the fire, but they are all critical to lessening the impact on the urban environment.

8.6.1.3 Waste Management

Smart city ecosystems also cannot function without having proper waste management. Here we have an overview of the waste management system and a few things about smart city ecosystems in short. The inefficiencies of traditional waste collection schedules and recycling are what plague the majority of our systems. IoT smart bins with fill-level sensors aggregate data that is transmitted back to central systems, enabling AI algorithms to derive optimized collection routes for waste, which in turn saves fuel for garbage trucks and lowers operational expenditure, to name one thing. By using AI capabilities systems, premium recycling systems can even additionally automate the categorization and sorting of streams of materials to enhance recycling rates. These support the circular economy model, minimize landfill dependency and are thus more sustainable.

8.6.2 Healthcare and Remote Monitoring

The interplay created by the emergence and integration of IoT device technology along with advanced AI is radically changing the business of treating ailments in patients by making real-time monitoring, predictive analytics, and more accurate diagnostics possible. Presently, some personal health data are maintained and tracked through IoT, such as wearables, smart medical devices, and remote monitoring solutions.AI analyzes this data to provide actionable insights, ensuring medical intervention at the right time for the right patients and enabling the right treatment. The quality, accessibility, and efficiency of health services have improved due to IoT and AI providing providers with relevant data for their decisions and patients with real-time feedback on their health [13].

8.6.2.1 Wearable IoT Devices

Wearables indeed represent the most reliable use of healthcare IoT, as they facilitates patients to observe vital parameters and even monitor them from afar. This includes a wide range of products, from fitness trackers and smartwatches, to medical-grade health monitors- these devices continuously track vital parameters such as heart rate, blood pressure, glucose levels, and oxygen saturation, besides keeping track of sleep patterns. An AI algorithm then analyzes and, simultaneously, recognizes variations, trends, or predicts possible health risks from it. An example is a smartwatch fitted with an AI-driven monitoring system, which will be able to identify irregularities in heart rhythms (for example, atrial fibrillation) and warn users to take medical advice before symptoms become serious.

Devices that can be worn act as indispensable aids in the management of chronic diseases like diabetes and hypertension while capturing parameters such as daily glucose and blood pressure levels. With chronic conditions, one can adjust to a real-time monitoring system that improves disease management to minimize complications. Most will come together with user-friendly apps that will relay the numerical data in easy-to-understand graphs, persuading users to take some action toward heeding their health [14].

8.6.2.2 Emergency Alerts

IoT enabled systems can detect emergencies and raise alerts in healthcare, which is the biggest game changer of all time. AI-powered wearables can detect life limiting events, such as heart attacks, serious declines in oxygen levels, or falls in the elderly. The devices then alert healthcare providers, emergency contacts (sometimes) and in some cases emergency services. Real-time location data and other pertinent health information alerts meanwhile are quick to arrive in these notifications. The smartwatch of an individual with fall detection, for instance, falls and gets stuck in immobile status. The AI within the device itself would detect this event and send an emergency alert with the person's GPS coordinates to a list of predispatched responders. For people with long-term medical conditions or the elderly living alone, this is an important functionality as it adds a safety barrier [15].

8.6.2.3 Enhanced Diagnostics

IoT, AI-driven diagnostic records an all-time high benchmark for accuracy that helps doctors diagnose diseases earlier and minimize false alarms for healthcare sites. State-of-the-art AI algorithms on large medical datasets can evaluate medical imaging data (X-ray, CT scan, MRI) for identifying lesions with an accuracy unparalleled by human competence. An AI-driven imaging system, for instance, can detect the smallest trace of a condition such as cancer or fracture/lung diseases that the human eye simply wouldn't spot. In certain settings where access to healthcare facilities is limited, such as in the case of remote or underserved areas, the potential value of portable IoT diagnostic devices has never been greater with AI. Some of these devices perform local image or sample analysis and send the diagnostic output to specialists for further processing. AI coupled with mobility, for example, an AI-enabled portable ultrasound device to diagnose pregnancy complications in rural settings, reduce maternal and neonatal mortality rates through early interventions. IoT and AI are thus democratizing access to high quality by connecting the dots between patients and healthcare resources.

8.6.2.4 Telemedicine and Remote Patient Monitoring

IoT- and AI-enabled telemedicine platforms have changed the landscape of the interaction of patients with healthcare providers. We have telemedicine for the patients to talk to physicians and specialists instead of driving to healthcare facilities. IoT sensors hold the key here, as they are in charge of real-time monitoring of the states of patients and sending the same to healthcare providers. A heart disease patient may be carrying a monitor that records his/her heart rate, blood pressure, and ECG readings. The data is processed by AI systems to look for any degradation in the system and this triggers doctors to act. AI makes sense of the data being fed from IoT devices in the back-end, which can help identify trends that might indicate worsening symptoms or the need for medication tweaks. This not only enhances the patient's outcome but it also lessens the overutilization of hospitals, thus making room for other patients who really need them. Telemedicine platforms also include an AI chat or virtual assistant to respond to patients queries first, which may be the most basic of medical queries or reminding once the patient is taking his medications. They improve the engagement and compliance of the patient with treatment plans for better end health results in the long term.

8.6.3 Industrial IoT and Predictive Maintenance

IIoT blends AI and IoT technologies to increase the efficiency of operations, reduce downtimes, and improve choices for sectors such as manufacturing, energy, and logistics. One of the principal applications of IIoT is predictive maintenance that employs live data and advanced analytics to predict equipment breakdowns before they happen, stealing time, money, and resources in the end system [8].

8.6.3.1 Real-Time Monitoring

In the IIoT systems, sensors are integrated within mission-critical machinery to measure the parameters of life (temperature, vibration) the pressure dashboards or humidity. Sensors are continuously sensing the data, this being a live data stream to gauge the status of industrial equipment performance. AI applications process this data and find patterns with respect to normal or deviations from operational limits. Our examples could be a rapid rise in vibration levels with a machine that may signal that a component is on the verge of failing or worse, a bearing is worn. Real-time monitoring of equipment enables timely identification of problems and hence, allows the preemptive actions to be taken prior to any huge production disrepute and associated costs.

8.6.3.2 Predictive Maintenance

Predictive maintenance is the most important step for achieving the longest life expectancy of industrial equipment hence concurrently striving to keep downtime to a minimum. Requesting IIoT systems to utilize AI models allows for predictions on when the machinery will fail – for both historical data and current real-time sensor inputs using the predictive nature mentioned above. This preventative measure equates to maintenance being scheduled and performed proactively, resulting in fewer losses due to unplanned maintenance and having to take a machine offline. For example, the use of historical data in assessing machinery failure trends: AI can gauge when something like motors or pumps is going to fail and predictive replacements (or maintenance) can be planned on components in time. Moreover, predictive maintenance reduces the necessity for downtime and thus equipment also fetches more ROI with a longer life cycle once implemented especially on costly industrial assets.

8.6.3.3 Operational Efficiency

Quasi-technically, AI-powered IoT systems serve, in additional ways rather than proactivity to maintenance, in optimizing industrial operations. AI may analyze production data so that bottlenecks in workflows can be determined or enhanced quality control may be characterized or those streamlined processes have been directed to maximize efficiency. For energy production, smart grids with IoT sensors warn of energy usage across facilities and forecast demand to ensure optimized distribution of energy resources. In this way, efficiencies are attained with savings in energy, reductions in costs of doing business, and better use of scarce resources.

8.6.3.4 Supply Chain Optimization

IoT sensors embedded in the warehouses, vehicles, and shipping containers keep a round-the-clock tab on inventory levels, the location of containers, and many environmental conditions such as temperature and humidity. This information is processed by AI that automates the supply chain operations – thoughtful inventory planning and routing, for instance. AI predicts shifts in demand and stocks the shelves just in time-reducing costs due to unnecessary storage and improving the availability of stock. IIoT systems can greatly increase operational efficiency and cut down delays in production and delivery through heightened visibility and control throughout the supply chain.

8.7 Challenges in Integrating AI, ML, and IoT

AI, ML, and the IoT unleash vast possibilities for industry revolution and efficiency enhancement. In this very juxtaposition, however, is posited the gargantuan challenge of first finding solutions before the mark is hit. Some of the critical concerns that IoT is facing include issues regarding data privacy and security; limited resources; constrained computational abilities; and the ergonomic issues in the use of AI-based IoT systems.

8.7.1 Data Protection and Security Challenges

One of the largest challenges facing AI and IoT systems is privacy and security, which are crucial to data privacy in a system. IoT devices often produce a constant flow of data, which is massive in quantity and much of it is quite sensitive, namely personal health records, financial transactions, and real-time location information. If we insist on passing this data over the network to the central system or cloud platform for the AI process, then the security issues we will face include cyberattacks, data breaches, and unauthorized access. Hackers are able to exploit these security gaps in IoT devices or communication networks and this ends up in criminals counterfeiting personal data and stealing sensitive information. In addition, privacy laws applicable to data include the General Data Protection Regulation and California Consumer Privacy Act requiring such companies to strictly comply with regulations on their personal data practices. These laws involve the organizations in issues related to the use of the data, they should inform the users on how data is collected and ask for their approval, and besides these they also must design strong encryption methods and anonymization methods. It is one of the most challenging issues to identify the harmony of building data applications that are AI-based and thus taking advantage of data and protecting privacy is AI as opposed to sectors where data are very sensitive like healthcare and finance.

8.7.2 Resource Constraints and Computational Limitations

IoT devices that have limited processing capabilities, memory capabilities, and battery life are effectively delivering the ideas of physical devices and resource mobility. IoT devices that have limited processing capabilities, memory capabilities, and battery life are effectively delivering the ideas of physical devices and resource mobility. It becomes an extraordinarily hard task to implement AI and ML algorithms in such devices when they are appropriated for real-time decision-making. For example, the mainly used deep learning models that are applied to image recognition or anomaly detection are the ones that need a giant joule of power and space, which is so far beyond the IoT gadgets.

Cloud solutions have been researched by different organizations for the purpose of taking the burden of heavy computations to centralized servers, thus enabling a better solution. However, the challenges that arise include the time required for data processing can be increased, the fact that the bandwidth must be increased and the fact that a stable internet connection must be maintained. Such limits are grave in cases where the workflow is required to be in no time, as is the case with autonomous vehicles or industrial automation. Edge computing emerged as the next step in alternative solutions to the edge-computing problem by bringing computation even closer to the IoT devices. However, the unresolved issue is the ways of achieving the lightweight AI model that can be executed on the edge devices and the action of the same devices won't be interrupted. The new IoT edge computing and AI processing recommendations through the old-age IoT devices updating will remain for some, however, many organizations will find that this is a barrier to them.

8.7.3 Ethical Considerations in AI-Enabled IoT

A lot of power is concentrated in AI, ML, and IoT to change businesses into lean and efficient mechanisms. However, that convergence also brings many problems before it can be mounted and implemented, and the most significant challenges include data privacy and security, resource constraints, computational limitations, and ethical considerations before one deploys AI-enabled IoT systems. Integrating AI into IoT systems brings to the table many ethical issues, such as surveillance, decision-making and bias. AI enabled IoT devices collect data continuously, so we have ubiquitous monitoring in smart cities, workplaces, and homes. Although these systems can make areas more secure and efficient, they can also infringe on individual privacy and autonomy. For instance, AI-enabled surveillance systems can lead to over-policing or misuse of data for inapt reasons and so deal with the debate on the dichotomy of security and civil liberties.

The issue of bias in AI algorithms is also an ethical one. Systems trained on biased data can maintain or even increase the existing inequalities. In IoT applications, such biases may be present in healthcare devices that do not work well for certain groups or smart home systems that cannot recognize diverse speech patterns or accents. Ensuring fairness and inclusivity in AI-enabled IoT systems is critical to eradicating unintended discrimination. Besides, more and more IoT projects are turning out to be machines with behavioral skills, and this might cause the users, who are legally being responsible, to have a question of, consequently, they publicly ask this question – who is to be responsible, that is, the right legal entity to be or the legitimate out-scale car transfer upon whom the liability distribution can be executed? Similarly, if a car equipped with an AI system is involved in a crash, the responsibility issue becomes thorny as it is difficult to resolve if the AI developer, the car manufacturer, or the user is the one responsible. Nevertheless, surely understandable, and accessible AI is highly appropriate in building up trust and, thus, in the adoption of whole and moral deployment.

8.8 Future Scope

The use of ML and AI in IoT systems is expected to grow significantly and provide transformational opportunities in several verticals. As IoT networks continue to develop, accomplishments will be focused on facilitating efficient data processing, forecasting models, and security. Edge and fog computing will help to reduce latency and provide quicker decision support in real-time situations. Self-learning and adaptive AI models will allow IoT systems to self-optimize performance and resource allocation in real time. Emerging technologies like federated learning and blockchain will help resolve privacy issues and establish secure data exchange in distributed IoT networks. The integration of AI and IoT will foster continuing growth, and transformations in healthcare, smart cities, and automation are anticipated to foster unprecedented progress in innovation and ultimately lead to a more intelligent, autonomous, and resilient system.

8.9 Conclusion

The synergistic application of ML and in IoT settings is changing the way things operate and interact with and respond to real-life situations. This interface has spawned applications of transformation – from predictive maintenance and real-time analytics to automation and user experience personalization. Certainly, being AI-driven now makes such insights and the addition of ML adaptability in IoT systems to provide smart and efficient solutions to some complex problems faced by industries like health, manufacturing, smart cities, and even agriculture – all of which witness this trend. In addition to the above, emerging challenges like limited device resources, data privacy issues, and the insatiable need for very robust algorithms have made edge computing, federated learning, and AI optimization likely paths for innovative development toward solutions to such issue areas. It is, therefore, a merger of AI, ML, and IoT that will bring an interconnected and intelligent tomorrow where systems will learn, evolve, and enjoy unprecedented value.

References

1. Bzai, J., Alam, F., Dhafer, A., Bojović, M., Altowaijri, S. M., Niazi, I. K., & Mehmood, R. (2022). Machine learning-enabled internet of things (IoT): Data, applications, and industry perspective. *Electronics, 11*(17), 2676.
2. Ghosh, U., Chakraborty, C., Garg, L., & Srivastava, G. (Eds.). (2022). *Intelligent Internet of Things for Healthcare and Industry*. Springer International Publishing.
3. Chen, Z., Liu, J., Shen, Y., Simsek, M., Kantarci, B., Mouftah, H. T., & Djukic, P. (2022). Machine learning-enabled IoT security: Open issues and challenges under advanced persistent threats. *ACM Computing Surveys, 55*(5), 1–37.

4. Ha, N., Xu, K., Ren, G., Mitchell, A., & Ou, J. Z. (2020). Machine learning-enabled smart sensor systems. *Advanced Intelligent Systems*, *2*(9), 2000063.
5. Djenouri, D., Laidi, R., Djenouri, Y., & Balasingham, I. (2019). Machine learning for smart building applications: Review and taxonomy. *ACM Computing Surveys (CSUR)*, *52*(2), 1–36.
6. Kumar, S., Tiwari, P., & Zymbler, M. (2019). Internet of Things is a revolutionary approach for future technology enhancement: A review. *Journal of Big data*, *6*(1), 1–21.
7. Ma, X., Yao, T., Hu, M., Dong, Y., Liu, W., Wang, F., & Liu, J. (2019). A survey on deep learning empowered IoT applications. *IEEE Access*, *7*, 181721–181732.
8. Baiju, B. V., Suresh, P., Sharmila, C., Deepa, M., Kirubha, D., & Solomon, F. A. M. (2025). Smart Monitoring of Parkinson's disease with Cloud-IoT technologies. In *Revolutionizing Healthcare Systems Through Cloud Computing and IoT* (pp. 205–234). IGI Global.
9. Din, I. U., Guizani, M., Rodrigues, J. J., Hassan, S., & Korotaev, V. V. (2019). Machine learning in the Internet of Things: Designed techniques for smart cities. *Future Generation Computer Systems*, *100*, 826–843.
10. Ambika, P. (2020). Machine learning and deep learning algorithms on the industrial Internet of Things (IIoT). *Advances in Computers*, *117*(1), 321–338.
11. Latif, S., Driss, M., Boulila, W., Huma, Z. E., Jamal, S. S., Idrees, Z., & Ahmad, J. (2021). Deep learning for the industrial Internet of Things (IIoT): A comprehensive survey of techniques, implementation frameworks, potential applications, and future directions. *Sensors*, *21*(22), 7518.
12. Stracener, C., Samelson, Q., Mackie, J., & Ihaza, M. (2019). The Internet of Things grows artificial intelligence and data sciences. *IT Professional*, *21*(3), 55–62.
13. Mastorakis, G., Mavromoustakis, C. X., Batalla, J. M., & Pallis, E. (Eds.). (2020). *Convergence of Artificial Intelligence and the Internet of Things*. Springer International Publishing.
14. Charef, N., Mnaouer, A. B., Aloqaily, M., Bouachir, O., & Guizani, M. (2023). Artificial intelligence implication on energy sustainability in Internet of Things: A survey. *Information Processing & Management*, *60*(2), 103212.
15. Singh, K., Singh, Y., Khang, A., Barak, D., & Yadav, M. (2024). Internet of Things (IoT)-based technologies for reliability evaluation with artificial intelligence (AI). In *AI and IoT Technology and Applications for Smart Healthcare Systems* (pp. 387–395). Auerbach Publications.

Chapter 9

Intelligent Machine Learning Approaches for IoT Network Threat Detection and Security Optimization

Somasundaram R, Roshini B,
Pavithraa D, and Nikil Aventhiha G

9.1 Introduction

As Internet of Things (IoT) technology rapidly expands across industries, the attack surface for cyber threats grows proportionally, creating urgent security challenges. The global IoT security market is projected to reach $59.16 billion by 2030, growing at a Compound Annual Growth Rate (CAGR) of 21.2% from 2023 [1]. This growth reflects the increasing recognition of security vulnerabilities within interconnected IoT ecosystems. Machine learning approaches have emerged as promising solutions for intrusion detection; however, implementing these techniques in real-world IoT scenarios presents significant challenges due to resource constraints and the unique characteristics of IoT networks.

This chapter investigates the application of various machine learning algorithms—including Random Forest, Decision Tree, Naive Bayes, Gradient Boosting, and k-Nearest Neighbors—to determine optimal approaches for IoT network security. The research specifically focuses on detecting critical threats such

DOI: 10.1201/9781003587859-9

as reconnaissance activities, Denial of Service (DoS) attacks, exploits, backdoors, fuzzing attacks, and worms that frequently target IoT devices.

The major contributions of this chapter include the following:

1. A comprehensive evaluation framework for comparing Machine Learning (ML) algorithms for IoT network threat detection
2. Implementation and assessment of Snort intrusion detection/prevention systems (IDS/IPS) for real-time threat prevention in IoT environments
3. Resource optimization techniques that balance security effectiveness with computational efficiency
4. Practical mitigation strategies for various attack types targeting IoT infrastructure

Using a comprehensive dataset of 82,332 network instances with 34 features—including metrics like packet counts, bytes transferred, and network states—this chapter effectively addresses IoT security challenges by leveraging machine learning for threat detection and mitigation, ensuring both accuracy and efficiency in resource-constrained environments. The chapter is organized as follows: Section 9.2 presents a literature review of current research; Section 9.3 details the methodology; Section 9.4 covers implementation approaches; Section 9.5 presents experimental results and discussion; and Section 9.6 concludes with insights, and Section 9.7 presents future research directions.

9.2 Literature Review

While cybersecurity is developing very rapidly, AI and machine learning are gaining more importance for threat detection today. It has been observed that the knowledge graph-based Hu's method can effectively detect multistep attacks [1]. Saminathan et al. presented an ANN-based model that reliably detects insider threats [2]. Akhtar and Feng studied several machine learning techniques, including Naive Bayes and SVM, for polymorphic malware detection [3], and Faruk et al. presented existing approaches toward malware detection and proposed AI-based improvements [4]. Thiziers et al. developed an 83%-accurate deep-learning model for malware detection [5]. Patil and Gedam proposed an 86%-accurate web-based tool for Android malware detection [6]. Lee et al. proposed an AI-SIEM system for the detection of cyber threats, which, however, is highly dependent on manual data labeling [7]. Tiwari et al. designed an intrusion detection system that monitors network activity and detects abnormal behavior [8]. Ashiku and Dagli designed a very effective deep learning-based IDS for identifying various types of attacks [9]. Nasri et al. enhanced detection against Android malware using machine learning classifiers [10].

The extensive literature survey implies progress in the evolution of ML within cybersecurity, but challenges still persist in the form of high computational costs and adaptation to changing threats. The summary of the literature review is presented in Table 9.1.

The literature review reveals significant progress in applying ML techniques to cybersecurity, but persistent challenges remain, particularly regarding computational efficiency and adaptation to IoT-specific constraints. This chapter addresses these gaps by focusing on resource-optimized ML approaches specifically designed for IoT network environments.

9.3 Methodology

This section outlines our comprehensive approach to IoT network threat detection and mitigation. The methodology follows a structured process comprising five key phases, as illustrated in Figure 9.1. It includes processes such as data collection and preprocessing, feature extraction, model training and evaluation, threat mitigation, and continuous monitoring and improvement.

9.3.1 Data Collection and Preprocessing

The research utilized a dataset containing over 2.5 million network traffic samples collected in a controlled laboratory environment using specialized network monitoring systems [15]. The dataset comprised 49 features capturing various aspects of network behavior and multiple attack types, including Fuzzers, DoS, Exploits, Backdoors, and Reconnaissance.

Preprocessing steps included:

- Handling missing values through appropriate imputation techniques
- Converting categorical variables into numerical representations using encoding methods
- Feature scaling to normalize data ranges
- Implementing data balancing techniques to address class imbalance issues
- Removing duplicate or redundant records to improve model efficiency

Ensuring the dataset was representative of actual network conditions by collecting samples from diverse network configurations and time periods. This comprehensive approach to data preparation established a solid foundation for robust model training and evaluation.

9.3.2 Feature Extraction

Feature extraction focused on identifying the most relevant attributes for distinguishing between normal and malicious network traffic. The dataset included critical features such as:

Table 9.1 Summary of the Literature Review

S.No.	*Journal Name*	*Methodology*	*Advantage*	*Disadvantage*
1	Knowledge Graph Based Large Scale Network Security Threat Detection Techniques [2]	Network threat Detection using Knowledge graph, Feature Template extraction and FT-CNN-BILSTM-CRF.	• High accuracy and F1-Score in detecting network threats, superior multistep attack detection compared to other methods.	• High computational resource demand limits scalability in large networks.
2	An Artificial Neural Network Autoencoder for Insider Cyber Security Threat Detection [4]	Network threat Detection using an unsupervised deep learning approach with an artificial neural network (ANN)-based autoencoder.	• This model is really good at spotting insider cyber threats because it looks closely at how users and systems behave. • It is very reliable and can catch these threats with just a few abnormal signs.	• Needs a lot of computing power and needs improvement to be faster. • Also, it could be better by analyzing different kinds of assets and using more advanced algorithms.
3	Malware Analysis and Detection Using Machine Learning Algorithms [6]	Involves using machine learning techniques, including Naive Bayes, SVM, J48, RF, and a proposed approach, to analyze and detect polymorphic malware, with a focus on measuring detection accuracy and comparing classifier performances.	• Machine learning algorithms like DT, CNN, and SVM show high accuracy in detecting malware, making them effective for cybersecurity.	• Machine learning models may require large amounts of labeled data and computational resources, making them resource-intensive to train and deploy.

(Continued)

Table 9.1 (*Continued*) Summary of the Literature Review

S.No.	*Journal Name*	*Methodology*	*Advantage*	*Disadvantage*
4	Malware Detection and Prevention using Artificial Intelligence Techniques [4]	Reviewing existing malware detection technologies, identifying weaknesses, and suggesting AI-based futuristic solutions for enhanced detection and prevention efficiency.	• Utilizing Artificial Intelligence (AI) for developing Anti-Malware Systems shows promise in effectively detecting and preventing malware attacks.	• Implementing AI-based solutions for malware detection may require significant computational resources and expertise, potentially increasing complexity and costs.
5	Malware Detection Using Deep Learning [5]	Proposed a deep learning-based model for malware detection using artificial neural networks trained on machine characteristics data, achieving an 83% accuracy rate.	• Developed a highly efficient malware detection model using deep learning and machine characteristics data.	• Limited by the reliance on machine characteristics data, potentially missing newer malware variants with different patterns.

(*Continued*)

Table 9.1 (*Continued*) Summary of the Literature Review

S.No.	*Journal Name*	*Methodology*	*Advantage*	*Disadvantage*
6	Malware Detection using Machine Learning [6]	Developed a web-based framework using feature selection and multiple machine learning algorithms to detect Android malware with an 86% detection rate.	• Provides a free and accessible solution for detecting malware, potentially reducing the risk of ransomware attacks and aiding users who cannot afford commercial software.	• Limited advancement compared to deep learning or natural language processing techniques may restrict accuracy.
7	Cyber Threat Detection based on Artificial Neural Networks using Event Profiles [7]	Developed an event profiling method involving data aggregation, decomposition, TF-IDF normalization, and vectorization for input into deep learning models.	• Proposed an AI-SIEM system using event profiles and artificial neural networks, improving cyber-threat detection and enabling efficient response to security alerts.	• Requires significant effort to manually label raw security events for supervised learning, potentially slowing down the process of dataset construction.
8	Intrusion Detection System [8]	Developed an IDS tool capable of monitoring network or system activities to detect and prevent malicious activity using various techniques, methods, and algorithms.	• Provides additional protection beyond firewall technology by monitoring and detecting intrusions, both externally and internally.	• Requires strong authentication, policy adherence, and human intervention, potentially increasing complexity and resource needs.

(*Continued*)

Table 9.1 *(Continued)* Summary of the Literature Review

S.No.	*Journal Name*	*Methodology*	*Advantage*	*Disadvantage*
9	Network Intrusion Detection System using Deep Learning [9]	Proposed deep learning architectures to develop an adaptive network intrusion detection system capable of detecting and classifying network attacks, demonstrated using the UNSW-NB15 dataset.	• Proposed deep learning-based network intrusion detection system achieved high accuracy in multiclass classification.	• Acknowledges the need for improvements, including feature reduction methods and handling zero-day attacks, which may require additional research and development.
10	Android Malware Detection System using Machine Learning [10]	Proposed a machine learning-based Android malware detection system trained with five classifiers and evaluated using Waikato Environment for Knowledge Analysis (WEKA), achieving high accuracy with Random Forest classifiers.	• Achieved high detection rates using machine learning classifiers for Android malware detection.	• Faces challenges with false alarms and selecting relevant features for improved detection performance.

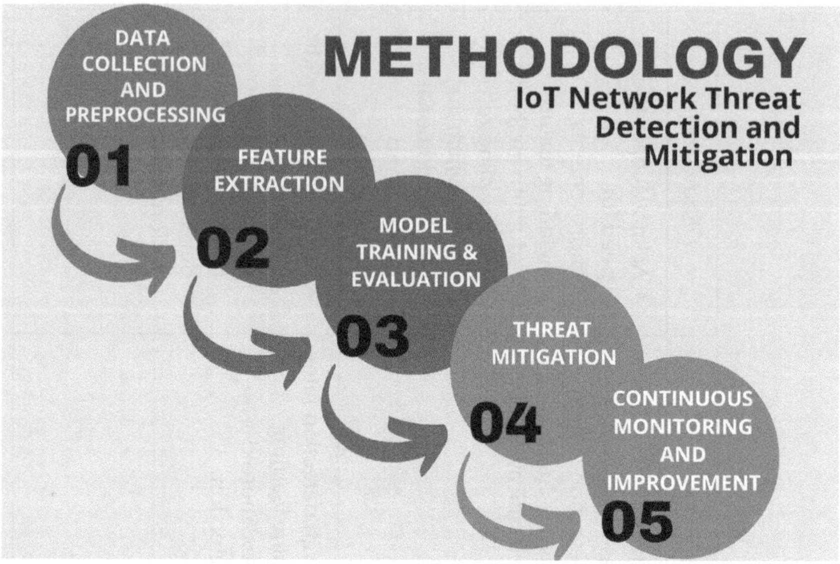

Figure 9.1 IoT network threat detection and mitigation in IoT network.

- Protocol types ('proto')
- Service types ('service')
- Packet-related metrics ('spkts', 'dpkts', 'sbytes', 'dbytes')
- Rate variables ('rate', 'sload', 'dload')
- Timing metrics ('sinpkt', 'dinpkt', 'sjit', 'djit')
- Connection attributes ('swin', 'tcprtt')
- Attack category labels ('attack_cat')

The feature importance analysis techniques, such as information gain and correlation analysis were used to identify the most discriminative features. This approach reduced dimensionality while maintaining the dataset's ability to effectively distinguish between normal traffic and various attack types.

The final feature set was carefully balanced to include both network performance indicators and attack signature patterns, ensuring comprehensive coverage of potential threat indicators while minimizing computational overhead.

9.3.3 Model Training and Evaluation

For model training, we utilized 50,000 network traffic samples distributed across different attack categories: DoS (40%), Exploits (25%), Reconnaissance (20%), and other malware forms, including Backdoors and Worms (15%).

The following machine learning algorithms were implemented and evaluated:

- Random Forest
- Decision Tree
- Naive Bayes
- Gradient Boosting
- k-Nearest Neighbors

Performance evaluation utilized standard metrics including:

- **Accuracy:** Overall correctness of classification
- **Precision:** Proportion of true positives among positive predictions
- **Recall:** Proportion of true positives identified correctly
- **F1-score:** Harmonic mean of precision and recall

The robustness and generalizability of results across different data partitions were done. Additionally, resource utilization metrics were recorded during model training and testing to assess computational efficiency—a critical factor for IoT deployments.

9.3.4 Threat Mitigation

Our threat mitigation approach incorporated multiple defensive layers:

- Real-time monitoring and blocking using Snort IDS/IPS [14]
- Rule-based detection for known threat signatures [13]
- Anomaly detection for identifying previously unseen attack patterns [12]
- Response automation for immediate threat containment [11]

Implementation involved deploying Snort in a test environment to evaluate its effectiveness against various attack types. Custom rules were developed to address IoT-specific vulnerabilities and attack vectors. Performance metrics tracked both detection accuracy and system resource utilization during mitigation activities.

The mitigation strategies were validated using over 13,000 samples representing diverse attack scenarios, ensuring comprehensive evaluation against realistic threat conditions.

9.3.5 Continuous Monitoring and Improvement

The final phase established a framework for ongoing security enhancement through:

- Real-time security alert monitoring
- Regular vulnerability assessments

- Periodic model retraining to adapt to evolving threats
- Security policy updates based on emerging attack patterns

This continuous improvement cycle ensures the security framework remains effective against evolving threats while maintaining optimal resource utilization in IoT environments. The tools and technologies used in this study are listed in Table 9.2.

9.4 Implementation of IoT Network Threat Detection

9.4.1 Detection Using ML

9.4.1.1 Dataset Loading and Data Preparation

- Loading the file from a Comma Separated Values (CSV) from the location. Using the functions head(), print(), and summary(), some preliminary sense of its structure and contents can be gained.
- Then the columns, selected by variable selected_columns will be used during further analysis. This involves features of IoT network traffic as well as the target variable, 'attack_cat', which is used to classify different categories of attacks.
- For the integrity of the data, missing values are identified through colSums(), so all differences are reflected and addressed. Furthermore, the 'attack_cat' variable is converted into a factor type to be used in the classification through as.factor().

9.4.1.2 Model Development and Assessment

- Different machine learning models are trained and tested on the selected IoT network traffic features to predict the categories of attacks. These models are designed to identify patterns corresponding to various attack types, like DDoS, Man-in-the-Middle, or malware.
- The randomForest and Naive Bayes libraries are used to implement the Random Forest, Decision Tree, Naive Bayes, Gradient Boosting, and k-Nearest Neighbors classifiers.
- Each classifier learns the relationship between input features and target attack categories from training data. Then the models are tested on another different test data to determine how well the model generalizes to new unseen data.

9.4.1.3 Model Evaluation Metrics

- It uses a custom function to compute key evaluation metrics that are essential for understanding the performance of machine learning models. That will

Table 9.2 Tools and Technology

Hardware/Software	*Developed by*	*Used in This Study*
R Programming Language	R Development Core Team	Data analysis, machine learning, and statistical computing tasks.
RStudio integrated development environment for R	RStudio, PBC	Used as a development environment for writing, executing, and debugging R code.
R packages/libraries (e.g., rpart, randomForest, e1071, class, caret, keras, Naive Bayes)	Various contributors within the R community	Utilized for implementing machine learning algorithms, performing data preprocessing, model evaluation, and other analytical tasks in R programming language.
Virtual Machine Environment	Morton L. Heilig	Utilized as a platform to host and run multiple operating systems and tools for IoT network security analysis.
Kali Linux operating system	Offensive Security	Provide preinstalled tools for IoT network reconnaissance, vulnerability assessment, and exploitation.
Ubuntu operating system	Canonical Ltd	Employed as an alternative operating system environment for certain tasks within the work.
Nmap (Network Mapper) tool	Gordon Lyon (Fyodor)	Utilized for IoT network exploration and auditing purposes, including port scanning, service enumeration, and information about IoT network hosts and services.
Snort intrusion detection and prevention system	Martin Roesch	Deployed as an intrusion detection and prevention system to monitor IoT network traffic in real time and detect suspicious activities.

be used to figure out such metrics as accuracy and precision, recall, and F1-score, which give a clear understanding of how well the model performs in correctly classifying instances across various attack categories. Accuracy gives an overall measure of correctness, precision assesses the accuracy of positive predictions, recall focuses on how well the model captures all relevant cases, and F1-score balances precision and recall for a more comprehensive performance evaluation.

- It will also measure the performance of the classifier as it predicts attack categories. Comparing these calculated metrics, the best-performing model will appear, so the selected classifier will have proof that it is effective in classifying different kinds of attacks, namely DDoS, Man-in-the-Middle, or malware.
- These discoveries allow for easier selection of the most reliable and efficient model for real-world applications that avoid false classifications and have better prediction accuracy.

9.4.1.4 Data Visualization with ggplot

- One custom function, 'compute_metrics', computes key performance metrics such as accuracy, precision, recall, and F1-score after each classifier output.
- These metrics also enable the evaluation of the model as to how much it is effectively classifying each attack category using accuracy, reflecting the overall performance measure, precision of avoiding false positives, and recall for identifying all positive cases.
- The calculated metrics enable detailed comparison of models and hence, the selection of the best-performing classifier for detecting and classifying network attacks.

9.4.2 Mitigation

9.4.2.1 Reconnaissance Attacks

Techniques used by attackers to gather information about the target IoT network or system, such as port scanning, vulnerability scanning, or network mapping.

Mitigation:

- Implement strict firewall rules to restrict unauthorized access and port scanning.
- Use IDS/IPS to monitor and block reconnaissance activities.
- Regularly update and patch software to eliminate known vulnerabilities.
- Employ techniques like IP address obfuscation, honeypots, and deception technologies to confuse attackers.

9.4.2.2 Backdoor Attacks

Malicious code or techniques that allow unauthorized remote access and control over a system or application.

Mitigation:

- Keep software up-to-date and apply security patches promptly.
- Use application whitelisting to prevent unauthorized software from running.
- Implement strict access controls and regularly review user privileges.
- Deploy host-based IDS to monitor for suspicious activities.

9.4.2.3 Denial of Service (DoS) Attacks

Attempts to disrupt a system, IoT network, or service by overloading it with too much traffic or too many requests.

Mitigation:

- Implement rate-limiting and traffic filtering mechanisms at the network level.
- Configure load balancers and web application firewalls (WAFs) to mitigate DoS attacks.
- Ensure redundancy in network infrastructure and server capacity.
- Have a documented and tested incident response plan for DoS attacks.

9.4.2.4 Exploit Attacks

Exploits take advantage of vulnerabilities in software or systems to achieve unauthorized access or execute harmful code.

Mitigation:

- Regularly update and patch software, operating systems, and applications.
- Deploy WAFs to detect and block exploit attempts.
- Implement secure coding practices and conduct regular code reviews.
- Implement address space layout randomization and data execution prevention to reduce the risk of memory-based exploits.

9.4.2.5 Fuzzing Attacks

Techniques that involve sending malformed or unexpected input to an application or system to identify and exploit vulnerabilities.

Mitigation:

- Implement input validation and sanitization mechanisms.
- Use secure coding practices and perform code reviews to identify and fix vulnerabilities.

- Deploy WAFs to detect and block fuzzing attempts.
- Regularly update and patch software and applications.

9.4.2.6 Worm Attacks

Self-replicating malware that spreads across IoT networks and systems, often exploiting vulnerabilities or leveraging social engineering tactics.

Mitigation:

- Deploy antivirus and antimalware solutions with up-to-date signatures.
- Implement IoT network segmentation and access controls to limit worm propagation.
- Regularly update and patch software and operating systems.
- Use IDS/IPS to monitor for worm activity.

9.4.2.7 Shellcode Attacks

Malicious code injected into a system or application to execute arbitrary commands or gain unauthorized access.

Mitigation:

- Deploy data execution prevention and address space layout randomization mechanisms.
- Implement strict input validation and sanitization measures.
- Use secure coding practices and conduct regular code reviews.
- Deploy WAFs to detect and block shellcode attempts.

9.4.2.8 Generic Attacks

A broad category that encompasses various types of attacks not specifically classified.

Mitigation:

- Implement defense-in-depth security measures, including firewalls, IDS/IPS, access controls, and secure configuration practices.
- Regularly update and patch software, operating systems, and applications.
- Conduct security awareness training for employees to recognize and report potential threats.
- Develop and test an incident response plan to effectively respond to and mitigate attacks.

By accurately classifying attack types, the predictive capabilities of the machine learning models inform targeted mitigation strategies. The models offer the ability to indicate not just the presence, but the presence of specific network threats such as DoS and processes such as exploit and reconnaissance; therefore specific defensive actions can be performed. Detection inherently permits faster responses to attacks, such as rate-limiting mechanisms when a DoS attack is detected, or shellcode detection that may signal an activation of input validation and the security protocols therein. It turns predictive insights into proactive, timely threat prevention.

9.4.3 Intrusion Detection System (IDS) and Intrusion Prevention System (IPS) Using Snort

Snort is a well-known open-source IDS/IPS which is lightweight and employs rule-based detection methods. Snort is a single-threaded IDS providing performance beneficial for securing low-bandwidth, low-powered IoT devices, with higher resource consumption than Suricata [16], which is multithreaded and better for security on a high-speed network. Unlike Zeek, which primarily analyzes and logs network traffic, Snort provides real-time packet inspection and intrusions into the network to detect and block attacks. These attributes, along with easy deployment, low computing requirements, and a robust community, make it practical for use in IoT network security.

9.4.3.1 Installation

Install Snort for network intrusion detection and prevention on Ubuntu (with Burp Suite) as shown in Figure 9.2.

9.4.3.2 Configuration

Configuring Snort on Ubuntu for effective intrusion detection using the Nano text editor as shown in Figures 9.3 and 9.4.

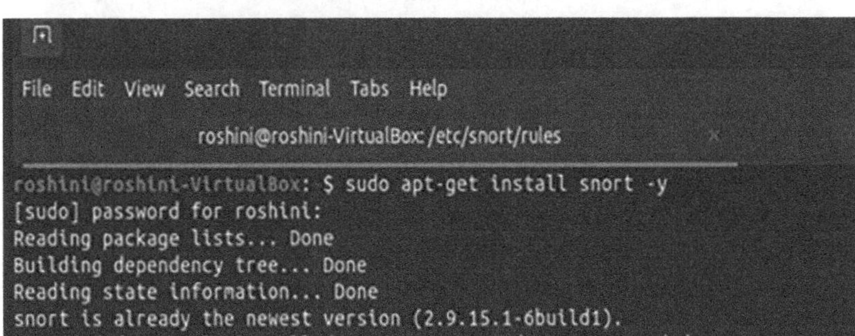

Figure 9.2 Setting up snort.

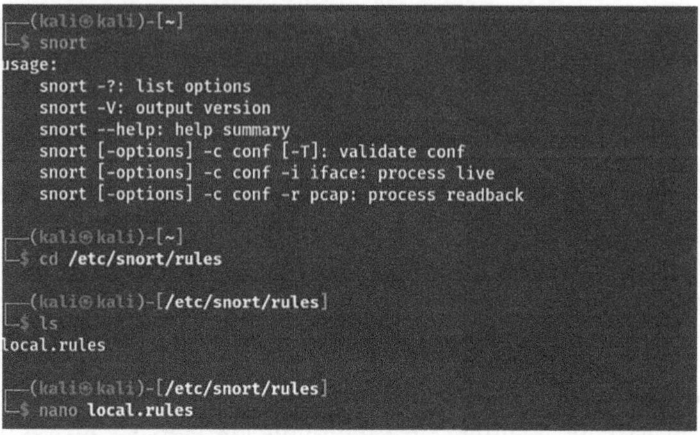

Figure 9.3 Snort configuration.

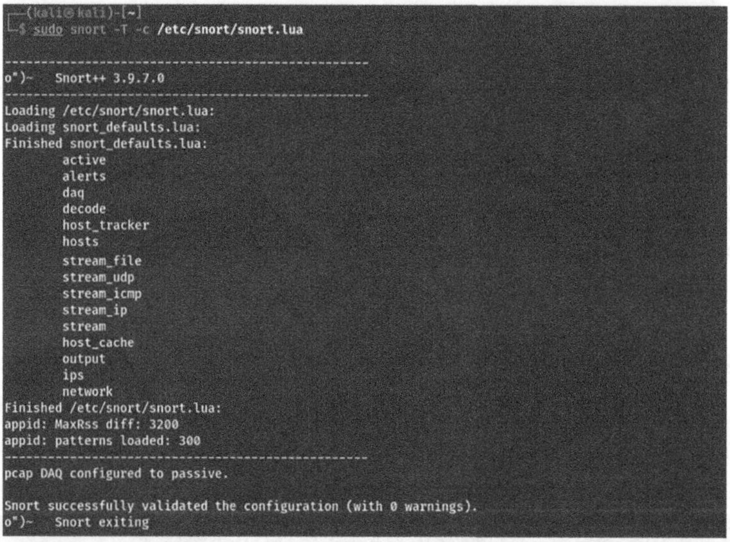

Figure 9.4 Threat detection.

9.4.3.3 Detecting Threats Using Snort

Beginning threat detection with Snort on Ubuntu to safeguard against potential security breaches, as shown in Figure 9.5.

9.4.3.4 Threat Simulation

- Sending attacks from Kali Linux to Ubuntu, as shown in Figure 9.6.
- Sending attacks from Windows to Ubuntu, as shown in Figure 9.7.

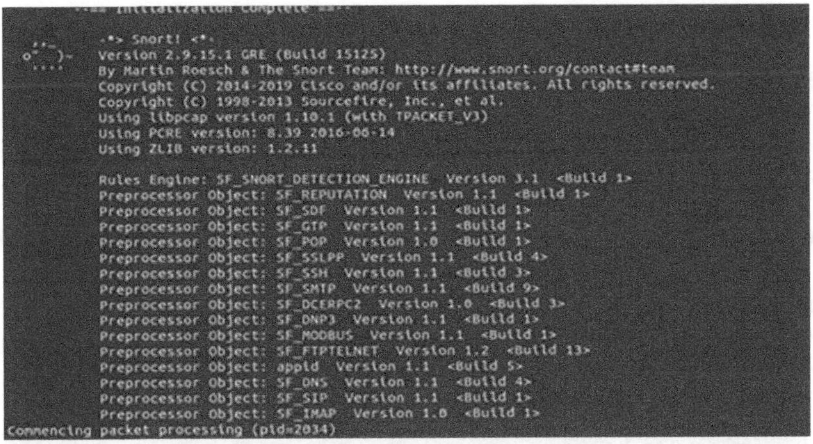

Figure 9.5 Threat detection.

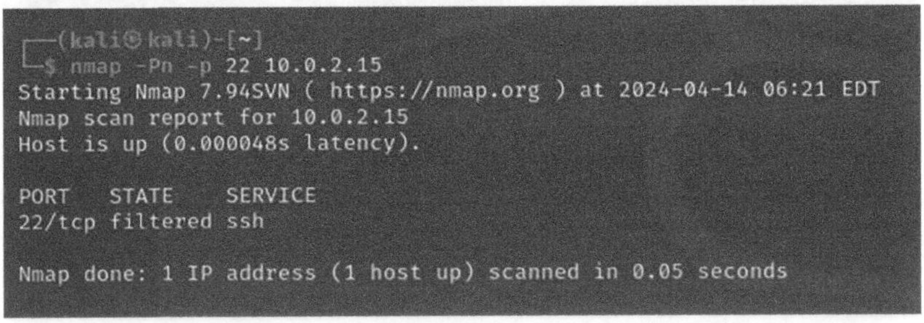

Figure 9.6 Threat simulation on Kali-Linux.

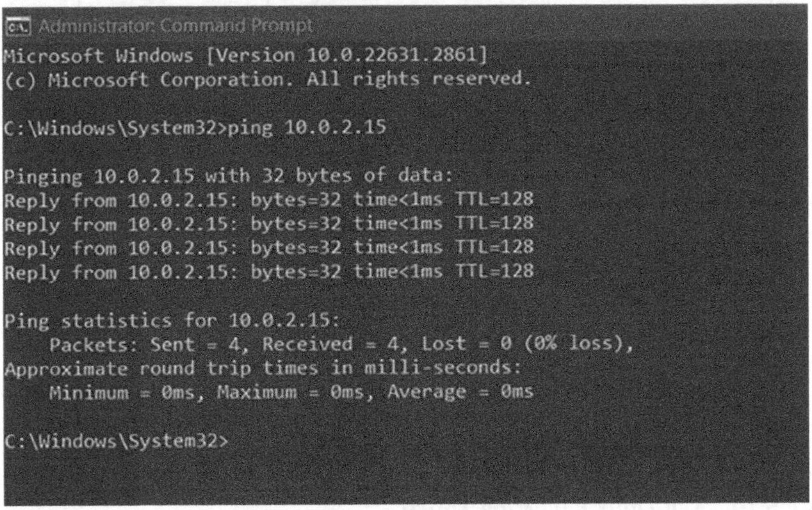

Figure 9.7 Threat simulation on Windows-Threat.

9.4.3.5 Threat Detected

Identification of attacks from Kali Linux and Windows on Ubuntu, as shown in Figure 9.8.

9.4.3.6 Repeat Threat Detection

- Uncovering the attacks from Windows on Ubuntu, as shown in Figure 9.9.
- Uncovering the attacks from Kali Linux on Ubuntu, as shown in Figure 9.10.

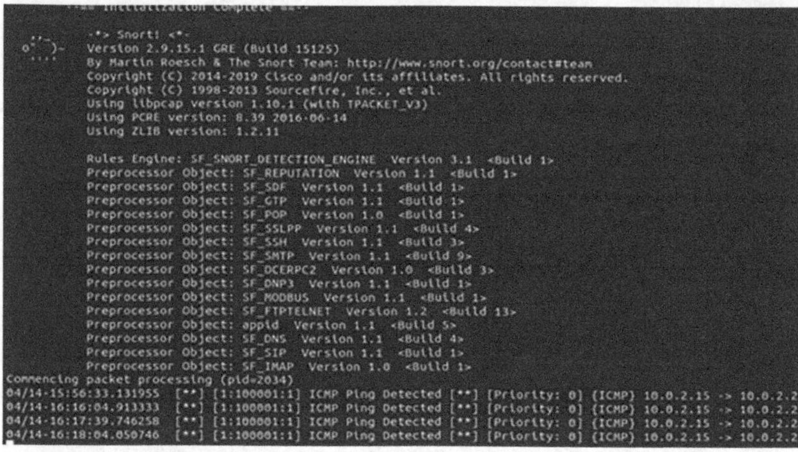

Figure 9.8 Detecting the Threat.

Figure 9.9 Windows Recurring Threat.

Figure 9.10 Kali Linux Recurring Threat.

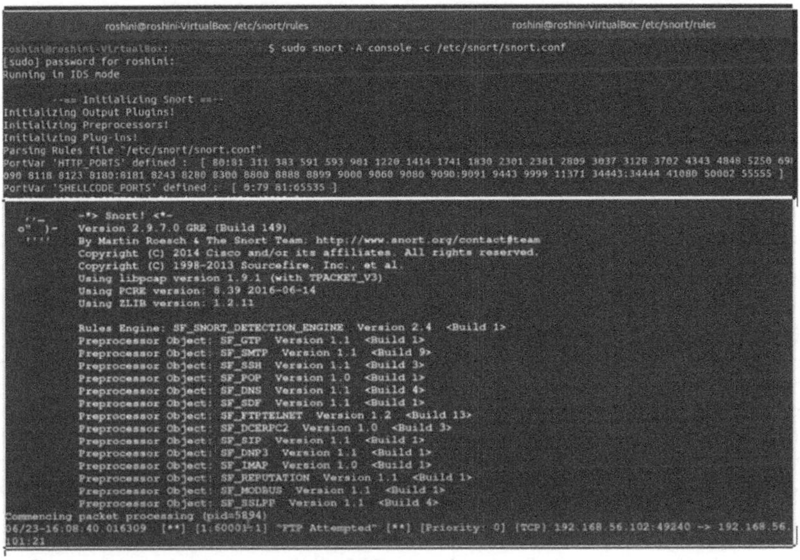

Figure 9.11 Threat-prevention in Ubuntu.

9.4.3.7 Threat Prevention

Ubuntu defended against the attacks successfully in both Kali Linux and Windows, as shown in Figure 9.11.

9.5 Results and Discussion

The code performs a thorough examination of the resource needs for several machine learning algorithms, including Gradient Boosting, Random Forest, Decision Tree, and Naive Bayes. It assesses both execution time and memory consumption to quantify their resource usage in the IoT network with IoT network malware dataset [11]. The code compares how well they perform in terms of accuracy, execution time, and memory usage to provide information about how effective and efficient they are in comparison. It uses graphic aids, such as bar plots and radar charts, to provide this comparison in a way that is visually engaging and helps the reader better understand the findings. The column dataset is presented in Figure 9.12.

Unlike rule-based systems that require constant manual updates, ML models continuously learn from new data. This enables better adaptation to emerging threats without relying solely on preexisting signatures. While traditional models can be computationally expensive, ML models optimized for IoT environments (e.g., lightweight classifiers and federated learning) balance security effectiveness with minimal resource consumption, making them ideal for resource-constrained

```
>names (data) #print colnames
[1] "X"                "dur"      "proto"    "service"  "state"    "spkts"    "dpkts"
[8] "sbytes"           "dbytes"   "rate"     "sload"    "dload"    "sloss"    "dloss"
[15] "sinpkt"          "dinpkt"   "sjit"     "djit"     "swin"     "stcpb"    "dtcpb"
[22] "dwin"            "tcprtt"   "synack"   "ackdat"   "smean"    "dmean"    "trans_depth"
[29] "response body_len" "ct_src_dport_1tm" "ct_dstdport_1tm" "is_ftp_login" "ct_ftp_cmd" "ct_flw_http thd"
[36] "attack_cat" "label"
```

Figure 9.12 Column-dataset.

Table 9.3 Classifier Performance Metrics

Classifier	*Accuracy (%)*	*Precision (%)*	*Recall (%)*	*F1-Score (%)*
Random Forest	91.25	97.8	96.5	97.1
Gradient Boosting	90.83	97.2	95.9	96.5
Decision Tree	86.84	72.5	92.4	81.3
Naive Bayes	45.67	51.8	39.6	44.8

Prediction \ Reference	**Analysis**	**Backdoor**	**DoS**	**Exploits**	**Fuzzers**	**Generic**	**Normal**	**Reconnaissance**	**Shellcode**	**Worms**
Analysis	6	1	7	8	0	0	0	2	0	0
Backdoor	0	2	4	10	7	2	0	2	0	0
DoS	23	31	410	518	199	13	0	2	9	0
Exploits	79	81	645	2350	269	70	12	135	17	16
Fuzzers	68	68	217	264	5531	32	0	119	0	1
Generic	0	0	2	3	47	76	7	11032	0	0
Normal	0	0	0	7	14	11	316	844	0	0
Reconnaissance	0	0	7	17	18	1	16	4	28	0
Shellcode	0	0	0	0	1	1	1	2	0	0
Worms	0	0	0	0	0	1	2	1	0	0

Figure 9.13 Confusion-matrix.

IoT devices (Table 9.3). The confusion matrix and the accuracy of attack using ML are shown in Figures 9.13 and 14, respectively. The plot of classifier performance metrics is presented in Figure 9.15.

Classifier	Accuracy	Precision	Recall	F1-Score
Random Forest	91.25%	97.8%	96.5%	97.1%
Gradient Boosting	90.83%	97.2%	95.9%	96.5%
Decision Tree	86.84%	72.5%	92.4%	81.3%
Naive Bayes	45.67%	51.8%	39.6%	44.8%

Figure 9.14 Accuracy of attack using ML.

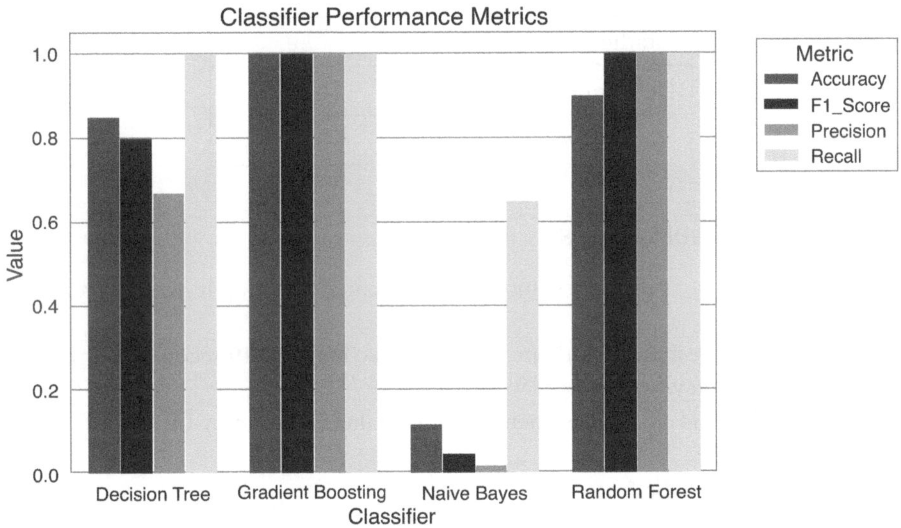

Figure 9.15 Classifier performance metrics.

9.5.1 Key Observations

- Random Forest and Gradient Boosting achieved the highest accuracy (91.25% and 90.83%), making them the most reliable for IoT network security.
- Decision Tree is fast but has lower precision (72.5%), which leads to more false positives.
- Naive Bayes struggles with network data (45.67% accuracy) but shows moderate precision (Figure 9.4).

Table 9.4 Execution Time & Memory Usage

Algorithm	*Execution Time (s)*	*Memory Usage (bytes)*
Random Forest	18.73	95,432
Gradient Boosting	19.89	100,472
Decision Tree	0.58	99,928
Naive Bayes	7.22	98,345

Table 9.5 Overall Model Performance (AUC Score)

Algorithm	*AUC Score*
Random Forest	0.91
Gradient Boosting	0.90
Decision Tree	0.76
Naive Bayes	0.50

9.5.2 Key Observations

- Decision Tree is the fastest model (0.58 second), making it ideal for real-time applications.
- Random Forest and Gradient Boosting take longer (~19 seconds) but provide better accuracy.
- Naive Bayes is efficient in memory but weaker in accuracy (Table 9.4).

9.5.3 Final Verdict

- **Best Overall Model:** Random Forest (Highest AUC: 0.91) (Table 9.5).
- **Best for Speed and Simplicity:** Decision Tree (86.84% Accuracy, Low Latency).
- **Alternative Choice:** Gradient Boosting (High Accuracy but Slightly Slower).
- **Not Recommended:** Naive Bayes (Low Accuracy, High False Positives).

9.6 Conclusion

This research effectively integrated machine learning techniques such as Random Forest, Decision Tree, Naïve Bayes, and Gradient Boosting for intrusion detection in IoT networks. By combining these models with Snort IDS/IPS, real-time threat detection and mitigation were achieved, addressing the computational limitations of IoT systems. The study also highlighted strategies for optimizing resource use, ensuring security solutions remain efficient and practical. Despite these advancements, challenges like scalability, evolving threats, and computational demands persist. Future work should focus on hybrid machine learning approaches, real-time anomaly detection, and federated learning to improve adaptability and robustness. Exploring lightweight ML frameworks and advanced neural networks could further enhance detection accuracy while reducing resource consumption. This study establishes a solid foundation for developing intelligent, scalable security systems capable of defending IoT ecosystems against emerging cyber threats.

9.7 Future Scope

Developing secure methods for sharing threat intelligence across IoT domains such as healthcare, industrial systems, and smart cities is a key area of research, as it can improve threat detection through collaboration while maintaining privacy. Future efforts should explore innovative techniques to detect and prevent adversarial attacks that target intrusion detection systems, ensuring robust defenses. Integrating blockchain technology could enhance data security and integrity, while quantum-resistant protocols are needed to safeguard against emerging risks posed by quantum computing. Autonomous response systems and self-healing networks could further bolster resilience by automatically mitigating threats and maintaining operations during attacks. Additionally, incorporating compliance verification tools into security frameworks is essential to meet evolving regulatory and ethical standards. These advancements aim to address current vulnerabilities and strengthen IoT networks against increasingly sophisticated threats.

References

1. AlSobeh, A.M., Gaber, K., Hammad, M.M., Nuser, M. and Shatnawi, A. Android Malware Detection Using Time-Aware Machine Learning Approach. *Cluster Computing*, 27(9) pp. 12627–12648, June 2024.
2. Hu, Z. Knowledge Graph-Based Large-Scale Network Security Threat Detection Techniques. *Applied Mathematics and Nonlinear Sciences*, 9(1), January 2024.
3. Thiziers, A.H., Tiémoman, K., and Kabir, T.T.Q. Malware Detection Using Deep Learning. *Open Journal of Applied Sciences*, 13(12), pp. 2480–2491, December 2023.
4. Saminathan, K., Mulka, S.T.R., Damodharan, S., Maheswar, R., and Lorincz, J. An Artificial Neural Network Autoencoder for Insider Cyber Security Threat Detection. *Future Internet*, 15(12), p. 373, November 2023.
5. Patil, P. and Gedam, M. Malware Detection Using Machine Learning. *IJRAR-International Journal of Research and Analytical Reviews (IJRAR)*, 10(2), pp. 418–423, April 2023.
6. Akhtar, M.S. and Feng, T. Malware Analysis and Detection Using Machine Learning Algorithms. *Symmetry*, 14(11), p. 2304, November 2022.

7. Faruk, M.J.H., Shahriar, H., Valero, M., Barsha, F.L., Sobhan, S., Khan, M.A., Whitman, M., Cuzzocrea, A., Lo, D., Rahman, A., and Wu, F. Malware Detection and Prevention Using Artificial Intelligence Techniques. *In Proceedings of the 2021 IEEE International Conference on Big Data (Big Data)*, Orlando, FL, USA, pp. 5369–5377, IEEE, December 2021.
8. Ashiku, L. and Dagli, C. Network Intrusion Detection System Using Deep Learning. *Procedia Computer Science*, 185, pp. 239–247, June 2021
9. Lee, J., Kim, J., Kim, I. and Han, K. Cyber Threat Detection Based on Artificial Neural Networks Using Event Profiles. *IEEE Access*, 7, pp. 165607–165626, November 2019.
10. Tiwari, M., Kumar, R., Bharti, A. and Kishan, J. Intrusion Detection System. *International Journal of Technical Research and Applications*, 5(2), pp. 38–44, April 2017.
11. Haddad Pajouh, H., Dehghantanha, A., Khayami, R., and Choo, K.-K.R. A Deep Recurrent Neural Network Based Approach for Internet of Things Malware Threat Hunting, *Future Generation Computer Systems*, 85, pp. 88–96, 2018. https://doi.org/10.1016/j.future.2018.03.007.
12. Somasundaram, R., and Thirugnanam, M. Review on Communication Security Issues in IoT Medical Devices. In B.K. Tripathy & J. Anuradha (Eds.), *Internet of Things* (*IoT*) (pp. 189–210). CRC Press, 2017.
13. Zhang, Z. K., Cho, M. C. Y., Wang, C. W., Hsu, C. W., Chen, C. K. and Shieh, S. IoT Security: Ongoing Challenges and Research Opportunities. In *Proceedings of the 2014 IEEE 7th International Conference on Service-Oriented Computing and Applications* (*SOCA 2014*), Matsue, Japan, (pp. 230–234). IEEE, November 2014.
14. Somasundaram, R. and Thirugnanam, M. IoT in Healthcare: Breaching Security Issues. In Jeyanthi & R. Thandeeswaran (Eds.), *Security Breaches and Threat Prevention in the Internet of Things* (pp. 174–188). IGI Global, 2017.
15. Dataset: https://www.kaggle.com/datasets/mrwellsdavid/unsw-nb15?select=UNSW_NB15_testing-set.csv.
16. Day, D. and Burns, B. A Performance Analysis of Snort and Suricata Network Intrusion Detection and Prevention Engines. In *Fifth International Conference on Digital Society*, Gosier, Guadeloupe (pp. 187–192), 2011.

Chapter 10

A Comprehensive Review of AI and IoT-Based Systems for Intelligent Accident Management and Response

Akhil Raju, D. Ajitha*, S. M. Prabin* ,
and Laxmi Shaw

10.1 Introduction

10.1.1 Accident Management Systems

An accident refers to an unforeseen and undesirable incident, particularly involving a vehicle, that occurs unexpectedly and results in harm or damage to people or property. The cause of an accident involves a mix of both concurrent and consecutive elements, where every element is essential for the accident to take place, yet none can independently cause it. The World Health Organization reports that road traffic accidents result in about 1.3 million deaths each year worldwide, in addition to inflicting non-fatal injuries on between 20 and 50 million people. As the world population reaches 8.1 billion, the demand for vehicles also escalates. This consequently leads to an increase in roadway collisions. Initially, the majority of these incidents are

* Corresponding Authors

DOI: 10.1201/9781003587859-10

nonlethal. Due to the delay in response time and lack of proper facilities, this can lead to a fatal mistake gradually. For a whopping 300 million vehicles in India, there is a vast network of roads that stretches over six million kilometers, and an incident may transpire at any juncture within this intricate network. This underscores the importance of a robust accident management system (AMS). An AMS represents a holistic and technology-oriented framework intended to effectively address and oversee road incidents. It integrates a variety of strategies, methodologies, and technological solutions aimed at mitigating the consequences of accidents, ensuring swift emergency responses, reducing traffic interruptions, and improving overall road safety.

This chapter makes key contributions to the field of Artificial Intelligence (AI)- and Internet of Things (IoT)-based accident management. It provides a comprehensive review of existing accident detection and alert systems, identifying their strengths and limitations. The study highlights the role of AI and IoT in enhancing real-time accident detection, response efficiency, and overall road safety. Additionally, it proposes a framework for integrating advanced AI models with IoT sensors to improve accuracy and minimize false alarms. The chapter is structured as follows: it begins with an introduction to AMSs, followed by an analysis of traditional and technology-driven approaches. Subsequent sections discuss the role of AI and IoT in accident detection, the various sensors and devices used, and the challenges faced in implementing such systems. Finally, the chapter concludes with a discussion on future directions and recommendations for improving AI-IoT-based accident management solutions.

In India, the concept of an AMS is increasingly recognized as essential, particularly as road safety and traffic regulations gain prominence. The country's varied road conditions, coupled with its high population density and persistent traffic congestion, render effective accident management imperative.

The major objectives of AMS are:

- **On-time Accident Detection:** one of the primary goals is to detect accidents promptly as they occur.
- **Prompt Emergency Response:** ensuring swift emergency response is crucial. The AMS should try to shorten the duration from when an accident is detected to when emergency services arrive, thereby lessening the seriousness of injuries and the likelihood of fatalities.
- **Traffic Management:** it also focuses on reducing traffic congestion and aims to ensure smooth traffic flow.
- **Minimum Impact:** the ultimate goal is to reduce the impact of accidents on human lives and infrastructure by facilitating quicker response and effective communication.
- **Maximum Road Safety:** By offering immediate data and insights, the system plays a role in building up safer road conditions. This includes preventing accidents, reducing risky behaviors, and educating the public about road safety.

- **Adaptation to Advancing Technologies:** AMS is adaptable enough to incorporate new technologies like 5G networks, edge computing, and sophisticated AI algorithms to remain relevant and efficient.
- **Continuous Updating:** As technology advances and more data is collected, the AMS should continually evolve and adapt to provide even more accurate accident detection, response, and traffic management.
- **Minimize Response Times:** By identifying accidents promptly and optimizing response procedures, the AMS intends to cut down the duration it takes for emergency services to arrive at accident locations.

The effect of efficient accident management on road safety, traffic efficiency, and emergency response cannot be overstated. Accidents may occur for various reasons like driver errors, actions of other road users, or mechanical failures in vehicles. It is essential to recognize that this issue poses a significant public hazard, with far-reaching effects on everyday life, including fatalities, loss of loved ones, and long-term disabilities. The repercussions can include both physical and psychological trauma, which can diminish the overall quality of life. Therefore, fast action in these situations is vital, and comprehensive support is necessary. In this context, technology plays a pivotal role. The implementation of an automated AMS can significantly enhance operational efficiency and workflow. Its impact extends across the domains of road safety, traffic management, and emergency services, fostering a safer and more agile road environment that is transforming the everyday lives of the common people.

- **Road Safety Enhancement:** Road safety is directly impacted by prompt and well-coordinated accident handling. Accidents that are promptly attended to reduce potential damage and injuries, which in turn lowers the number of fatalities and long-term health effects.
- **Uninterrupted Traffic Flow:** Accidents frequently result in traffic jams that impede the efficient movement of automobiles. In addition to reducing traffic jams and guaranteeing that the road network operates at its best, efficient accident management helps quickly clears accident scenes.
- **Quick Emergency Response:** Emergency response is sparked by effective accident management. Law enforcement, rescue teams, and medical professionals respond more quickly when there is prompt detection and prompt alarms. This ultimately results in fewer fatalities and less severe injuries.
- **Fewer Additional Accidents:** Because of decreased visibility and distracted driving, traffic jams brought on by accidents can worsen and result in additional collisions. Such secondary events are significantly reduced when accidents are managed well.
- Accurate and timely accident management enables emergency services to distribute resources with precision. To maximize response effectiveness, the appropriate people and tools are sent to the appropriate areas.

- **Data-Based Decision-Making:** Authorities can make informed decisions by using real-time data from AMSs. This includes determining the most effective diversion routes, allocating resources based on the accident's severity, and improving general road safety tactics.
- **Economic Impact Reduction:** Prompt accident response reduces financial costs from medical bills, auto repairs, and lost production. Effective management lessens these financial consequences by reducing the severity of accidents.
- **Perception of Safety and Public Trust:** Effective AMSs promote public confidence in traffic safety protocols. People feel safer on the roads and have greater confidence in the ability of the authorities to protect their safety when they believe that accidents are handled well.

AMSs have demonstrated significant potential in reducing accidents and fatalities across various sectors by leveraging advanced technologies and data-driven approaches. These systems not only enhance safety but also improve operational efficiency and environmental outcomes. In the oil and gas sector, the Driving Journey Management System transformation has resulted in a 25% decrease in its related to driving, even though driving activity has increased by 500%. By using data analysis and intervention techniques, traffic infraction instances also decreased by 75%, and 13% of high-risk drivers were remediated to lower-risk categories [1]. Advanced safety features like terrain impact prevention and upset prevention might potentially cut fatalities in general aviation by 66.5%. In particular, terrain impact prevention alone may reduce fatal accidents by 30.7%, underscoring the vital role that technology plays in improving aviation safety [2]. A 6% reduction in travel time, a 9% reduction in average stop delay, and a 27% reduction in vehicle stops are just a few of the encouraging outcomes of integrating Car2X technology into Traffic Incident Management systems. The environmental advantages of such systems are demonstrated by the 16% reduction in fuel usage and carbon monoxide emissions that result from these enhancements [3]. By speeding up emergency response times, India's Smart Accident Fatality Reduction System seeks to lower the number of fatalities from traffic accidents. The significance of prompt intervention in accident management is shown by the fact that a one-third decrease in the chance of mortality is linked to a 10-minute reduction in medical response time [4]. Even though these systems have a lot of potential, there are still issues with infrastructure compatibility, technology integration, and regulatory compliance. By addressing these problems, the efficiency of the AMS could be further improved.

10.1.2 Traditional vs Technology-Driven Approaches

Numerous facilities have been established all over the place to mitigate the consequences of accidents. The evolution of AMSs has been substantial, with conventional strategies serving as the groundwork for contemporary solutions for a long time. Historically, these traditional methods depended heavily on manual procedures and human involvement. Typically, accidents were reported by witnesses, victims, or law enforcement officials through telephone calls or direct notifications. Upon receiving information, emergency services such as ambulances and police were dispatched to accident scenes based on the reported location. Police personnel were responsible for directing traffic away from accident sites to minimize congestion. After the accident was resolved, authorities conducted investigations to determine causes and faults, often involving interviews and examination of evidence. The lack of real-time data and communication technology made it challenging to promptly respond to accidents.

While these methods were working somehow, traditional methods had their limitations. Relying on manual reporting led to delayed emergency response times, impacting the severity of injuries and overall accident outcomes. Reports could be inaccurate or incomplete, making it challenging for emergency services to adequately prepare for the scene. The lack of real-time traffic management often resulted in traffic congestion around accident sites, causing further delays and increasing the risk of secondary accidents. There was no way to capture comprehensive accident data for analyzing the incident and adopting preventive measures. Misallocation of resources could happen due to the lack of real-time information.

Traditional methods have become the foundation of modern systems to build upon. Since the only way to tackle the problem was to make the public aware, effective awareness of public road safety and reporting has happened. Manual protocols for the same have become the standardized procedures adopted in modern systems. Also, the limitations of traditional approaches fueled the drive to integrate technology and paved the way for technology-driven AMSs. Despite the advancements in technology, road safety management systems still rely significantly on manual data collection, visual inspections, and subjective evaluations by professionals to assess their effectiveness. However, this approach is expensive, time-intensive, and occasionally inadequate due to issues like incomplete reporting and data of insufficient quality.

Some of the methods implemented and established to tackle road accidents in India are mentioned below. National emergency numbers that aim to provide integrated emergency services, including accident response are important among them. This helpline connects callers with police, fire services, and medical assistance. There are many trauma care schemes in India, such as [5]:

- National Highway Trauma Care Project (NHTCP)
- National Highways Accident Relief Services Scheme (NHARSS)
- NHAI
- Incident Management System (IMS)
- Emergency Medical Service Systems (EMSS)

There are also control rooms that monitor major roads 24x7, acting as traffic management centers. Another step taken is the introduction of CCTV cameras in most of the important areas that are monitored. Various Indian states have initiated projects to enhance road safety and accident management. These initiatives often include improved road signage, better lighting, and stricter enforcement of traffic rules. States such as Kerala in South India have established a network of AI cameras that can automatically alert the authorities if there are any traffic violations and incidents.

While these initiatives contribute to accident management in India, there is still room for advanced technology integration. Various advancements present the opportunity to deliver more thorough and efficient data collection and analysis, with the aim of enhancing road safety [6]. Modern technologies like AI, Machine Learning (ML), Image Processing, IoT, Smartphone applications, Geographic Information Systems, Global Positioning Systems (GPS), Drones, Social Media, Virtual Reality, Simulators, Radar, Sensors, and Big Data provide useful means for identifying and providing information on the road safety, use behavior, road characteristics, and accident management. As mentioned above, technologies such as AI, image processing, and IoT have been widely applied to enhance efficiency due to their ability to automate the whole process with high accuracy and less time-consuming compared to manual work [7]. Table 10.1 gives an overview of the key differences between traditional and technology-driven approaches in AMSs.

Table 10.1 Comparison of Traditional vs. Technology-Driven Approaches

Aspect	*Traditional Approach*	*Technology-Driven Approach*
Reporting	Manual (calls, witnesses, and police)	Automated (Artificial Intelligence, Internet of Things sensors, and mobile apps)
Response Time	Delayed	Real time
Traffic Management	Manual redirection	Automated rerouting via GPS and AI
Data Collection	Interviews and physical evidence	Digital data, sensors, and real-time monitoring
Resource Allocation	Often inaccurate	Optimized through data analytics
Accuracy	Prone to errors	High accuracy with automation
Cost and Time	High	Reduced due to automation
Preventive Measures	Limited	Advanced predictive analytics

10.1.3 Challenges in Current Accident Management Systems

In this digital era, automation is streamlining complex processes, and AMSs are a significant area of research benefiting from modern technologies. However, real-life implementation remains challenging due to technical, infrastructural, and societal barriers. Many smart technologies are still in development, and breakthroughs often arise from addressing limitations in existing methods. Identifying these challenges is essential to advancing accident management solutions. AMSs face delayed emergency responses, often caused by inaccurate reporting and communication bottlenecks, leading to more severe outcomes [8]. Data collection remains unreliable, as it predominantly relies on witness accounts rather than real-time monitoring, undermining decision-making and resource allocation [9]. Traffic congestion near accident sites further complicates response efforts, increasing the risk of secondary accidents, while integration issues between agencies hinder coordination and data sharing [10].

The absence of real-time data affects decision-making and results in poor resource allocation, limiting the ability to analyze accident trends and implement preventive measures [11]. Technical and infrastructural barriers also limit AI-IoT adoption in accident management. Many accidents in remote areas go unnoticed, especially when vehicles are hidden by geographical features or victims are unconscious, which delays emergency response [12]. Cybersecurity threats, high costs, and data privacy concerns add further complexity to AI-IoT implementations [13]. Additionally, scalability issues make it difficult to adapt AMSs across urban and rural settings. Public awareness and compliance with accident reporting and traffic regulations remain insufficient, reducing the effectiveness of automated systems. Addressing these challenges through AI- and IoT-driven innovations can enhance real-time data collection, optimize emergency response, and improve overall accident management, reducing risks and potentially saving lives. This chapter explores various AI-IoT approaches aimed at minimizing these risk factors and improving the efficiency of accident response systems. Figure 10.1 provides a general algorithm for working on a modern AMS in real time with the integration of AI and the IoT.

10.2 Introduction to AI and IoT

The evolution of AI and IoT technologies represents a remarkable journey marked by crucial achievements. The origins of AI can be traced back to the early 1940s, with the significant contributions of Warren McCulloch and Walter Pitts, who proposed the idea that artificial neurons could have a lasting impact on the field. In the following years, pivotal developments occurred, including Donald Hebb's introduction of Hebbian learning in 1949 and Alan Turing's renowned Turing test in 1950, which assesses the ability of machines to exhibit intelligent behavior comparable to that of humans. The phrase "Artificial Intelligence" was first introduced

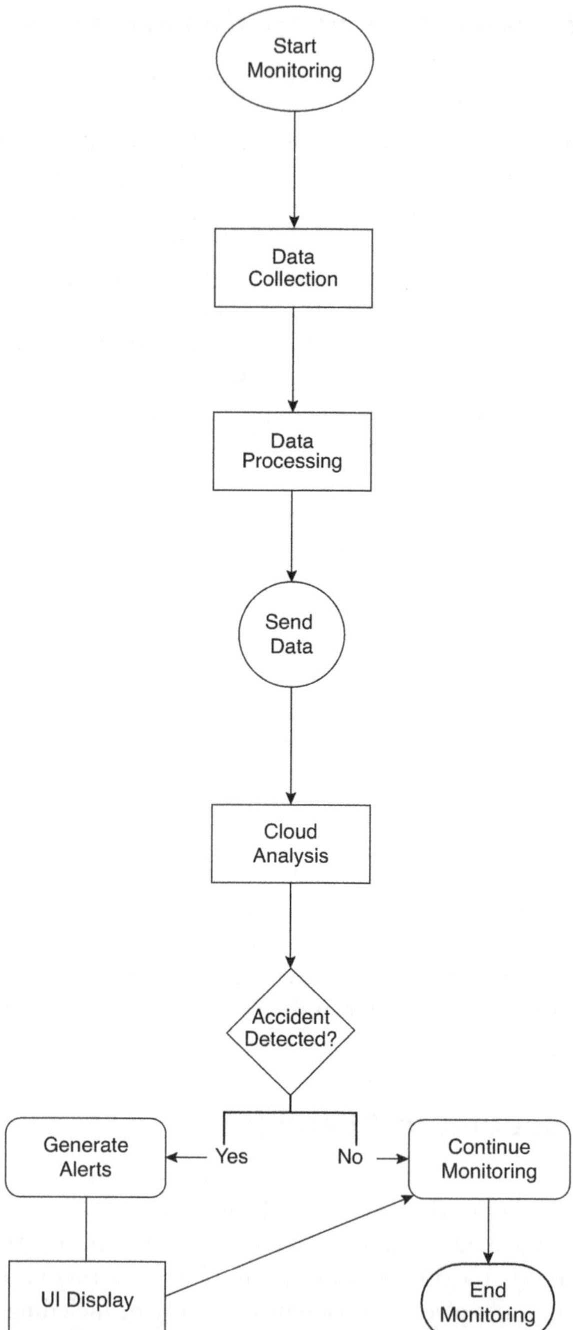

Figure 10.1 Accident monitoring system.

by John McCarthy in 1956, signifying the formal recognition of this domain as an academic discipline. The first origins of the IoT can be traced back to the late 1960s, when researchers began to conceptualize methods for linking computers and systems, leading to the development of ARPANET, which served as a foundational model for the Internet even in modern times. The twentieth century also witnessed the rise of advanced software applications and humanoid robotics, illustrating the expanding capabilities of both AI and IoT. Although there were challenges, including the so-called AI winters, the recent convergence of AI and IoT has significantly advanced these fields. Currently, the integration of deep learning, big data, and artificial general intelligence underscores the symbiotic relationship between AI and IoT, setting the stage for a future characterized by transformative innovations and enhanced connectivity [14].

10.2.1 Artificial Intelligence

AI is the ability of digital computers or computer-controlled robots to perform tasks typically associated with human intelligence. It involves cognitive processes such as reasoning, understanding, and learning from past experiences. Since the advent of digital computers in the 1940s, AI has evolved to execute complex operations, including mathematical problem-solving and strategic gameplay like chess. Despite advancements in processing power and memory, AI struggles to replicate human adaptability across diverse tasks requiring extensive real-world knowledge. However, in specialized domains, AI has achieved human-expert-level performance, significantly impacting medical diagnosis, search engines, voice and handwriting recognition, and chatbot technology. As AI continues to evolve, it pushes the boundaries of technological innovation, enhancing automation and decision-making across industries [9,10].

10.2.2 Key Components of AI

The advancement of AI is driven by key components such as ML, Neural Networks, and Natural Language Processing, each enhancing AI's capabilities. ML enables systems to analyze data patterns and improve predictions over time. Traditional ML relies on structured datasets, while deep learning autonomously processes unstructured data, uncovering complex insights [15]. Neural Networks, inspired by the human brain, consist of interconnected layers that process information, allowing for pattern recognition, classification, and decision-making in images, videos, and speech [15]. Natural Language Processing enables machines to comprehend and generate human language, facilitating applications like chatbots, translation, and sentiment analysis [15]. The integration of ML, Neural Networks, and Natural Language Processing forms the foundation of AI, enhancing its adaptability, intelligence, and communication abilities. Combined with computer vision, these elements drive AI-driven advancements that optimize processes, transform industries, and improve human-computer interactions [16].

10.2.3 Internet of Things

The IoT constitutes an expansive ecosystem encompassing physical entities embedded with sensors and software [15]. These intelligent gadgets necessitate minimal human intervention, autonomously amassing and exchanging data through network connections. Presently, the IoT envelops a diverse range of commonplace items, commonly known as "smart" gadgets. This category spans from smartphones, household appliances, thermostats, and illumination systems, to more intricate constructs like irrigation installations, surveillance cameras, automobiles, and even urban infrastructure. Wearable smartwatches monitor physical activity, voice-controlled intelligent speakers simplify daily routines, and vehicle transponders expedite toll transactions via electronic processing. The IoT revolutionizes our interaction with our surroundings, streamlining and automating once-complex undertakings that exceed human capabilities. It has a vast scope, encompassing countless interconnected devices that seamlessly operate to elevate our lifestyles and amplify the efficiency of diverse industrial applications.

10.2.4 Components and Elements of IoT

The IoT encompasses a complex ecosystem of components and elements that collectively enable the seamless interaction of devices and data. Sensors and devices that function as the system's sensory apparatus are the foundation of the IoT. These intelligent sensors possess the capability to gather real-time information from their environment, capturing variables such as temperature, light levels, pressure, and other pertinent data points. Without the need for human oversight, these devices are interconnected, forming a network that facilitates communication and data exchange autonomously. This interconnectivity is crucial and is often enabled by wireless technologies that allow for real-time collaboration and information sharing among devices.

The data collected from these interconnected devices is related to a cloud-based infrastructure. The cloud acts as a centralized storage and processing facility for the vast quantities of data produced by IoT devices. Within this environment, sophisticated analytical techniques, including ML algorithms, can be employed to derive valuable insights from the amassed data. The insights gained from this analytical process can inform decision-making and enhance automation across a variety of sectors [16].

A user interface (UI) is essential for facilitating effective communication and control within an IoT system. This UI serves as a portal through which users can observe and engage with the system, providing valuable insights and enabling the management of device behaviors and functionalities. The UI functions as a connection between the intricate technology that underpins the system and the user's intuitive interactions.

The security and integrity of the IoT system are critical considerations. Protecting the system entails defending devices and data against malicious threats, unauthorized access, and potential data breaches. This protection strategy includes the implementation of encryption, authentication protocols, and ongoing monitoring to identify and address possible vulnerabilities from both inside and outside the system [17].

For the IoT to be widely adopted, the idea of network interconnection is pivotal. The core of a connected ecosystem is the smooth communication between devices made possible by various wired and wireless technologies that come together as a single unit.

Together, the sensors, devices, cloud infrastructure, connectivity, UIs, security features, and network interconnections that make up the IoT enable a revolutionary network of smart devices that improve automation, efficiency, and decision-making in all sectors and industries that utilize the applications of IoT along with other technologies.

10.2.5 Role of AI and IoT in Enhancing Accident Management Systems

The integration of AI and the IoT is transforming road safety by enabling real-time data collection, predictive analytics, and automated response mechanisms [16]. AI-driven sensors and cameras help detect accidents, while IoT enables seamless communication between vehicles and infrastructure, reducing accident frequency and severity. Various industries benefit from this synergy: healthcare uses AI for driver behavior analysis, finance optimizes traffic flow, manufacturing applies predictive maintenance, and retail forecasts high-risk zones [17]. However, challenges such as data security and ethical concerns must be addressed for effective implementation. IoT devices, including accelerometers, gyroscopes, and smoke sensors, gather and transmit real-time data to analytics platforms for processing [18]. AI, particularly ML, enhances big data analysis by identifying patterns and making predictions more efficiently than human evaluation [19,20]. Combining AI and IoT in accident management ensures real-time detection, automated alerts, and rapid emergency response, significantly increasing victims' chances of survival [21]. Figure 10.2 shows a general workflow of a system when the IoT and cloud platform are integrated.

10.3 IoT in Accident Management

10.3.1 Sensors

10.3.1.1 Accelerometer

An accelerometer measures acceleration, detecting changes in speed, direction, and vibrations [22]. It quantifies acceleration in meters per second squared (m/s^2) or G-forces, with Earth's gravity equal to approximately 9.8 m/s^2 [23]. Accelerometers

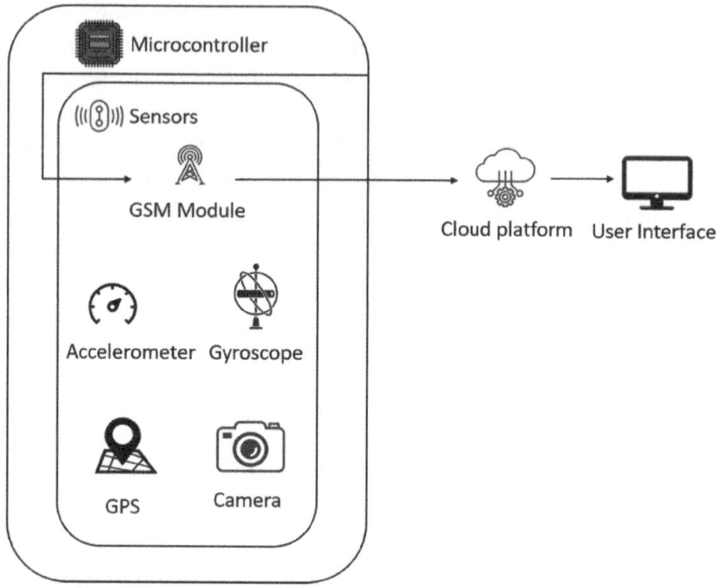

Figure 10.2 Integration of cloud platform into the accident management architecture.

operate along one, two, or three axes, using capacitive plates or piezoelectric materials to measure acceleration. They communicate via analog, digital (SPI/I2C), or PWM interfaces, with low power consumption making them ideal for battery-powered applications. Selection depends on range (±1 g to ±250 g), power needs, and additional features like tap detection and temperature compensation. Inertial Measurement Units, integrating accelerometers with gyroscopes, enhance motion tracking and orientation determination [24].

10.3.1.2 Gyroscope

A gyroscope is an angular velocity sensor that measures rotational speed and determines an object's orientation [25]. Micro-Electro-Mechanical Systems (MEMS) gyroscopes, widely used in autonomous systems, detect angular motion by measuring shifts in resonating mass [26]. Key parameters include range, which affects measurement sensitivity [27], and bias drift, which requires calibration for accuracy [28]. Integrating gyroscopes and accelerometers enhances accident detection by analyzing motion patterns in real time. Accelerometers detect sudden acceleration changes, aiding accident identification [21,29], while gyroscope sensors improve accuracy by detecting irregular rotational movements. Studies using the MPU-6050 sensor—which combines both gyroscope and accelerometer—have improved motion tracking and reduced errors in accident detection systems [30,31]. Additionally, the "DeepCrash" Internet of Vehicles (IOT) system utilizes MEMS sensors for cloud-based accident detection.

10.3.1.3 GPS

The GPS is a satellite-based navigation system that provides precise location and time data using a network of satellites. Alongside Russia's GLONASS, the EU's Galileo, and China's Beidou, GPS plays a key role in positioning and navigation [21]. Integrated with IoT, GPS enhances applications such as location tracking, geofencing, asset management, and smart city development. In accident management, GPS is essential for determining incident locations, especially in remote areas, ensuring timely emergency response. Studies have used GPS with AI-IoT setups to detect accidents and optimize ambulance routing. The Neo-6M module is commonly employed for precise location tracking [32], while the U-Blox GPS module facilitates real-time detection with fast data retrieval [33]. Some studies explore the Local Positioning System as an alternative, using beacons for location determination. Additionally, geocoding techniques convert GPS coordinates into addresses, aiding emergency services.

10.3.1.4 GSM Module (Global System for Mobile Communications)

The Global System for Mobile Communications (GSM)/GPRS module utilizes a SIM card for accessing an access point. Through relevant protocols, it establishes a reliable connection with various websites [18]. This technology is employed to create a portable and mobile IoT-based device capable of transmitting data to a designated web server and allowing access from anywhere across the globe.

The prototype work using Arduino Nano [19] uses the SIM800L. The SIM800L wireless GSM/GPRS module finds application in prototyping boards like Arduino, enabling remote data transmission, phone calls, and SMS messages. This compact module offers efficient wireless communication, boasting a small power footprint and even featuring a power-saving mode that can lower current consumption to as little as 1 mA. The utilization of enhanced AT commands facilitates MQTT requests for server communication. While data transmission causes the module's current consumption to rise to about 2 Amps, it generally operates with a DC power supply within the range of +3.7 V.

SIM900 GSM module is used for working in [20]. The SIM900 GSM module, in combination with the ATmega328p, represents a high-performance and energy-efficient 8-bit AVR microcontroller as mentioned in the article.

In the project [21], a direct 12V power supply is provided from a battery source. The unit is equipped with VCC, Tx, Rx, and GND pins. It features three LEDs: one indicating power status, another indicating network connectivity, and a third indicating operational status. The unit operates on a 2G network. A GSM modem or module functions as a device that utilizes GSM mobile technology to establish a wireless data link with a network. Such modems find applications in mobile phones and other devices communicating with mobile networks, and they utilize SIM cards to authenticate their identity within the network.

A GSM module enables communication between the accident detection system and external parties, such as emergency services, authorities, and individuals. When an accident is detected, the GSM module can send out alerts, notifications, and other relevant information. This real-time communication is crucial for fast response and assistance during emergencies of any kind. Therefore, a GSM module can be highly important in an accident detection and alert system nowadays.

10.3.1.5 Camera

A camera plays a crucial role in accident detection by capturing visual data that AI systems analyze to identify incidents, hazardous conditions, and collisions. It continuously monitors surroundings and records images or videos when triggered by sudden movements or environmental changes, providing critical context for incident response. Real-time transmission of this data to a cloud platform or central server allows for immediate analysis and decision-making. In [22], a front-camera setup captures images for deep learning-based accident detection, while [30] uses a Raspberry Pi to photograph the driver and relay images to the hospital for trauma preparedness. The model by Khaliq [22] installs a vehicle-mounted camera to document accident moments. Additionally, [23] employs a Pi camera with a servo motor to capture and transmit accident footage to the cloud, where deep learning algorithms assess severity and extract relevant insights.

10.3.1.6 Miscellaneous

Apart from the above-mentioned sensors, there are a variety of other sensors also that are used in different AMSs. A temperature sensor is used in many situations to measure the engine temperature and alert them or to contact the fire and rescue if it detects fire in case of an accident. The study by Ahmed [24] uses a DS18S20 sensor for detecting overheating in the engine. Similar to this, this proposed model uses a temperature sensor, DS18B20, for detecting the temperature of the vehicle [25]

In the model proposed in [22], a sound sensor is integrated. If the noise detected in the sensor exceeds a particular threshold value, then the alert is set. Also, we can see the use of force sensors for detecting any anomalous force. [26], shock sensors to detect any shock to the vehicle [23,27], MQ3 sensor to detect alcohol in the breath [23], and also the integration of medical sensors such as a pulse sensor [22] Biomedical sensors, which detect the individual's heart rate, temperature, and pressure [28].

These sensors are capable of collaborating to collect real-time information about the vehicle's environment and its own performance. They enable the system to monitor and respond to various environmental and vehicle-related factors that might indicate an accident.

10.3.2 Data Collection Methods

10.3.2.1 Raspberry Pi

The Raspberry Pi, developed by the Raspberry Pi Foundation in the UK, is a credit card-sized computer board that offers full-fledged computing capabilities when connected to a TV or monitor. While its primary goal is to promote computer education among younger students at an affordable cost, its versatility makes it an ideal platform for programming, computing basics, and diverse project-building endeavors.

The Raspberry Pi is a member of a family of compact yet powerful single-board computers, with its initial launch occurring in 2012. Since then, various versions and models have been released, each featuring a Broadcom system on a chip that includes an integrated Advanced RISC Machine (ARM)-compatible CPU and GPU for graphics processing on the chip.

Various models of Raspberry Pi have emerged, with processing speeds ranging from 700 MHz to 1.2 GHz and memory capacities spanning 256 MB to 1 GB RAM. The device stores its operating system and program memory on Secure Digital cards. While Raspbian OS, a Linux-based operating system, is the recommended choice by the Raspberry Pi Foundation, alternative third-party systems such as RISC OS Pi, Diet Pi, and Kali Linux can also be employed [34].

One of the key attributes of the Raspberry Pi is its collection of general-purpose input/output (GPIO) pins, which allow for the manipulation of electronic components, making it ideal for physical computing and delving into the IoT. The diagram of the computer illustrates its configuration and components.

The Raspberry Pi family encompasses several models, including both Model A and Model B variations. Model A typically offers reduced RAM and fewer features, such as USB and Ethernet ports.

There are several models developed for accident management that utilize the capabilities of a Raspberry Pi single-board computer. The paper by [25] used the Raspberry Pi Zero, which was the most popular single-board computer at that time, consisting of a Secure Digital card slot, video outputs, audio outputs, an HDMI mini slot, a USB port, and a GPIO header. Another work that introduces an integrated accident detection and reporting system [26] used the Raspberry Pi as a master controller for performing all tasks that a desktop or laptop can achieve. They added a Raspberry Pi 3B+ and connected it to a camera, which can send the videos and photos to the cloud to measure the accident's severity. Other models employ a two-phase Accident Detection and Reporting System. The paper by [23] used Raspberry Pi to link the IoT devices and work as a computer. The proposed vehicle crash detection system, which incorporated deep learning technology, [27] also connects the sensors to the Raspberry Pi. The microcontroller is programmed to collect data from the sensors, process it, and alert if the specified criteria are met.

The accelerometer sensor sends data through the I2C and SPI interfaces. The Raspberry Pi connects to the accelerometer by linking its SDA and SCL pins to GPIO2 and GPIO3 on the Raspberry Pi, respectively. Since the accelerometer operates at 3.3 volts, its VCC pin is connected to physical Pin 1 of the Raspberry Pi, while the ground pin is connected to physical Pin 6. The vibration sensor SW-420, known for its high sensitivity and nondirectional capabilities, operates at 5 volts; consequently, its VCC pin is attached to the physical Pin 2 of the Raspberry Pi, the ground pin is connected to the physical Pin 9, and the Digital Output pin is linked to GPIO17. The Digital Output pin from another vibration sensor is connected to GPIO27 on the Raspberry Pi. These sensors are installed at the front and rear sections of the vehicle. The GPS module retrieves the current location and operates on 5 volts, so its VCC pin connects to physical Pin 4 of the Raspberry Pi, the ground pin connects to physical Pin 14, and the TX pin is connected to GPIO18 [29,32].

10.3.2.2 Arduino

The Arduino microcontroller stands as an open-source platform offering programmability and the flexibility to update code at any point. Its inception dates back to 2005, introducing a versatile microcontroller designed for professionals and students to build interactive devices utilizing environmental sensors.

With inputs and outputs, Arduino microcontrollers facilitate information retrieval and output based on incoming data, including internet-based communication through HTTP requests. A notable example of this is the Expressif Systems Platform (ESP) board, capable of connecting to Wi-Fi networks or functioning as a server.

The Arduino platform consists of two fundamental aspects: hardware and software. The hardware element involves the utilization of Arduino development boards. On the software side, the Arduino Integrated Development Environment serves as the programming medium. Powered by 8-bit Atmel AVR microcontrollers or 32-bit Atmel ARM, coding these microcontrollers is facilitated through C or C++ languages within the Arduino IDE [35]

Various models of Arduino boards exist, each catering to specific project requirements. The cofounder of Arduino, Massimo Banzi, highlights several key reasons for employing Arduino boards:

- **Active User Community:** Arduino fosters a collaborative community where users can share experiences and receive solutions to challenges.
- **Affordability and Accessibility:** Arduino microcontrollers are economically priced, making them an excellent starting point for newcomers.
- **Inexpensive Hardware:** The Arduino platform itself is open-source, while users only pay for the physical hardware.

- **Multiplatform Compatibility:** The Arduino Integrated Development Environment operates across various platforms, such as Microsoft, Linux, and Mac OS X.

Arduino boards come in diverse types, each with specific microcontrollers, clock speeds, and capabilities. They range from the Arduino Uno to the Arduino Nano, offering various specifications to suit project demands. Arduino's hardware encompasses components such as the microcontroller, external power supply, USB port for programming, analog and digital pins for input/output, and power and ground pins [36]. Table 10.2 Is a summary of AMS components and the function they perform in brief.

Table 10.2 Accident Management System Components and Their Roles

Category	*Subdivision*	*Component/ Technology*	*Role in Accident Management Systems*
Artificial Intelligence	Data Analysis and Prediction	Deep Learning Algorithms	Analyze images and videos to detect accidents.
		Machine Learning	Predict high-risk zones and optimize traffic flow.
		Classification Algorithms (e.g., Convolutional Neural Network)	Classify objects and detect accidents with high accuracy.
		Ensemble Machine Learning Models	Combine multiple algorithms to improve prediction accuracy.
	Route Planning and Optimization	Multihop Optimal Forwarding Algorithm	Determine the optimal route between the accident vehicle and the ambulance using vehicle-to-vehicle communication.
		Optimal Route Planning Algorithm	Plan the most efficient route from the accident vehicle to the hospital using GPS data.

(Continued)

Table 10.2 (*Continued*) Accident Management System Components and Their Roles

Category	*Subdivision*	*Component/ Technology*	*Role in Accident Management Systems*
Internet of Things	Sensors	Accelerometer	Detect sudden changes in acceleration, indicating a possible accident. Can also determine the direction of impact.
		Gyroscope	Measure rotational changes, helping to determine the vehicle's orientation and detect rollovers.
		GPS	Determine the precise location of the accident for efficient emergency response. This data can be used for geocoding and reverse geocoding.
		Global System for Mobile Communications Module	Send alerts and notifications to emergency services and designated contacts.
		Camera	Capture images and videos of the accident scene for analysis and evidence.
		Temperature Sensor	Detect fire or overheating in case of an accident.
		Sound Sensor	Detect loud noises, such as a collision.
		Force Sensor	Detect anomalous forces experienced by the vehicle.

(*Continued*)

Table 10.2 (*Continued*) Accident Management System Components and Their Roles

Category	*Subdivision*	*Component/ Technology*	*Role in Accident Management Systems*
		Shock Sensor	Detect impacts and vibrations associated with accidents.
	Data Collection Methods	Raspberry Pi	Act as a central processing unit, collecting data from sensors, communicating with other devices, and potentially running AI algorithms.
		Arduino	An alternative microcontroller platform for data collection and processing.

10.4 Artificial Intelligence in Accident Management

In the last decade, AI has grown rapidly, enabling the processing of large datasets and transforming various fields, including accident management. One of the primary functions of AI in AMSs is analyzing data gathered through IoT devices and making predictions using advanced algorithms. AI-driven AMSs rely on real-time accident detection, where sensor integration plays a key role in ensuring accurate detection. Various sensors, including accelerometers, GPS, and force-sensitive resistors, are used to detect accidents as they occur [11,12]. Once an accident is detected, critical data—such as the location and vehicle details—is transmitted instantly to emergency responders, facilitating swift intervention [11,12]

When discussing algorithms, [28] proposed two useful models: the Multihop Optimal Forwarding Algorithm, which utilizes vehicle-to-vehicle communication to determine the best route for ambulances, and the Optimal Route Planning Algorithm, which leverages GPS data to map the shortest path from an accident site to the hospital. These algorithms aim to optimize resource allocation, reduce transportation costs, and improve response times [30]. Additionally, AI-powered predictive analytics plays a crucial role in accident prevention. ML models analyze accident patterns and trends, contributing to the development of proactive safety measures [13,31].

Deep learning has significantly advanced accident detection. The "deep-crash" model, implemented in [33], integrates a cloud-based deep learning training server with an Inception V3 network-based binary image classification model, achieving 96% accuracy in traffic collision detection. AI's ability to mimic human cognitive functions enhances its decision-making capabilities. Another study combined IoT and deep learning to improve accident detection and reporting systems. This study utilized transfer-learning-based pretrained models, ResNet-50 and InceptionResNetv2, to classify accidents more accurately, reducing false alarms. It was found that ResNet-50 performed better due to its higher accuracy and recall rate. Classification algorithms have also been widely adopted. In [30], a Convolutional Neural Network model was employed for object classification and accident detection, achieving nearly 97% accuracy. Another study, [32], proposed an ensemble ML model incorporating multimodal data and gradient boosting, further improving classification accuracy. Despite these advancements, AI and IoT-based AMSs face ethical considerations and challenges. Data privacy remains a significant concern, as accident detection systems rely on continuous real-time data collection. Ensuring secure data transmission and compliance with privacy regulations is critical for responsible deployment [13]. Implementation challenges, such as sensor calibration errors and high costs of AI-integrated infrastructure, need to be addressed to maximize the effectiveness of these systems. The integration of AI and IoT in accident management has already demonstrated substantial improvements over traditional methods. While early IoT-only approaches faced high false positive rates and detection errors, AI-enhanced models have significantly improved accuracy, efficiency, and scalability. Ongoing research and technological advancements will continue to expand the capabilities of these intelligent systems, making accident detection and response more reliable and effective.

10.5 Conclusion

This study reviewed various research papers and publications to analyze advancements in AI and IoT for accident management and the rapid evolution of these technologies. Since the inception of technology, humankind has continuously sought improvements, and the integration of AI and the IoT in accident management has significantly enhanced efficiency while reducing errors. By leveraging a combination of sensors including thermal, speed, and impact sensors along with ML and deep learning algorithms, accident detection and response systems have become more effective.

Despite these advancements, AI-IoT-based AMSs still face several challenges. Lack of standardization remains a major issue, as the AI-driven operations domain lacks consistent frameworks for data management and implementation, leading to fragmented research efforts. Additionally, sociotechnical risks are not yet fully understood, increasing the likelihood of failures in autonomous AMSs. Many AI-driven incident management solutions are still in their early development stages, requiring further research to fully explore their potential.

Other limitations include concerns about cybersecurity, implementation costs, and data storage. AI-IoT systems store large volumes of accident-related data, often in cloud platforms, raising concerns about data privacy and security vulnerabilities. The risk of hacking must be minimized to ensure safe and reliable AMSs. The cost of implementing AI-IoT technologies in vehicles remains a barrier to widespread adoption. From a physical safety perspective, additional hardware or sensors must not interfere with critical vehicle safety features such as airbags and automatic locks, nor should they pose a risk to occupants during accidents.

10.6 Future Scope

The future of AI and IoT-based AMSs holds great promise, offering enhanced efficiency, response time, and accuracy in emergency services. Real-time data transmission will be improved using advanced sensors along with GPS and accelerometers, which will instantly detect accidents and transmit critical information to emergency responders. AI-driven severity assessment models will further enhance emergency response by analyzing sensor data to prioritize intervention based on accident severity. AI-powered automated alerts integrated with mobile applications will significantly reduce response times by notifying emergency contacts, hospitals, and first responders in real time. Additionally, AI-driven resource optimization will improve the allocation of emergency services, ensuring better efficiency in handling multiple incidents. Continuous data collection and accident pattern analysis will help identify trends, assess risk factors, and implement data-driven policy changes to prevent accidents. However, for successful deployment, challenges such as data privacy, ethical concerns, and the need for standardized protocols must be addressed. Future research must focus on developing standardized frameworks for AI-driven operations to enhance consistency and reliability. Additionally, integrating sociotechnical factors into AI systems will help mitigate risks and improve system resilience. Further advancements should explore large language models to enhance accident detection accuracy and scalability. While no system is perfect, continuous advancements in AI and IoT applications will lead to more robust, reliable, and scalable accident management solutions. Future research should emphasize enhancing accuracy, reducing false positives, and improving emergency response efficiency. With ongoing innovation, AI-IoT-based AMSs will play a crucial role in improving road safety and reducing accident-related fatalities.

Data Availability

All the datasets used in this study are publicly available.

Conflicts of Interest

The authors assert that there are no conflicts of interest. The sponsors did not contribute to the study's design, data collection, analysis, interpretation, manuscript preparation, or the choice to publish the findings.

References

1. A. Budi and B. Raid, "Driving & Journey Management Transformation, Systematic Automotive Risk Reduction Framework," 2024, doi: 10.2118/220253-MS.
2. J. G. Fuller and L. R. Hook, "Effectiveness of Automatic Safety Systems in Reducing General Aviation Fatalities," *J. Aerosp. Inf. Syst.*, vol. 20, no. 5, pp. 1–11, 2023, doi: 10.2514/1.I011069.
3. S. G. Farrag, F. Outay, A. U. H. Yasar, D. Janssens, B. Kochan, and N. Jabeur, "Toward the Improvement of Traffic Incident Management Systems Using Car2X Technologies," *Pers. Ubiquitous Comput.*, vol. 25, no. 1, pp. 163–176, 2021, doi: 10.1007/S00779-020-01368-5.
4. D. B. Joseph et al., "Smart Accident Fatality Reduction (SAFR) System," In: Kumar, S., Sharma, H., Balachandran, K., Kim, J.H., Bansal, J.C. (eds) Third Congress on Intelligent Systems. CIS 2022. *Lecture Notes in Networks and Systems*, vol 613. Springer, Singapore. https://doi.org/10.1007/978-981-19-9379-4_38.
5. N. Roy et al., "Consensus Recommendations for Acute Trauma Care & Outcomes in LMICs from the Transdisciplinary Research, Advocacy & Implementation Network for Trauma in India," *Indian J. Med. Res.*, vol. 159, pp. 274–284, 2024, doi: 10.25259/IJMR_2417_23.
6. A. Rahane, P. Rahane, S. Rahane, K. Lungade, V. Aher, and M. A. Jawale, "Prescriptive Analytic and Machine Learning Based Solution for Avoiding Accidents Based on Weather Conditions," *2023 4th Int. Conf. Comput. Autom. Knowl. Manag. ICCAKM 2023*, pp. 01–06, 2023, doi: 10.1109/ICCAKM58659.2023.10449505.
7. M. Sobhana, G. S. S. V. Mendu, N. Vemulapalli, and K. K. Chintakayala, "Optimized Feature Selection Approaches for Accident Classification to Enhance Road Safety," *IAES Int. J. Artif. Intell.*, vol. 13, no. 3, pp. 3283–3283, 2024, doi: 10.11591/ijai.v13.i3.pp3283-3290.
8. Y. Remil, A. Bendimerad, R. Mathonat, and M. Kaytoue, "AIOps Solutions for Incident Management: Technical Guidelines and A Comprehensive Literature Review," *ACM Trans. Softw. Eng. Methodol.*, vol. X, 2024, Accessed: March 17, 2025. [Online]. Available: https://arxiv.org/abs/2404.01363v1
9. C. Macrae, "Learning from the FAIlure of Autonomous and Intelligent Systems: Accidents, Safety, and SocIoTechnical Sources of Risk," *Risk Anal.*, vol. 42, no. 9, pp. 1999–2025, 2022, doi: 10.1111/RISA.13850.

10. P. Hamadanian et al., "A Holistic View of AI-driven Network Incident Management," *HotNets 2023- Proc. 22nd ACM Work. Hot Top. Networks*, pp. 180–188, 2023, doi: 10.1145/3626111.3628176.
11. R. U. Khattak and Abdullah, "Advancing Road Safety through Intelligent Vehicle Accident Detection and Reporting Enabled by IoT Innovation," *NUML Int. J. Eng. Comput.*, vol. 3, no. 1, 2024, doi: 10.52015/NIJEC.V3I1.66.
12. G. Sujithra, P. Kiruthika, S. S. Rathinam, and A. Sruthi, "Smart IoT based accident monitoring and rescue system," *J. IoT Soc. Mobile Anal. Cloud*, vol. 6, no. 2, pp. 188–198, 2024, doi: 10.36548/jismac.2024.2.009.
13. J. Park and D. Kang, "Artificial Intelligence and Smart Technologies in Safety Management: A Comprehensive Analysis across Multiple Industries," *Appl. Sci.*, vol. 14, no. 24, 2024, doi: 10.3390/APP142411934.
14. A. S. Anurag, "Early beginnings of AI: The field of research in computer science," IGI Global Scientific Publishing, pp. 1–20, 2024, doi: 10.4018/979-8-3693-2643-5.ch001.
15. G. Paolone, D. Iachetti, R. Paesani, F. Pilotti, M. Marinelli, and P. Di Felice, "A Holistic Overview of the Internet of Things Ecosystem," *IoT*, vol. 3, no. 4, pp. 398–434, 2022, doi: 10.3390/IOT3040022.
16. P. P. Jayaraman, C. Perera, D. Georgakopoulos, S. Dustdar, D. Thakker, and R. Ranjan, "Analytics-as-a-Service in a Multi-Cloud Environment through Semantically-Enabled Hierarchical Data Processing," *Softw. Pract. Exp.*, vol. 47, no. 8, pp. 1139–1156, 2017, doi: 10.1002/SPE.2432.
17. D. Y. Perwej, S. Q. Abbas, J. P. Dixit, D. N. Akhtar, and A. K. Jaiswal, "A Systematic Literature Review on the Cyber Security," *Int. J. Sci. Res. Manag.*, vol. 9, no. 12, pp. 669–710, 2021, doi: 10.18535/IJSRM/V9I12.EC04.
18. R. K. Ghosh, "GSM, GPRS and UMTS," in Wireless Networking and Mobile Data Management, Springer Singapore, 2017, pp. 55–94, doi: 10.1007/978-981-10-3941-6_3.
19. S. Ur Rehman, S. A. Khan, A. Arif, and U. S. Khan, "IoT-Based Accident Detection and Emergency Alert System for Motorbikes," AIMS 2021- Int. Conf. Artif. Intell. Mechatronics Syst., pp. 0–4, 2021, doi: 10.1109/AIMS52415.2021.9466055.
20. G. Chiddarwar, S. Dhivar, A. Kulkarni, B. Gajbhiye, and N. Chaudhari, "Accident Alert System Using IoT," *Int. J. Sci. Res. Comput. Sci. Eng. Inf. Technol.*, vol. 3307, pp. 171–175, 2022, doi: 10.32628/cseit2282125.
21. A. Beheramali, "Accident Detection and Alert System GPS & GSM on IOT Based," *Adv. Appl. Sci. Res.*, vol. 16, no. 1, pp. 5–?, 2023, doi: 10.36648/0976-8610.16.1.59.
22. K. A. Khaliq, O. Chught Ai, A. Shahwani, A. Qayyum, and J. Pannek, "Road Accidents Detection, Data Collection and Data Analysis Using V2X Communication and Edge/Cloud Computing," *Electronics*, vol. 8, no. 8, 2019, doi: 10.3390/electronics8080896.
23. V. Patil, A. More, M. Mahajan, and H. Gholap, "AI and IOT Based Road Accident Detection and Reporting System," *Int. J. Res. Appl. Sci. Eng. Technol.*, vol. 11, no. 5, pp. 6977–6982, 2023, doi: 10.22214/ijraset.2023.53315.
24. V. Ahmed and N. P. Jawarkar, "Design of Low-Cost Versatile Microcontroller Based System Using a Cell Phone for Accident Detection and Prevention," *Int. Conf. Emerg. Trends Eng. Technol. ICETET*, pp. 73–77, 2013, doi: 10.1109/ICETET.2013.17.
25. D. Vijendra Babu, M. Harish, M. Azarudeen, R. S. K. Reddy, and K. Jose, "Raspberry Pi Based Real-Time Vehicle Accident Intimation with an Alert Message and Image Capture," *IOP Conf. Ser. Mater. Sci. Eng.*, vol. 993, no. 1, pp. 0–7, 2020, doi: 10.1088/1757-899X/993/1/012081.

26. N. Pathik, R. K. Gupta, Y. Sahu, A. Sharma, M. Masud, and M. Baz, "AI Enabled Accident Detection and Alert System Using IoT and Deep Learning for Smart Cities," *Sustainability*, vol. 14, no. 13, 2022, doi: 10.3390/su14137701.
27. C. V. S. Babu, N. S. Akshayah, P. M. Vinola, and R. Janapriyan, "IoT-based smart accident detection and alert system," in Handbook of Research on Deep Learning Techniques for Cloud-Based Industrial IoT, *IGI Global*, 2023, pp. 322–337, doi: 10.4018/978-1-6684-8098-4.ch019.
28. Y. R. B. Al-Mayouf, O. A. Mahdi, N. A. Taha, N. F. Abdullah, S. Khan, and M. Alam, "Accident Management System Based on Vehicular Network for an Intelligent Transportation System in Urban Environments," *J. Adv. Transp.*, vol. 2018, 2018, doi: 10.1155/2018/6168981.
29. W. A. Kusuma, Z. Sari, and A. T. Sari, "Sensor Fusion Accelerometer dan Gyroscope untuk Pengukuran Perubahan Kinematik Pergelangan Kaki," *Kinet. Game Technol. Inf. Syst. Comput. Network, Comput. Electron. Control*, 2018, doi: 10.22219/kinetik.v1i1.8.
30. F. B. Baseme, D. Hanyurwimfura, and C. Twizere, "Real-time Alert AI and IoT Based Accident Prevention and Detection," *ACM Int. Conf. Proceeding Ser.*, pp. 275–286, 2024, doi: 10.1145/3651781.3651824.
31. G. Roopini, P. P. Nagraj Rao, V. Dankan Gowda, B. S. Ingole, S. Pandey, and S. H. Chandra, "AI-Driven IoT Framework for Vehicle Accident Avoidance and Detection with Cloud Integrated Energy Efficient Solutions," *2024 1st Int. Conf. Innov. Commun. Electr. Comput. Eng. ICICEC 2024*, 2024, doi: 10.1109/ICICEC62498.2024.10808555.
32. P. Cheng and B. Oelmann, "Joint-angle measurement using accelerometers and gyroscopes—A survey," *IEEE Trans. Instrum. Meas.*, vol. 59, no. 2, pp. 404–414, Feb. 2010, doi: 10.1109/TIM.2009.2024367.
33. W. J. Chang, L. B. Chen, and K. Y. Su, "DeepCrash: A Deep Learning-Based Internet of Vehicles System for Head-on and Single-Vehicle Accident Detection with Emergency Notification," *IEEE Access*, vol. 7, pp. 148163–148175, 2019, doi: 10.1109/ACCESS.2019.2946468.
34. S. J. Johnston and S. J. Cox, "The Raspberry Pi: A Technology Disrupter, and the Enabler of Dreams," Electronics, vol. 6, p. 51, 2017, doi: 10.3390/electronics6030051.
35. S. Thu and H. H. T. Khaung. Technol, and undefined 2016, "Construction of Android and Arduino for Home Appliances Switching System," ijeast.com, vol. 1, pp. 66–71, 2016, Accessed: October. 30, 2024. [Online]. Available: https://www.ijeast.com/papers/66-71,Tesma111,IJEAST.pdf
36. A. S. Ismallov and Z. B. Jo'rayev, "Study of Arduino Microcontroller Board," *Sci. Educ. Sci. J.*, vol. 3, no. 3, pp. 172–179, 2022.

Chapter 11

Navigating the Future of IoT Security: Emerging Trends, Challenges and Strategic Solutions

Raghu N, Niranjan Kannanugo,
and Ben Othman Soufiene

11.1 Introduction

The Internet of Things (IoT) is growing rapidly due to the new trends and the possible innovations that are influencing its future. Moreover, many things are now part of the IoT network, meaning that perfect data transfer and communication can be done. This interconnectivity is providing a myriad of different ways to use this technology across many industries like healthcare, smart cities and homes, industrial automation [1]. The adoption of IoT devices using machine learning (ML) and artificial intelligence (AI) methods is a major research area within the IoT [2]. Thus, there may be a situation in which the application's capabilities may be getting modified by environmental factors and be doing its self-learning from data collections. As a consequence, IoT platforms are becoming more intelligent, more predictive, and can optimize processes by themselves. Another major trend is the use of edge computing in IoT settings. Through moving processing power closer to the data source, edge computing brings latency down low and allows faster response times [3]. More efficient systems, bandwidth conservation, and processing of the data at the

DOI: 10.1201/9781003587859-11

edge may be possible with IoT devices [4]. However, the development of safe IoT networks remains the most important point to face in the future.

The data exchanged between connected devices should be kept secure to an increased standard due to their exponential growth in numbers. The cyberattacks depend on development of encryption, authentication systems and safe communication protocols [5]. IoT devices' lifespan and their power saving are also being advanced as a result of the technologies in energy capturing and power management. A greener IoT scenario is being created by the energy-efficient IoT devices that can be powered by a small amount of power or renewable energy sources only [6]. All things considered, IoT has great power to revolutionize sectors, increase efficiency, and raise standards of living. The IoT ecosystem is set for ongoing development and innovation by embracing new trends, harnessing AI capabilities, giving security top priority, and stressing sustainability [7].

11.2 Literature Review

Hussain et al., [8] have stated that the (IoT in the future will profoundly affect our life in terms of economy, business, and society. Usually with limited resources, the participating nodes in IoT networks attract targets for cyberattacks. In this sense, great efforts have been made to solve the security and privacy concerns in IoT networks mostly by conventional cryptographic methods. Nevertheless, the special qualities of IoT nodes make the current solutions inadequate to cover the whole security range of the IoT systems. Different security issues can be addressed using ML and Deep Learning (DL) technologies, which can supply embedded intelligence in IoT devices and networks. The security needs, attack paths, and present IoT network security solutions are methodically reviewed in this article. We then focus on the holes in these security solutions requiring ML and DL techniques. At last, we go in great length on the current ML and DL approaches for handling various security issues in IoT systems. We also address several prospective avenues of inquiry for IoT security based on ML- and DL-based technologies.

Srivastava et al., [9] have explained that the security problems influencing the future IoT standards have attracted interesting attention from many research groups in the recent past. Under this perspective, multiple future IoT-centric issues coupled with threat modelling, intrusion detection systems (IDSs), and several emergent technologies were offered under several assessments in the form of surveys. On the other hand, in this paper we have concentrated just on the newly discovered IoT-related flaws. This paper is a multifold survey stressing on the knowledge of the main causes of fresh vulnerabilities in IoT paradigms and problems in current research. First, we have focused on several layers of IoT architecture and underlined the important problems of each layer together with the main concerns of many IoT systems. Second, we go into IoT malware-enabled distributed denial of service, Sybil, and collusion attack capabilities' exploitation, detection, and defence mechanisms.

We have also covered many cutting-edge techniques for intrusion detection and approaches for IDS configuration in next IoT systems. Third, based on various IoT-enabled cyberattacks, we have briefly categorized the current IoT authentication systems and conducted a comparison study of such protocols. We have provided some developing blockchain options for real-time future IoT research. We have also included a comparison of several recently created simulation tools and IoT test beds distinguished by various IoT infrastructure layers. We also help readers by comprehensive classification of current surveys in this field that target numerous scopes connected to the IoT paradigm and by outlining some of the open concerns and future research paths.

Singh et al., [10] have mentioned that the explosion of IoT gadgets has transformed our interaction with technology and ingrained connectivity into all aspects of contemporary life. But this explosive expansion has brought a number of security issues endangering IoT ecosystems' integrity, privacy, and usefulness. From device vulnerabilities to data breaches and advanced cyberattacks, this study offers an abstract survey of the convoluted terrain of IoT security issues. Rising solutions present interesting paths to strengthen IoT settings' security posture among these difficulties. While hardware-based security systems increase device resistance against attacks, blockchain technology has the ability to improve data integrity and create trust. Novel approaches including AI-powered anomaly detection help to identify real-time threats; privacy-preserving methods try to balance data utility with secrecy. Furthermore, changing the basic method of IoT network security is the idea of zero trust systems. This study emphasizes not only the seriousness of IoT security issues but also the proactive actions forming IoT security's direction.

Kumar et al., [11] have mentioned that the IoT has great possibilities for transforming uses in many different fields, but major security issues prevent its general acceptance. This work offers a thorough study of the IoT security scene today, pointing out main challenges and suggesting future solutions to overcome them. We look at IoT device and network weaknesses and investigate the consequences of any security lapses. Analysing current security policies and their constraints helps us emphasize the great necessity of strong security solutions catered to the particular features of IoT ecosystems. Moreover, this work suggests a fresh approach to address growing concerns and protect IoT installations with improved authentication techniques, safe communication protocols, and IDSs. Our study helps to clarify IoT security concerns and offer insightful analysis that will help create reliable IoT systems going forward.

Sultan et al., [12] have emphasized the research on response strategies, ongoing monitoring, and fast firmware updates. Ensuring compliance and creating a safer IoT ecosystem are both aided by enterprises adhering to established norms and standards. This research study addresses the challenges, best practices, and future possibilities of IoT security systems. New ways of interacting with technology have emerged as a result of the proliferation of interconnected devices made possible by the IoT. However, these interconnected ecosystems also present significant security risks that require comprehensive solutions. The specific challenges and the development of reasonable solutions to decrease hazards are the focus of this investigation into IoT security systems. Discovering potential vulnerabilities and threats to data confidentiality and integrity requires an analysis of the various IoT network and protocol topologies. It further examines emerging trends and technologies like distributed identity management and blockchain-based solutions that can fortify the security of the IoT. This study provides a comprehensive guideline for both academics and practitioners.

Prasad et al., [13] have described that the rapid growth of the IoT has revolutionized technology by connecting smart devices and sensors to get data-driven insights across several industries. Still, this revolutionary development has resulted in security issues as well since equipment left open to possible cyberattacks and exploitation are linked. The several difficulties, current solutions, and future trends in IoT cybersecurity are investigated in this research study. It addresses privacy issues and resource limits as well as strong authentication and data encryption as fixes; it also sees blockchain and AI improving security. Encouragement of cooperation among stakeholders will help to create a safer and more robust IoT ecosystem, therefore guaranteeing the IoT's whole potential and tackling security issues.

Rahman et al., [14] have illustrated that the IoT' explosive expansion has transformed connectivity and presented major security concerns. The limited processing power and energy resources of some IoT devices make them easy targets for cybercriminals. Customized security solutions for next-generation IoT networks are in high demand, and this research satisfies that demand by focusing on issues like device authorization, private data, and network integrity in distributed situations. Lightweight cryptography for secure communication, anomaly detection based on ML for real-time threat elimination, and distributed security management using blockchain are all areas that are being studied. Combining several techniques is advised using a multilayered strategy to provide strong security all through the IoT lifecycle. The study also emphasizes the need for industry cooperation and consistent standards to raise security across several platforms. It underlines the need for regulatory systems in setting strict security criteria and supports a cooperative approach to guarantee IoT networks. This paper provides insightful analysis of IoT security issues and workable ideas for a more robust digital future.

Rozlomii et al., [15] have explained that including the IoT into many different application fields not only increases possibilities but also creates certain difficulties. These issues centre on IoT device security; many of them are typified by constrained resources including memory, battery consumption, and computational capability. Key issues related to guaranteeing IoT device security are investigated in this paper together with suggested tactics and solutions fit for limited resources. Development and research of lightweight cryptographic techniques that are able to offer strong data security with minimum resource consumption are given great importance. Crucially to guarantee the robust and continuous operation of IoT devices, strategies for effective energy management and memory use are also discussed. The paper emphasizes the need for creating flexible security systems able to react to changing operational situations and limited resources. It underlines the main need of always updating security systems to fit evolving circumstances and to protect against fresh and future cyber threats. Apart from technological features, the need for strategic planning and creativity in IoT security is also highlighted. Further study and development should concentrate on developing integrated solutions combining hardware, software, and administrative features to maximize general efficiency and security of IoT systems. This paper helps IoT devices running under limited resources to comprehend and solve security challenges. It offers a general picture of the present possibilities and difficulties as well as guidance for next study and progress in this continually changing topic.

Chowdhury et al., [16] have illustrated that security is a major issue in the expanding IoT ecosystem since the wide range of IoT device capabilities is reflected in the several sectors. This paper examines the complex IoT architecture, revealing the typical defects and traceable security events that provide context for the value of having consistent security systems. Simultaneously, the study paper identifies the enormous commercial opportunities resulting from these problems and emphasizes the fact that they can be seized by means of the development and implementation of innovative security systems and consulting services. Depending on its present assessment and empirical data by means of literature analysis to evaluate new technologies and market trends, the report forecasts the direction of IoT depending in which future advances in IoT security find place. Generally speaking, this study suggests that actively interested actors that are frightened of the developing security concerns have chances to leverage the expansion and creativity in creating robust IoT systems. As such, the ideas presented in this study fit the researchers as well as the industry players.

Karie et al., [17] have stated that in 2025, the estimated 38.6 billion connected IoT devices will increase to; by 2030, the count is expected to be 50 billion. The growing use of IoT devices in many spheres of our lives has brought us major advantages, including job automation and better quality of life. But every time a new IoT device is installed, fresh and distinctive security risks surface or enter the environment where the device has to run. It can be quite difficult to instantly identify and reduce every security risk brought about by various IoT devices installed. This is because many of the IoT gadgets are produced without thinking through their security consequences. With an eye toward the several IoT security issues as well as the present efforts toward countering cybersecurity threats in IoT networks, we evaluate the existing literature and present IoT threat detection research advancements in this study. This report does, however, also draw attention to various IoT future directions.

Raghavendra et al., [18] have explained that the IoT has turned common place objects into smart, linked gadgets, therefore creating fresh monitoring and control opportunities. Still, security is a major issue for IoT technology to be adopted widely on scale. The present IoT security scene is reviewed in this study together with ideas for next studies. First, we give a general picture of the IoT architecture and then examine its fundamental security objectives of confidentiality, integrity, availability, and authentication. We compile main IoT threat models including application attacks, network invasions, and physical manipulation. We then introduce a taxonomy of cutting-edge ideas suggested for access control, trust management, anomaly detection, and hardware attack resilience. Ultimately, given the scale, limits, and variety of IoT ecosystems, we draw attention to open issues in creating lightweight, scalable security architectures. Promising future facilitators for increasing IoT security are also new technologies including blockchain, AI, and 5G networks.

Singh et al., [19] have stated that remarkable developments in the IoT in recent years have caused a paradigm change in the digital scene. These technical advancements have, however, presented fresh difficulties, especially in cybersecurity. Naturally linked to the internet, IoT devices are vulnerable to several kinds of attacks. IoT services also sometimes manage private user data, which could be used by illegal service providers or hostile parties. The junction of conventional and cloud-based systems creates special security concerns due to the lack of consistent rules as IoT ecosystems grow. Enabled by Platform-as-a-Service and Infrastructure-as-a-Service models, cloud-based IoT systems present scalability and flexibility but also increased security vulnerabilities. The complex interaction among these systems and conventional IoT devices calls for all-encompassing plans to safeguard user privacy and data integrity. The urgent security issues connected to the general acceptance of IoT devices and services are underlined in this work. We suggest workable answers to close current security weaknesses and foresee and get ready for next threats. Our method calls for thorough investigation of the main security issues IoT solutions are now confronted with. We also propose proactive solutions to reduce these hazards, therefore enhancing the general safety of IoT products and systems.

Xu et al., [20] have illustrated that once more on the verge of changing its scope to enable fresh design revolutions is computer-aided design. Following both historical and modern technology and application trends, one can find various developing research and development paths in which computer-aided design approaches and techniques may have substantial influences. Among these, the IoT stands out since it can drastically change daily living as well as how science and engineering systems are built and run. IoT also presents a remarkable system full of technological and conceptual difficulties. For example, significantly lowered quantitative limits on allowable area and energy measurements depend on qualitative design and optimization advances. Security is most certainly the most demanding of criteria for the general fulfilment of many IoT ambitions. IoT security spans at least four different dimensions and has quite a broad reach. Regarding security breadth, it covers rarely discussed chores such as trustworthy sensing, computing, communication, privacy, and digital forgetfulness. It also seeks for fresh and improved methods considering the possibility of physical access to IoT devices for the safety of hardware, software, and data. Common parts of IoT devices, sensors and actuators provide various special security issues, including the integrity of physical signals and acting events. At last, one can imagine several semantic threats during data processing. Our strategic goal is to stimulate the evolution of IoT computer-aided design security methods. We begin by outlining, with an eye on security concerns, a brief assessment of IoT prospects and difficulties. We next go through the possibilities of hardware-based IoT security solutions. Finally, we draw to attention many case studies supporting the use of reliable Physical Unclonable Functions and digital Physical Unclonable Functions (PPUFs) for several IoT security protocols.

Akhunzada et al., [21] have described the future smart cities recently since they promise to significantly raise the quality of living. Managing a city's assets securely still depends much on IoT being combined with their matching service delivery models. Different IoT technologies, many architectural elements, and new entities of evolving ICT systems create new security risks and vulnerabilities by their deployment. Large-scale, smooth communication among several IoT technologies depends much on the operations of the fundamental wireless access technologies like Wireless Sensor Networks (WSNs), Software Defined Radio (SDR), Cognitive Radio (CR), and Radio Frequency Identification (RFID). We emphasize the possible security flaws, threats, and difficulties of important IoT enabling technologies behind the development of smart cities by means of topical layered taxonomies. We also spot important needs and main enablers that are absolutely essential for the growth of safe smart cities. At last, we go over several open problems that must be resolved if we are to fully utilize 5G in the next smart cities.

Zhang et al., [22] have explained that the wearable gadgets, home appliances, and software to share and transmit data on the Internet allow the IoT to present possibilities. Preserving information security on the shared data is a crucial problem that cannot be overlooked given the abundance of private information in the shared data. This article starts with a broad overview of the information security background of IoT and proceeds with information security-related issues IoT will face. At last, we will also highlight areas of future study that can help to address security issues related to IoT.

11.2.1 First Early Advancements

The IoT originated in the early 1980s when the first research on linking objects to the internet started. Kevin Ashton first employed RFID technology to enhance supply chain management while working at Procter & Gamble in 1999, hence coining the phrase "Internet of Things" [23]. The logistics and industrial automation sectors were early adopters of the IoT, with sensor and networked devices serving to monitor and manage assets. The early deployments laid the groundwork for the wide variety of IoT applications as shown in Figure 11.1. One of the earliest and most well-known examples of an IoT device was the "smart" Coca-Cola vending machine installed at Carnegie Mellon University in 1982. This machine could check the temperature of newly filled drinks and keep track of inventory [24].

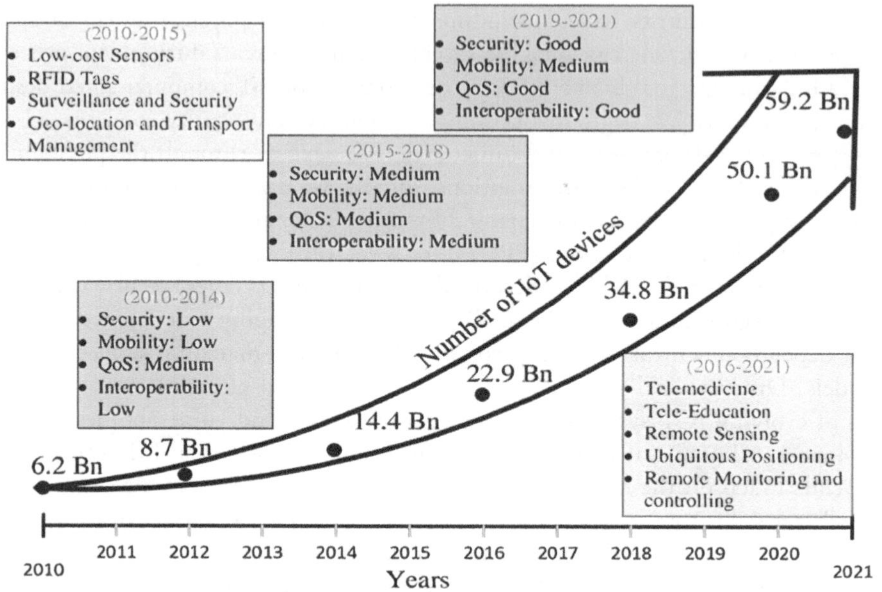

Figure 11.1 Evolution of Internet of Things.

This basic yet creative application showed how connected devices might offer real-time data and increase operational effectiveness [25].

11.2.2 Development and Broadening

The technology improvements in sensor development, cloud computing, and wireless communication have been Connected gadgets that initially became commonplace in the late aughts and early aughts. Release of IPv6, which substantially increased the total number of available IP addresses, was a critical turning point that allowed for the broad deployment of IoT devices. The increased strength of IoT is now possible for any company. This is the result of the price of sensors and connections falling. A rapid increase in the number of IoT-enabled devices and systems in every sector, from homes to factories, is what the driving force is. Smart devices make up the IoT e.g., a thermostat that can be virtually operated or smart home appliances, for example. Industrial sectors can apply the Industry 4.0 principles and create smart factories with the help of the IoT [26]. By connecting software, machinery, and tools, producers can improve operations, foresee possible maintenance problems, and monitor manufacturing processes in real time. This leads to an increase in productivity, less downtime, and better-quality products. Also, the development of the IoT has affected city infrastructure to the extent that smart cities have started to emerge. Cities have benefited from IoT technology by using it for traffic management, public service expansion, and energy efficiency. The IoT used in a smart grid helps to allocate power effectively, and the intelligent traffic signals can ease the congestion by responding to the drivers' demands in real time [27].

11.2.3 IoT Current Situation

The modern IoT has become a massive network of connected devices. The number of IoT unit was expected to be around 10 billion by 2021, and this number would further grow in the year after. This technology is evolving due to the increasing need for connectivity in a wide range of industries, and the ever-increasing pace of innovation in technology. However, the rapid expansion of the IoT has also some challenges. The rise in the frequency of cyberattacks and data breaches affecting IoT devices has made security and privacy issues the main concern [28]. Data privacy and security in transmission between the devices must be ensured. The other problem with interoperability between systems and IoT devices is the fact that various manufacturers are using different proprietary protocols and standards. IoT development is being facilitated through the hope of benefits in spite of these bumps on the road. The adoption of the IoT may take place by merging latest so-called technologies such as blockchain, edge computing, 5G, and AI into existing IoT systems [29].

11.3 Emerging Trends in IoT

11.3.1 Edge Computing: Accelerating Data Processing and Decrease Latency

The IoT is edge computing, which moves data processing and storage closer to the devices doing the actual data production and management. This localized method greatly improves data processing efficiency and drastically decreases latency. We achieve this by making data travel shorter paths to processing. IoT devices that can react faster and run more reliably are crucial for time-sensitive applications. This is made feasible since the device can handle data processing at the network's periphery. One of the most important outcomes of recent technological advancements that have occurred during our lifetime is the use of edge computing in the IoT as shown in Figure 11.2. The IoT has a greater impact because edge computing has the potential to address some of the most pressing issues of our day, such as the scarcity of food and water, the effects of climate change, and the health concerns that are facing the entire world [30].

Critical for making judgments in secure mobility and preventing disasters in real time, edge computing substantially decreases latency by enabling real-time data analysis from sensors and cameras. In manufacturing, lower latency helps machines respond quicker to control commands and adjustments, which in turn improves the accuracy and quality of their output. It is crucial to note that in case of an emergency, wearable gear and medical sensors can monitor vital signs and provide

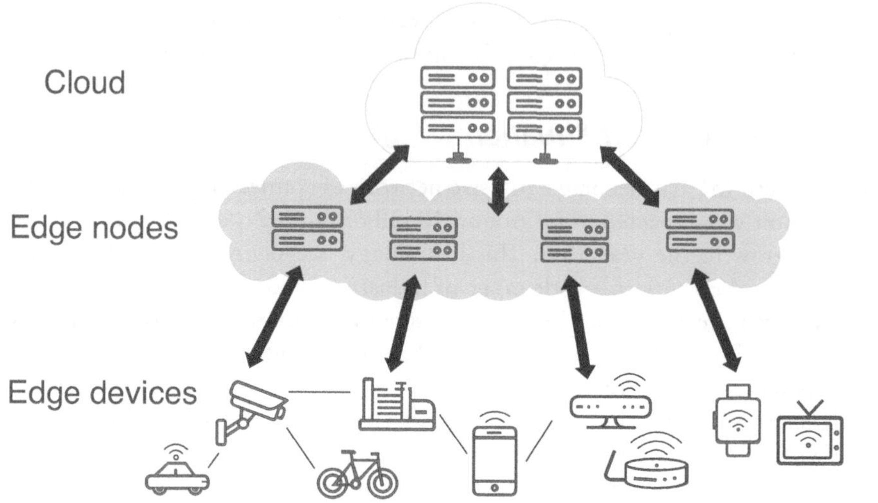

Figure 11.2 Edge computing.

doctors and patient's quick feedback. Edge computing maximizes bandwidth usage for local data processing, lowering the amount of information transferred as well as reducing transfer costs, by only transferring data that is absolutely necessary to centralized cloud servers [31].

Consolidating data and doing early data analysis on the edge devices allows for a reduction in the amount of data transferred to the cloud, as they only transmit summarized or aggregated data. The use of cutting-edge computing for local processing of data enhances privacy and security by storing sensitive information close to its point of origin and reducing the likelihood of breaches of data happening during transmission. Organizations can achieve better data management by minimizing their dependency on foreign cloud services, assessing data on edge devices, and developing strong security measures tailored to local needs. A wide variety of uses can be made of edge computing. IoT cutting-edge computing in manufacturing enables continuous monitoring of processes and machines. The machinery operations are optimized by sensors, which collect the data and do the processing in real time to detect shortages. Using predictive maintenance and real-time data analysis is a way to find machine problems before the system develops them, which would shorten the machinery lifecycle, less the downtime, and stop the loss of material costs in the future. The edge computing method that enables quality assurance is used for monitoring and to make sure that the produced products are in high quality in real time. Apart from the production of sustainable high-quality products, edge computing is a powerful tool for fast detection and removal of defective products [32]. The edge computing method is based on the quick and efficient processing of such critical data as heart rate, glucose levels, and blood pressure, which is then transmitted to medical wearable devices. Going by this dimension, the valuable information and timely notices can be delivered to patients and doctors. As a result of the local real-time data analysis technique, critical health changes can be detected and treated, which leads to better patient performance and a better remote patient monitoring experience. Besides, hospitals will also be optimized by the lessened traffic brought about by better public transportation. Security cameras and environmental sensors can work together with edge computing to identify and react to issues like fires, accidents, and poor air quality. As a result, communities are safer, responses to emergencies are faster, and disaster management is improved [33]. Smart electrical networks and systems that handle supply and demand in real time greatly benefit from edge computing's ability to regulate energy use. It lowers costs, improves energy efficiency, and facilitates the integration of renewable energy sources. Data analysis from different medical devices and systems can help with healthcare management, allocation of resources, and delivery in general [34].

11.3.2 5G Integration: Increasing Capabilities in Networking and Connectivity Provision

The integration of 5G technology, which improves connection and network capabilities, might radically alter the IoT. Massive device connectivity, reduced latency, and lightning-fast speeds are all possible with 5G. It changes the way people interact with technology and serves many industries, making it a crucial enabler for the next version of IoT applications [35].

The efficiency of IoT devices and apps is greatly improved by 5G's key features, which include ultra-low latency, network slicing, and high speed and capacity. Figure 11.3 shows that 5G networks are essential for the transmission and reception of enormous amounts of data by a variety of IoT devices, including connected cars,

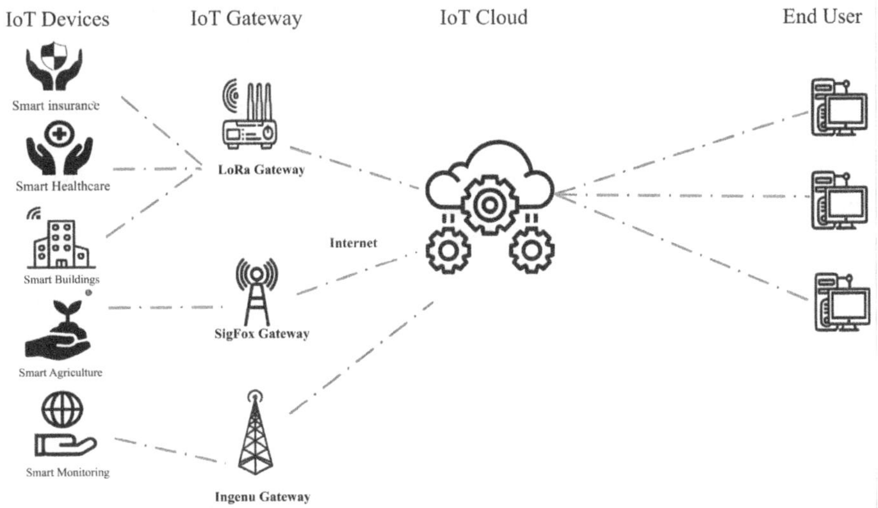

Figure 11.3 5G communication integration.

industrial sensors, and high-quality video surveillance cameras. The elimination of congestion during data transfer allows for much faster download and upload rates, which in turn improves streaming quality, gaming responsiveness, and accessibility to cloud-based applications. Applications requiring virtually immediate response times are essential for 5G's ultra-low latency. As an example, patient safety is guaranteed via less harmful and precisely performed remote procedures. Autonomous vehicles utilize data collected in real time from sensors and other sources to reduce the likelihood of accidents and make split-second judgments [9]. With 5G, industrial automation can control manufacturing processes with pinpoint accuracy, allowing for modifications and coordination across robotic systems in real time, which boosts efficiency and safety. One physical 5G network can support many virtual networks thanks to network slicing. The optimal performance for numerous IoT applications may be ensured because each slice can be tailored to specific requirements, such as latency, bandwidth, security, and more [10]. This functionality enables several use cases to run concurrently on the same network infrastructure, including critical applications like healthcare and emergency services as well as high-bandwidth entertainment services, as shown in Figure 11.3.

IoT applications for 5G include smart cities, healthcare, and agriculture, among others. The 5G, smart city traffic control centers, vehicles, and traffic lights can all communicate in real time, which improves traffic flow, allows for dynamic traffic regulation, and ultimately reduces congestion. Updates on traffic conditions and alternate routes for linked vehicles in real time Smart grids that use 5G to dynamically balance supply and demand improve energy management and distribution, leading to less energy waste and cheaper prices. Public safety systems are aided by more rapid and consistent communication among emergency services, which is facilitated by the real-time transmission of high-definition video from security cameras to law enforcement and first responders. With 5G's high-speed, low-latency capabilities, patients and healthcare professionals may have high-quality video consultations, making healthcare more accessible, especially in remote areas. By continually monitoring patients' vital signs and transmitting data in real time to healthcare practitioners, wearable gadgets and home health monitors enable early identification of health problems and timely therapies. This improves patient outcomes and lowers hospital readmission rates. By connecting patients with specialists using 5G-enabled mobile health devices, patients have access to better, on-demand medical care in the form of remote diagnostics and treatment regimens [36].

The farming precision in agriculture has been made possible by the 5G technology through the use of IoT sensors that monitor the soil health, crop development, and weather conditions. The successful installation of this system could not only bring us a more sustainable agriculture but also could result in more production efficiency. This is usually done by cloud seeding, which involves artificial raindrop nuclei into clouds. In the case of cloud seeding, it is considered a suspicion of artificial rainfall. This kind of activity is a common way to solve future environmental problems. The purpose is to make new varieties of crops that produce enough materials for the biological breakdown of foods. If newer breeds are developed then the need for the husks [37].

11.3.3 Blockchain Technology: Protection of Internet of Things Transactions and Data Integrity

The technology of blockchain is getting more and more known for its potential to secure the transactions which are being done on IoT and also provide the data protection [38]. The worries of the security and privacy of the IoT can be greatly solved with the blockchain technology, this gives a distributed ledger that is not able to be changed. In this article we're going to look deeper into the benefits of blockchain technology in the context of the IoT, unfolding how it might enhance security and ensure the authenticity of data.

Enhanced security, data integrity, trust, and transparency are the main pluses that the blockchain technology introduced to the IoT as shown in Figure 11.4. Together, these aspects of the IoT systems not only significantly boost the performance but also make them more reliable. Blockchain are built using distributed architectures, which makes them very secure and provides resistance to manipulation, as they are next to impossible to break or tap. This is because changing one node can't kill the whole system, which is the main shield of the system from threats [39]. When a blockchain technology records a transaction, it cannot be altered or reversed since it is immutable. As a result, the transaction becomes nonreversible and cannot be altered. This aims at prevention of fraudulent acts as well as the

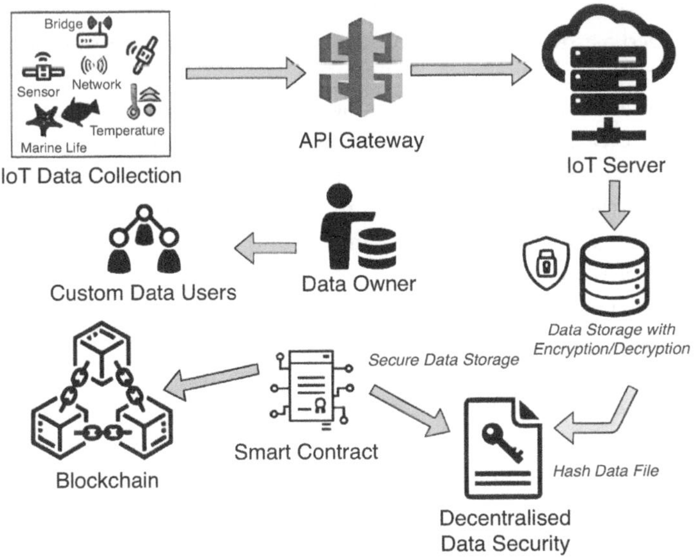

Figure 11.4 Blockchain Technology used in IoT data collection.

protection of personal data. To be safer and to be more difficult to be hacked, cryptographic technologies have been invented to encrypt each transaction and then link them. Blockchain technology's open ledger, which records all transactions in a way that can be viewed by all authorized parties, is the source of both the data integrity and transparency [40].

The gathering of data and its subsequent processing through the use of IoT devices require that recorded data be unchangeable in nature, which a responsibility is born by the blockchain technology. Data security depends on integrity that is guaranteed by storage and processing by blockchain, and thus its immutability is a useful feature. What is key in supply chain management, along with the track and trace origin and destination of the commodities to ensure their legality, is the full traceability of a transaction made possible by blockchain technology [41]. When blockchain is used for the creation of a treaty between various parties, the truthfulness of records of transactions will be increased and interactions will be fully clear, hence leading to a higher level of trust and accountability. It can help when there are a number of parties and the data, they rely on to transact business. Because it ensures the quick exchange of information and does not involve as many costs as manual trading transactions do. If all the parameters are met, smart contracts can carry out transactions with the help of automation, thus the transactions will be made without any intermediaries and people will trust the entire process. To begin with, the conditions of these contracts are programmed into the code, which is the main mechanism that enables them to be carried out. The main benefit of blockchain technology is decentralized trust, which is capable of providing IoT devices with the veracity of data and the operations they carry out, without use of a centralized authority. In this respect, the greatest benefit is when no human input is needed as the devices communicate frequently with a number of different industrial sectors.

An immutable and publicly available ledger detailing all links in the supply chain can be created using blockchain technology. By recording each purchase and shipment, supply chain management can be enhanced, leading to improved traceability. In the long run, this aids in supply chain management by revealing bottlenecks and reducing wait times. Smart contracts allow for automatic and safe interactions between devices that are part of the IoT. One example is the ability of smart meters in smart homes to automatically pay for energy usage in real time. This leads to better efficiency and lower costs by automating transactions and doing away with middlemen. Since blockchain records energy transactions between customers and producers, distributed autonomous energy grids can profit from it in terms of energy management. Energy equalization and better tracking of generation and consumption are both made possible by this. Users are able to purchase and sell energy directly with one another through peer-to-peer energy trading. Another application of blockchain technology is the decentralization of power generation and consumption occurs simultaneously with increased capacity utilization of renewable energy sources. Blockchain technology ensures the secure sharing of medical records at all times, putting the minds of doctors, patients, and insurance companies at ease. Patients can safeguard their privacy while gaining access to trustworthy folks with the ability to manage their own data. The adoption of blockchain technology allows for the tracking of pharmaceuticals and medical devices from their site of production all the way to the hospital.

11.3.4 Artificial Intelligence: Making IoT Smarter with Artificial Intelligence and Data Analytics

The IoT relies on AI to power more intelligent and autonomous systems through data analytics and ML. Through the analysis of massive amounts of data created by IoT devices, AI can uncover patterns and insights that can inform wise decision-making. Efficiency, adaptability, and reactivity to changing circumstances are all enhanced by this integration, which boosts the capabilities of the IoT as shown in Figure 11.5.

The most important ways in which AI has impacted the IoT are through data analytics, automation, and better decision-making. These three areas collectively enhance the efficiency and effectiveness of IoT systems. Smart home energy efficiency and security can be enhanced by analysing usage patterns with the help of AI algorithms that identify patterns and correlations in the massive datasets generated by IoT devices. Using historical data, ML models may foretell when things will happen, allowing for preventative maintenance to cut down on downtime and equipment failures in industrial settings. The performance of AI-powered autonomous driving depends on the technology's ability to perform real-time data analysis and processing, provide insights, and quick answers to new or changing conditions.

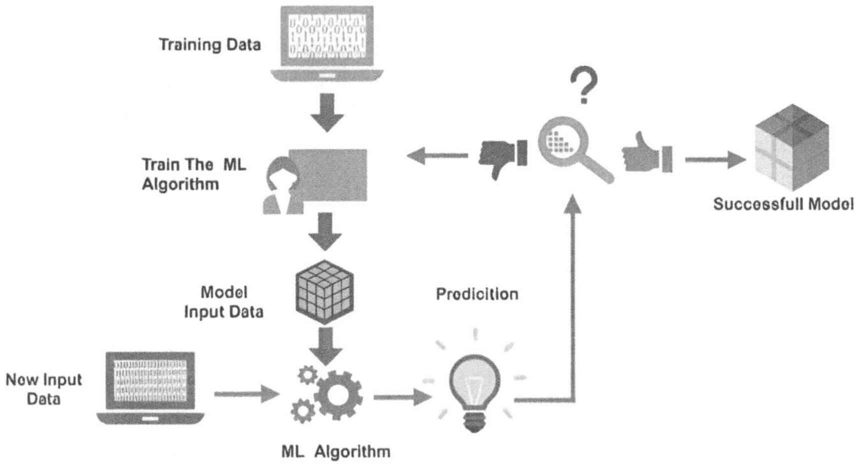

Figure 11.5 AI and machine learning integration.

ML can improve the drama by not only creating the most effective output but also by reducing the percentage of human mistakes by automating the most monotonous, repetitive jobs. AI-powered drones will be able to measure the leaf color index of plants, either independently or in coordination with humans, and decide which map should be uploaded. The HVAC system in a smart building, for instance, uses an AI system to acquire data, as well as to learn and adjust itself based on it, thus the building can become more comfortable with lower energy expenditure, while dependent on the consumption patterns and future weather predictions. Technology made those things possible and become more accurate through automation using AI.

This refers to management and inventory control that is part of this. Insights powered by AI can help businesses make smarter decisions. You can design personalized marketing strategies that are people-oriented by analysing customer data from the web together with the help of IoT devices and AI. ML can be the driver of better products and services' development by doing a study of consumer reviews and product metrics. AI could back-up industrial process data mining and thus, make it possible to unearth the potential for innovation and development. Among the use cases of AI in the IoT are healthcare, smart homes, and the detection of fraudulent financial transactions, or the prediction and prevention of health hazards from patient data in nursing. AI-driven intelligent virtual assistants like Apple Siri, Google Home, and Amazon Alexa are the new trend in the smart homes that can be an all-in-one tool at home. By replicating human actions, AI creates more advanced home automation solutions that lead to the perfect regulation of temperature, lighting, security, and entertainment.

ML is a study of energy consumption and a technology of suggesting new methods of energy saving. For example, it can be temperature or time-based by switching off appliances during the peak-time to cut down the energy consumption. Other than getting information from public health databases, electronic health records, and the health IoT monitors, the AI system is now able to close the gap by using big data to prevent the onset of health-related epidemics. AI analysts are able to engage the patient through the electronic patient file and the use of raw data which can be easily and very quickly converted to drug therapy programs that are specific to the patient by the evaluation of the patient's profile and referred data. AI-led IoT devices allow health care professionals to continuously monitor their patients' vital signs and the health indices as the events occur. This is because technology facilitates the early treatment of chronic diseases and thus helps step in whenever there are emergencies. The anticipated period of time when Industrial Internet of Things (IIoT) machines will malfunction is monitored by an AI system and the data that are data tubes are the sensors and the records of maintenance. The stops in the product process are reduced through preventive maintenance and, as a result, the service life of the machines is prolonged. AI is leveraged to streamline the manufacturing process by using efficient data analysis from production to come up with new production methods for figures which results in more production and less waste materials and high-quality end products. Eventually, every single customer manages to attain the goal of their businesses and companies through the use of AI in the fields of logistics, inventory control, demand predicting, and cutting costs.

11.4 Emerging Trends in the Internet of Things

The swift progression of technology consistently drives the IoT domain. The IoT settings give great opportunity for transformation through increased security standards, new sensor technologies, and integration with developing technologies. Ensuring effective security measures is vitally crucial for securing private data and minimizing cybersecurity threats as IoT installations develop and are increasingly integrated. Two potential advancements in IoT security are quantum-resistant encryption techniques and decentralized identity management systems. These policies guarantee long-term data security by way of safe and tamper-proof solutions for processing digital IDs.

- **Improvements in Sensor Technology:** With the ability to gather data in real time from the real world, sensors play a pivotal role in IoT systems. Novel sensor technologies have the potential to revolutionize IoT applications by enhancing data precision, reliability, and efficiency. Improvements in energy collection methods, smaller sensors with greater sensitivity and resolution, and new battery technologies are all possibilities for the future of sensors.
- **Suggestion:** Richer data collection enabled by advanced sensor technologies follows in the footsteps of improved decision-making, analytics for prediction, and optimization of IoT systems. Companies will be able to take advantage of new opportunities for growth, efficiency, competitiveness, and development by deploying state-of-the-art sensors, which will lead to disruption and change in many areas.
- The convergence of the IoT with emerging technologies like virtual reality and augmented reality opens up new avenues for immersive and interactive experiences. Businesses may create completely full immersion that superimpose digital information onto the physical environment in real time by merging IoT data with augmented reality and virtual reality technology. By enabling workers to access real-time data from the IoT and instructional content through augmented or virtual reality goggles or headsets, this link improves efficiency and cuts down on downtime in industries like remote service and training.
- **Recommendations:** Enhancing security measures is crucial for establishing trust in IoT installations, particularly in critical sectors such as healthcare, infrastructure, and finance. Businesses may reduce the risk of data breaches and cyberattacks, encourage innovation, and hasten the adoption of the IoT by addressing security concerns.

11.5 Challenges and Considerations

IoT has great potential to change sectors, increase efficiency, and raise quality of living. Along with these possibilities, although, a number of issues and ethical questions have to be resolved to guarantee the appropriate implementation of IoT technologies.

- The consistent gathering, processing, and transferring of data represents a potent invasion of privacy and is one of the main components of the web of things, which is why they are a main concern. According to the IoT, the collection of small amounts of data about the users' daily life turns to be one of the biggest issues in cyberattack, while the data retrieval, profiling, and even unauthorized access are some of the main issues facing the users.
- The problem of data security and regulation in the area of the IoT is very complex. One of the biggest problems is the fact that the IoT devices can produce so much data that it becomes difficult to manage it. A problem with data distribution, ownership, control, and exploitation appears where IoT devices are concerned. The disagreements between the stakeholders, like the suppliers, service providers, and end-users, about who owns the data are hard to solve, and these issues are most common in IoT systems with multiparty connectivity.
- Disparities in access to and proficiency with digital technologies (such as the IoT) are known as the digital divide. Inequality is exacerbated as the digital divide widens as a result of infrastructure constraints, socioeconomic status, and geographical location, all of which contribute to the explanation of inequalities in access to IoT technology. Since those without IoT devices risk falling behind in an increasingly interconnected society, this impacts economic opportunities, social inclusion, healthcare, and education.
- Ethical norms and standards must be established and adhered to promote the responsible development and implementation of IoT technology. It is the responsibility of industry organizations, regulatory agencies, and standards-setting bodies to ensure that IoT installations adhere to ethical principles, best practices, and compliance mechanisms that prioritize privacy, accountability, transparency, and human rights (Table 11.1).

11.6 Conclusion and Future Scope

The current state of the IoT is being shaped by new trends and possible innovations that could revolutionize several industries, improve people's quality of life, and increase efficiency. The upcoming blockchain technology, together with other important trends in cloud computing, AI, 5G connection, and the IoT landscape,

Table 11.1 Comparative Analysis Emerging Trends in IoT

Aspect	*Emerging Trends*	*Challenges*	*Strategic Solutions*	*Reference*
Device Authentication	Zero Trust Architecture, AI-based authentication	Weak credential management, unauthorized access	Multi-factor authentication, blockchain-based identity verification	Srikanta Kolay et al. [37]
Data Privacy	Edge computing for decentralized processing	Data breaches, lack of encryption in transit and storage	End-to-end encryption, privacy-preserving computation	Garcia Lopez et al. [38]
Network Security	5G security enhancements, Software-Defined Networking	Distributed denial of service attacks, lack of standardization	AI-driven intrusion detection, network segmentation	Prabakaran et al. [39]
AI and IoT Security	AI-powered anomaly detection, predictive threat intelligence	AI adversarial attacks, model poisoning	Federated learning, explainable AI security models	Jyothsna et al. [27]
Regulatory Compliance	General Data Protection Regulation (GDPR), California Consumer Privacy Act (CCPA), National Institute of Standards and Technology (NIST) IoT Cybersecurity Framework	Compliance complexity, cross-border data laws	Unified security policies, automated compliance checks	Diamantopoulou et al. [26]
Hardware Security	Trusted Platform Modules, Physical Unclonable Functions	Firmware vulnerabilities, supply chain attacks	Secure boot mechanisms, hardware-based encryption	Singh [25]
Cloud and IoT Security	Hybrid cloud security models, Confidential Computing	Cloud misconfigurations, insecure APIs	Secure Access Service Edge, Zero Trust Cloud Security	Zhu et al. [24]

is causing a rapid transformation. Due to the huge amount of data produced by the IoT, decision-making can now take place in real time, and response times can be improved thanks to the merging of AI and edge computing. The ability of 5G technology to deliver reliable, high-speed, and high-capacity connectivity enables the smooth integration of critical applications. Blockchain technology opens the door to new forms of cooperation and novel business models that can strengthen the integrity, honesty, and reliability of IoT networks.

The convergence of these developments will propel the IoT industry to unprecedented levels of development and innovation, resulting in better user experiences will follow suit. Due to the convergence of several technologies, the IoT environment is experiencing several changes. Because of this, progress is being accelerated, and new opportunities are being created for businesses and consumers alike.

References

1. Sundaravadivel, P., Kougianos, E., Mohanty, S.P., & Ganapathiraju, M.K. (2017). Everything you wanted to know about smart health care: Evaluating the different technologies and components of the Internet of Things for better health. *IEEE Consumer Electronics Magazine*, 7, 18–28.
2. Sharma, V., You, I., Andersson, K., Palmieri, F., Rehmani, M. H., & Lim J. (2020). Security, privacy and trust for smart mobile- internet of things (MIoT): A survey. *IEEE Access*, 8, 167123.
3. Kim, H.-S., Yun, S., Kim, H. et al. (2018). An efficient SDN multicast architecture for dynamic industrial IoT environments. *Mobile Information Systems*, 11, 8482467. https://doi.org/10.1155/2018/8125126.
4. Keele, S. (2007). *Guidelines for performing systematic literature reviews in software engineering*. Technical Report, EBSE, Goyang-si, South Korea.
5. Li, C.P., Jiang, J., Chen, W., Ji, T., & Smee, J. (2017). 5G ultra-reliable and low-latency systems design. In *Proceedings of the 2017 European Conference on Networks and Communications (EuCNC)*, Oulu, Finland, 12–15 June 2017, pp. 1–5.
6. Noura, M., Atiquzzaman, M., & Gaedke, M. (2019). Interoperability in internet of things: Taxonomies and open challenges. *Mobile Network and Applications*, 24, 796–809.
7. Kitchenham, B., Pretorius, R., Budgen, D. et al. (2010). Systematic literature reviews in software engineering - a tertiary study. *Information and Software Technology*, 52 (8), 792–805.
8. Malatji, M. (2023). Management of enterprise cyber security: A review of ISO/IEC 27001:2022. In *2023 International Conference on Cyber Management and Engineering (CyMaEn)*, Bangkok, Thailand. https://doi.org/10.1109/CyMaEn57228.2023.10051114
9. Hussain, F., Hussain, R., Hassan, S., & Hossain, E. (2019). Machine learning in IoT security: Current solutions and future challenges. *IEEE Communications Surveys & Tutorials*, 22, 1686–1721. https://doi.org/10.1109/COMST.2020.2986444.
10. Srivastava, A., Gupta, S., Quamara, M., Chaudhary, P., & Aski, V. (2020). Future IoT-enabled threats and vulnerabilities: State of the art, challenges, and future prospects. *International Journal of Communication Systems*, 33. https://doi.org/10.1002/dac.4443.
11. Singh, D. S. (2023). IOT security challenges and emerging solutions: A comprehensive review. *International Journal of Scientific Research in Engineering and Management*, 7(09). https://doi.org/10.55041/ijsrem25662.

12. Kumar, M., Yadav, U., Raghav, P., & Kumar, J. (2024). Securing the Internet of Things (IoT): Current landscape, obstacles, and future strategies. *Conference Proceeding*. https://doi.org/10.62919/yewq1232.
13. Sultan, M. (2023). Securing the internet of things: Challenges, strategies, and emerging trends in IoT Security Systems. *International Journal of Research in Engineering and Innovation*. https://doi.org/10.36037/ijrei.2023.7607.
14. Prasad, J., Parvateesam, C., Nagulmeera, S., & Avinash, V. (2023). Enhancing Iot security: Addressing challenges, implementing solutions, and envisioning cybersecurity trends for the future. *International Journal of Engineering Applied Sciences and Technology*. https://doi.org/10.33564/ijeast.2023.v08i06.006.
15. Rahman, M., & Laskar, A. (2024). Securing IoT networks: Challenges and solutions for next-generation smart devices. *Journal of Information Technology and Sciences*. https://doi.org/10.46610/joits.2024.v10i03.002.
16. Rozlomii, I., Yarmilko, A., & Naumenko, S. (2024). Data security of IoT devices with limited resources: Challenges and potential solutions, *Proceedings of the 4th Edge Computing Workshop* (*DOORS*), 85–96.
17. Chowdhury, S., Hossain, Z., Rana, M., Hossain, A., Faisal, M., Wahid, S., & Karim, M. (2024). Security challenges and business opportunities in the IoT ecosystem. *Advanced International Journal of Multidisciplinary Research*. https://doi.org/10.62127/aijmr.2024.v02i05.1089.
18. Karie, N., Sahri, N., & Haskell-Dowland, P. (2020). IoT threat detection advances, challenges and future directions. *Emerging Technologies for Security in IoT (ETSecIoT)*, 22–29. https://doi.org/10.1109/ETSecIoT50046.2020.00009.
19. Raghavendra, G. S., & Yesaswini, A. M. (2024). Design and implementation of Internet of Things (IoT) framework for governing modern cyber attacks in computer network. *International Journal of Safety & Security Engineering*, 14(5), 1385–1390.
20. Singh, N., Buyya, R., & Kim, H. (2024). IoT in the cloud: Exploring security challenges and mitigations for a connected world, *arXiv*, 2402, 1–27.
21. Xu, T., Wendt, J., &Potkonjak, M. (2014). Security of IoT systems: Design challenges and opportunities. In 2014 IEEE/ACM, *International Conference on Computer-Aided Design (ICCAD)*, pp. 417–423. https://doi.org/10.1109/ICCAD.2014.7001385.
22. Akhunzada, A., Islam, S., & Zeadally, S. (2020). Securing cyberspace of future smart cities with 5G technologies. *IEEE Network*, 34, 336–342. https://doi.org/10.1109/MNET.001.1900559.
23. OjaroudiParchin, N., Alibakhshikenari, M., Jahanbakhsh Basherlou, H., AAbd-Alhameed, R., Rodriguez, J., & Limiti, E. (2019). MM-wave phased array quasi-Yagi antenna for the upcoming 5G cellular communications. *Applied Sciences*, 9, 978.
24. Zhu, J., Hou, R., Wang, X., Wang, W., Cao, J., Zhao, B., ... & Meng, D. (2020). Enabling rack-scale confidential computing using heterogeneous trusted execution environment. In *2020 IEEE Symposium on Security and Privacy (SP)* (pp. 1450–1465). IEEE. SAN FRANCISCO, CA.
25. Singh, A. (2025). Hardware-assisted security of smart IoT applications. *In Hardware Security: Challenges and Solutions* (pp. 51–70). Edited by Ashutosh Mishra, Mrinal Goswami, Manoj Kumar and Navin Singh Rajput. Cham: Springer Nature Switzerland.
26. Diamantopoulou, V., Tsohou, A., & Karyda, M. (2019). General Data Protection Regulation and ISO/IEC 27001: 2013: Synergies of activities towards organisations' compliance. In *Trust, Privacy and Security in Digital Business: 16th International Conference, TrustBus 2019*, Linz, Austria, August 26–29, 2019, Proceedings 16, pp. 94–109. Springer International Publishing.

27. Jyothsna, V., Sandhya, E., Kamalapuram, K. B., & Bhasha, P. (2025). AI-driven threat detection in cloud environments. *In Convergence of Cybersecurity and Cloud Computing* (pp. 261–284). IGI Global Scientific Publishing.
28. Jara, A.J., Belchi, F.J., Alcolea, A.F., Santa, J., Zamora-Izquierdo, M.A., Gómez-Skarmeta, A.F. (2010). A pharmaceutical intelligent information system to detect allergies and adverse drugs reactions based on Internet of Things. In *Proceedings of the 2010 8th IEEE International Conference on Pervasive Computing and Communications Workshops (PERCOM Workshops)*, Mannheim, Germany, 29 March–2 April 2010, pp. 809–812.
29. Wang, A., Wang, P., Miao, X. et al. (2020). A review on non-terrestrial wireless technologies for Smart City Internet of Things. *International Journal of Distributed Sensor* Networks, 16 (6).
30. Qadri, Y. A., Nauman, A., Zikria, Y. B., Vasilakos, A. V., & Kim, S. W. (2020). The future of healthcare internet of things: A survey of emerging technologies. *IEEE Communications Surveys & Tutorials*, 22 (2), 1121–1167.
31. Mendez Mena, D., Papapanagiotou, I., & Yang, B. (2018). Internet of things: Survey on security. *Information Security Journal: A Global Perspective*, 27 (3), 162–182.
32. Hassija, V., Chamola, V., Saxena, V., Jain, D., Goyal, P., & Sikdar, B. (2019). A survey on IoT security: Application areas, security threats, and solution architectures. *IEEE Access*, 7, 82721–82743.
33. Obaidat, M. A., Obeidat, S., Holst, J. et al. (2020). A comprehensive and systematic survey on the internet of things: Security and privacy challenges, security frameworks, enabling technologies, threats, vulnerabilities and countermeasures. *Computers*, 9 (2), 44.
34. Ferrag, M. A., Shu, L., Yang, X., Derhab, A., & Maglaras, L. (2020). Security and privacy for green IoT-based agriculture: Review, blockchain solutions, and challenges. *IEEE Access*, 8, 32031–32053.
35. Waltman, L. & Van Eck, N. J. (2012). A new methodology for constructing a publication-level classification system of science. *Journal of the American Society for Information Science and Technology*, 63 (12), 2378–2392.
36. Zhang, Z., Cho, M., Wang, C., Hsu, C., Chen, C., & Shieh, S. (2014). IoT security: Ongoing challenges and research opportunities. *2014 IEEE 7th International Conference on Service-Oriented Computing and Applications*, pp. 230–234. Massachusetts Ave., NW Washington, DC, United States. https://doi.org/10.1109/SOCA.2014.58.
37. Kolay, S., & Hiwarkar, T. (2023). IoT security: Issues, best practices, and open challenges. *International Journal of Information Security Engineering*, 01 (02), 7–13.
38. Garcia Lopez, P., Montresor, A., Epema, D., Datta, A., Higashino, T., Iamnitchi, A., … & Riviere, E. (2015). Edge-centric computing: Vision and challenges. *ACM SIGCOMM Computer Communication Review*, 45 (5), 37–42.
39. Prabakaran, D., Nizar, S. M., & Kumar, K. S. (2021). Software-defined network (SDN) architecture and security considerations for 5G communications. *In Design Methodologies and Tools for 5G Network Development and Application* (pp. 28–43). IGI Global Scientific Publishing.

40. Kiran, B., Raghu, N., Maniunatha, K. N., & Girish, P. (2021). Design of IoT based Instrument Landing System. In 2021 *International Conference on Disruptive Technologies for Multi-Disciplinary Research and Applications (CENTCON)*, 1, pp. 207–212. IEEE.
41. Veena, V., Manjunath, R., Asha, V., Gangaraju, V., Swetha, G., & Raghu, N. (2025). Smart homes with IoT technology provide safety and security for elderly individuals. In S. Mallik, S. Mathivanan, S. Sangeetha, & B. Soufiene (Eds.), *Real-World Applications of AI Innovation* (pp. 425–450). IGI Global Scientific Publishing. https://doi.org/10.4018/979-8-3693-4252-7.ch020

Index

For Product Safety Concerns and Information please contact our EU representative GPSR@taylorandfrancis.com Taylor & Francis Verlag GmbH, Kaufingerstraße 24, 80331 München, Germany